Oxford EAP

A course in English for Academic Purposes

ADVANCED / C1

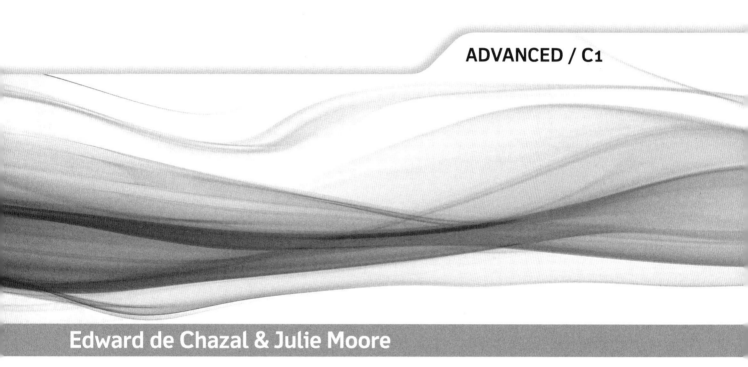

Edward de Chazal & Julie Moore

Teacher's Handbook

OXFORD

UNIVERSITY PRESS

Great Clarendon Street, Oxford, OX2 6DP, United Kingdom

Oxford University Press is a department of the University of Oxford.
It furthers the University's objective of excellence in research, scholarship,
and education by publishing worldwide. Oxford is a registered trade
mark of Oxford University Press in the UK and in certain other countries

© Oxford University Press 2013

The moral rights of the author have been asserted

First published in 2013

2017 2016 2015 2014 2013

10 9 8 7 6 5 4 3 2 1

ISBN: 978 0 19 400181 6   Book
ISBN: 978 0 19 400182 3   Pack

Printed and bound by Gráfica Maiadouro S. A. in Portugal

This book is printed on paper from certified and well-managed sources

Contents

Course introduction *Page 004*

Teaching notes, answers, and suggestions for extension tasks and further practice

1 BEHAVIOUR *Page 008*

2 SUSTAINABILITY *Page 019*

3 CREATIVITY *Page 029*

4 INFORMATION *Page 038*

5 PATTERNS *Page 050*

6 RESPONSIBILITY *Page 061*

7 DATA *Page 073*

8 INFLUENCE *Page 083*

9 VARIATION *Page 095*

10 GLOBALIZATION *Page 105*

11 OBSERVATION *Page 117*

12 RESEARCH *Page 127*

Audio CD track listing *Page 135*

COURSE INTRODUCTION

WHAT IS EAP AND *OXFORD EAP*?

English for Academic Purposes (EAP) is a fast-developing area of English language teaching. Like other English for Specific Purposes (ESP), it is characterized by working out what students' needs are, then creating a syllabus and programme of study to meet them. Every student has slightly different needs, depending on their chosen discipline, language and cognitive level, cultural background, and other factors. Similarly, within different disciplines there are varying approaches to teaching, learning, and assessment. However, there are also core skills, tasks, and academic language that are common to most disciplines and are therefore relevant to the needs of most students preparing to study English at university level.

Oxford English for Academic Purposes, as a 'general' EAP course, accommodates such different needs by focusing on core tasks relevant to all students, such as working out the main points of an academic text or lecture. It requires them to approach the course content from different perspectives (e.g. economic, technological, legal, social, business), and to write and speak about these in relation to what they know and – as far as possible – to their own discipline. This practice of discussing and analysing an issue from several perspectives is a recurrent feature of the course. Also common to all EAP students is the need to develop critical thinking skills; these are integrated into relevant tasks throughout the course.

HOW CAN *OXFORD EAP* HELP STUDENTS AND TEACHERS?

Oxford EAP is an accessible and effective course in EAP for students from a variety of cultural and educational backgrounds whose first language is not English. It addresses the needs of adult learners who are planning to study, or are already studying, at university level in English, whether on a preparatory foundation course, or a degree or diploma. The course material is suitable for students from any academic discipline and does not require any specialist subject knowledge. Students will engage with a broad range of texts and topics which are presented for the non-expert user. Through their engagement with this material, students systematically and progressively develop their academic skills, language, and critical thinking.

For teachers, *Oxford EAP* offers a carefully structured syllabus which supports both classroom and independent learning, and enables teachers to deliver integrated, effective, and varied EAP classes and programmes. Within each unit, the skills modules are interrelated, but not interdependent. This means that different modules can be taught by different teachers independently of each other. To study the speaking module in a unit, for example, does not require students to have studied the preceding reading, writing, or listening modules for that unit. The units, then, maintain a 'horizontal' coherence with the different modules unified by theme and academic focus. The individual skills are also developed progressively in each 'vertical' strand throughout the book: for example, writing skills build incrementally from sentences, to paragraph structure, and then to types of essay and timed writing tasks.

All the units and modules have clearly stated aims and learning outcomes. These are reflected in the task headings. The rubrics are written to be concise but complete, and to give a clear indication of what is intended to happen at each stage of each task. This Teacher's Handbook adds further explanations, rationales, answers, and suggestions for extension tasks and further practice.

HOW IS *OXFORD EAP* ORGANIZED?

Each unit is based around a theme. Unit 1, for example, is organized around the theme of *Behaviour*, which leads to more specific topics for each skills module: different aspects of human behaviour such as social and political (Reading); motivating factors in human behaviour (Writing); educational behaviour and learning in universities (Listening); a discussion and application of behaviour (Speaking). The aim of the topics is not for students to learn topic-based vocabulary, but to offer contexts for the development of academic skills and language. The order of the modules moves from the orthographic skills of reading and writing into the oral skills of listening and speaking. Units 1–6 end with a one-page Vocabulary module, which looks at key aspects of academic vocabulary using content from the unit in question, and at useful vocabulary-learning strategies. Units 7–12 continue with half a page of vocabulary, together with half a page covering the Research Project. The Research Project offers an opportunity for students to read more widely around a topic of their choice within their subject area, leading to a 2,000-word essay.

The academic focus underpins all the skills work within each unit, and relates closely to the learning objectives of each module. For example, Unit 5, based around the theme of Patterns, deals with the academic focus of *citation and referencing*. In Unit 5A Reading, students practise quotation, paraphrase, and summary, and learn to use a content or author focus. Unit 5B Writing requires students to introduce citations using appropriate language, while Unit 5C Listening continues the focus of citation and referencing by referring to people, works, and ideas in spoken texts. In the Speaking module, 5D, students put this work into practice as they refer to source material in their spoken work. Finally, Unit 5E Vocabulary looks at various lexical patterns including verb and clause patterns. By the end of this unit, students should be familiar with what citation and reference is, why it is important, understand the language related to it, and how to recognize and use citation and reference in academic texts.

The striking opening photo on the first page of each unit illustrates the theme, and provides a key insight into the academic focus as well as informing a short discussion task on these pages. In Unit 6, for example, the photo shows peacekeeping forces delivering aid. This leads into the unit theme of responsibility and academic focus of selecting and summarizing from sources. A recurrent notion within the unit is the extent to which different agents, such as academics in universities and international staff in global organizations like the United Nations, should be responsible for global issues such as human rights. The opening photo also serves as a way into the unit theme, and some prompts can help students access the theme, for example: *Describe in detail what you see in the photo. How can it be connected to the unit theme and the academic focus? What aspect or interpretation of the theme does it emphasize? Can you suggest any alternative images? Why?*

The organization of the course aims to orientate the student in Unit 1 with opportunities for personalization within the unit theme of Behaviour, moving through to the theme of Research in Unit 12. This final unit offers students opportunities to reflect on their learning and consider what their next steps are in their academic journey.

At the back of the book, there are over forty pages of related resources including:

- **Glossary** of grammatical and academic terms used in the Student's Book. Students can be directed here to check meanings quickly, but also to clarify distinctions between essential items of academic and EAP terminology which they may find confusing (e.g. *cohesion* and *coherence*).

- **Language reference** with in-depth information organized by academic function and form, such as noun phrases and comparison and contrast. Primarily, this supports and extends the Academic Language which appears in each module, but it can also function as a free-standing reference tool for independent study.

- **Additional reference material** with checklists such as evaluation criteria for essays and presentations, which can be used in a wide range of academic contexts.

- **Additional material from units**, for example pre-lecture handouts and further reading texts.

- **Video and audio transcripts** for increased support while listening, checking of answers, and modelling aspects of pronunciation and spoken English.

At the teacher's discretion, these resources can be used at any time and repeatedly throughout the course.

HOW DOES *OXFORD EAP* WORK IN THE CLASSROOM?

Within *Oxford EAP*, the approach to each module varies according to the unit and module objectives. There is no single, formulaic approach; there are, however, certain consistent aims and features.

The **Rationale** at the head of each module explains what the academic focus is, why it is important, how it relates to the particular module skill, and what students need to do in order to apply it. Together with the teacher, students should carefully read and understand the rationale before starting work on the module, so that everyone in the classroom knows what they are aiming to do, and why.

Learning objectives for each module are presented as bullet points, below the Rationale. They introduce the module by showing students what they will learn, and can act as a checklist once the module is completed. Students can evaluate the success of their learning by saying what they feel they can and cannot do well.

Tasks build up in most cases to a clear outcome or outcomes, and in doing so allow students to replicate the process they will go through in their real academic studies. The main activity and outcome of each task is given as the heading, e.g. *TASK 1 Presenting an argument at paragraph level*. Within tasks, there are a number of sub-tasks or activities, each with its own rubric or instruction. There is built-in variety in format: students carry out some tasks individually, and others in pairs or in groups.

Skills are organized into separate modules of Reading, Writing, Listening, and Speaking. Each module has learning objectives relating to one particular skill, and to realize these objectives, more limited instances of other skills are needed. For example, a speaking module may have a listening stage, in which students listen to an extract from a presentation as preparation for giving one themselves. This serves as a sample for students to familiarize themselves with the type of task, and to develop their confidence in doing this task. Similarly, a reading module may require students to write a summary of a text; a listening module could involve reading a pre-lecture handout. While the skills modules develop the unit theme, academic focus and learning objectives, they do not have to be done in order. To suit particular programmes, each skills strand can be taught separately, and it is not necessary for students to have studied, for example, the reading module in a unit before studying the writing module. However, the skills development is graded by level of difficulty, becoming more challenging as the course progresses, and some caution would be needed if planning to cover the units in a different order.

Reading texts are all authentic texts sourced from material published by Oxford University Press. They are chosen for their currency, variety, and interest, and to support and exemplify the academic focus of the module. The reference and page numbers of the source are given at the end of each text extract.

The writing tasks take students through the academic practices needed to write academic texts, which students put into practice in a range of texts including essays. The second half of the book has an additional writing strand, the research essay. Students write this 2,000-word essay following the staged guidelines presented through Units 7–12. This process enables students to personalize their essay by selecting and refining a topic from their chosen discipline.

Listening tasks are developed from authentic lectures given by academics at Oxford University. Students follow structured note-taking tasks and respond to the lecture material. There are DVD and audio recordings, plus transcripts at the back of the book.

Speaking tasks are based around seminars and discussions, plus presentations, including a poster presentation. As with the other skills, a wide range of topics relating to the unit theme are explored.

Academic Language sections in each module support the effective development of skills. Academic language is extensive and complex, and students need to gradually notice and learn the most important patterns, structures, functions, and notions – and relate these to meanings and uses. For example, noun phrase structures are complex and extremely frequent in academic texts; *Oxford EAP* examines noun phrase forms with multiple postmodifiers including relative clauses, and uses such as expressing information concisely, or presenting alternative arguments. What underlies this approach is the connection to context: students are presented with frequent noun phrase patterns, they link these to particular uses in a text, and then transfer the language to new contexts. Rather than attempting to explain every grammatical possibility, this course focuses on meanings, forms, and uses of frequent and useful language which is widely found in academic texts. The information on academic language given in the modules is designed to be brief and useful, with further, more detailed description in the Language reference at the back of the book.

Independent study is developed throughout the course, with independent research tasks integrated into units. In particular, the research essay in the second half of the book requires students to spend a considerable amount of time studying independently. While doing so, students can collaborate, for example through discussing and exchanging ideas on a topic or how to approach their written texts. Many tasks require access to an external resource such as a library or the internet.

Critical thinking is a defining characteristic of EAP, and students need to engage critically with the texts they read, the lectures they listen to, and the material in discussions they participate in. What this means in practice is that students need to question what they read, look for assumptions and weaknesses, make connections, respond, and evaluate. Tasks which foreground critical thinking in *Oxford EAP* indicate this in the task heading. A characteristic of these tasks is that the answers are 'unkeyable', i.e. the responses are open to interpretation and cannot always be predicted in advance. An example of critical thinking in an early module (Unit 1B) is for students to evaluate their writing ability using given criteria. Later, in Unit 6, students have to identify assumptions and ask critical questions about a text. In many critical thinking and other tasks, checklists or lists of criteria are given as guidelines to help students complete the task; these are also given at the back of the book. A major aim of critical thinking tasks is to promote student autonomy.

UNIT 1 Behaviour

INTRODUCTION

Unit 1 aims to introduce a number of key characteristics of academic contexts, practising navigating texts in each of the four skills modules. By the end of this unit, students should be familiar with different academic text types and ways of approaching them to meet their needs. Before starting each module, ask students to read the module rationale, which introduces the key terms and aims of the module. A Glossary of the key terms in bold can be found on page 199.

1A Reading introduces and practises several key ideas in academic reading, including the genre, audience, and purpose of a text, and perspectives in texts. The structure of the module reflects the navigational process of reading: students encounter a reading list, a number of text extracts from different genres, and elements of a text such as a cover and contents page. The module concludes with an independent study task which both looks back at the work done in the module and looks ahead to consolidate this work.

1B Writing focuses on essay introductions. The module follows a process of pre-writing (evaluating writing ability), through reflection on the writing process, to a sequenced analysis of sample essay introductions, and culminating in a productive task in which students plan and write their own introductions. As introductions need to be concise and information-rich, there is a focus on complex noun phrases in order to express information concisely.

1C Listening introduces an authentic academic lecture. Using extracts from different parts of the lecture – beginning, middle, and end – students practise navigating the lecture. They identify the function of signposting language and learn to link it with the lecturer's main points. Students also use visuals to help them predict and access the lecturer's material.

1D Speaking covers discussions arising from material in the lecture (1C Listening). Students prepare for two discussions in different ways, first individually, then collaboratively. These processes enable students to evaluate their performance in the discussions, in particular the way they prepared for them. Academic discussions are typically based around both students' ideas and material in texts (reading texts and/or lectures), which is reflected in this module.

1E Vocabulary focuses on the ability to use vocabulary flexibly, switching easily between different word forms to achieve the best phrasing in a particular context. Using the key set of perspective vocabulary, students work on recognizing and using different word forms to improve their range of expression.

DISCUSSION

1 As the first Discussion task in the course, this gives students the opportunity to learn more about each other through a series of brief presentations. Groups can be of any size, though if time is short, smaller groups will be quicker. Allow a short preparation stage, but limit this to a few minutes – students should know the information or can simply say they haven't decided yet (e.g. what to study).

2 Keep the same groups for the rest of the discussion. You could start by writing *behaviour* on the board, and asking students which academic subjects particularly relate to it and how (e.g. *psychology* relates to rationales for cognitive behaviour and motivations; *economics* relates to how people respond to external factors such as the supply and price of goods). The discussion should illustrate that any discipline can relate to behaviour, though with some, e.g. zoology, it may be animal rather than human behaviour.

3 Ask students to select the three most important factors individually, which can then form the basis of the discussion. Encourage students to add further motivating factors and give examples. Stress that they should aim to reach agreement in the discussion.

4 Allow a fixed time for each student or group to present their ideas to the class. Encourage questions by asking some yourself first. *Why ...?* is usually a good starting question. Encourage students to offer reasons and evidence to support their ideas.

1A **Reading** Academic texts

As with all modules, start by going through the rationale (or asking students to read this beforehand to prepare for the module). Ask students to check key terms in bold in the Glossary on page 199, e.g. *Which term refers to a way of looking at something?* (Answer: perspective).

TASK 1 Understanding genre, audience, and purpose in texts

1 This task aims to familiarize students with the important concepts of genre, audience, and purpose (GAP). You can adopt either an inductive approach, where students do the task and work out the characteristics of GAP, or a deductive approach, where you present and explain these characteristics before setting up the task. Go through the completed example, then elicit the audience and purpose for the second item, university textbooks. Make sure that students understand that academic textbooks go beyond the 'objective' presentation of information into argument and stance (a person's subjective view of something). Students could work individually at first, before discussing their answers. Encourage students to reach agreement through discussion of the points.

Sample answers

Genre (What?)	Audience (For whom?)	Purpose (Why?)
1 subject-specific dictionary - *lists short definitions in alphabetical order for key concepts in a discipline (e.g. medicine)*	*students / staff of the subject*	*to define technical terms / explain key concepts*
2 university textbook - *information based around chapters with different themes relating to the discipline*	*students, academic tutors*	*to present and explain key information on an aspect of the topic; to argue for and against certain positions and theories*
3 abstract of a journal article - *a text of about 200 words at the beginning of an academic article*	*students, academics, researchers*	*to summarize a whole article in order to enable the reader to decide whether to read it or not*
4 journal article - *research-based, peer-reviewed (i.e. academics in the field critically review articles before publication) conventional texts (i.e. based around accepted structures and conventions)*	*academics, students studying at a higher level (e.g. Master's / research level)*	*to present the results of research; to present arguments; to give overviews of current thought on a specific topic*
5 newspaper article - *a text of up to about one page in length, often shorter*	*the general public*	*to inform and entertain through a mixture of facts and opinion*
6 encyclopaedia entry - *a concise text giving information on a factual topic related to the world or universe*	*anyone looking for information*	*to present key facts about a topic*
7 essay - *a text usually of 500+ words usually written by a student in response to a task or question*	*tutor, examiner*	*to demonstrate familiarity with and understanding of a subject*
8 review / critique - *a text of a few hundred words, in a journal, which assesses published work or a book, or more generally, in a newspaper or magazine, which assesses a book, exhibition, film, etc.*	*the general public or specialists interested in what is being reviewed*	*to offer (mainly subjective) evaluation*

9	scientific report – an extensive academic or professional text, usually conventionally structured	specialists in the field such as students, researchers, professors, professionals	to present a piece of ongoing or completed research, including its limitations and main findings
10	Master's dissertation – a text of 10-20,000 words usually written by a student to achieve a degree award, e.g. a Master's or Doctorate	a student's tutor and an external examiner, research students who consult it in a library	to present the results of research; to provide evidence that the student has reached the required level

2 This activity enables students to apply the material to their own situation. Monitor the discussions, and ask questions where appropriate.

Answers

2 Academic genres: subject-specific dictionary, university textbook, abstract of a journal article, journal article, scientific report, Master's dissertation. Student essays and reviews / critiques can be academic depending on how they are written and referenced.

Newspaper articles and encyclopaedia entries are not academic.

TASK 2 Understanding reading lists and references

1 This task aims to familiarize students with a reading list. Explain that lecturers and course leaders often give out reading lists to students at the beginning of a course, in order to guide their reading. Briefly elicit what information is given for each title (e.g. publisher and date of publication). Give a short time limit, e.g. 1 minute, for students to complete the matching activity.

Answers

a subject-specific dictionary   b journal article
c review   d university textbook

2 and 3 This activity aims to clarify the different parts of each publication reference. Mention that there are many variations in style: some referencing styles require the country as well as the place (city) of publication to be stated; some referencing styles ask for the author's full first name, not just their initial. Ask students to say how they arrived at their answers, especially the more difficult items such as volume and page numbers.

Sample answers

2	author surname(s)	Black, Gleeson
	author initial(s)	G.D., K
	edition	3e, 2e
	page numbers	351-366, 1447-1449
	place of publication	Oxford
	publisher	Oxford University Press
	title of article	What assumptions about human behaviour underlie asylum judgments?
	title of book	Oxford Dictionary of Economics, Health and Human Behaviour
	title of journal	International Journal of Refugee Law
	volume number	22, 38
	year of publication	2009, 2010

TASK 3 Identifying and comparing features of a genre

1 and 2 This task presents extracts from different genres so that students can compare typical features of each. Set a time limit for the first activity and do not answer any language questions at this point. There are clues to help students match the extracts with the texts in Task 2, such as the title which is given for Text 2. Allow a short time for discussion in pairs or groups, then conduct whole-class feedback. Possible information which helps to identify the genre includes: title, style, purpose of the text, how the content is presented, e.g. a definition (Text 3), or an explanation (Text 1).

Answers (3.1 and 3.3)

Text 1: Reference - d, Jones, K. & Creedy, D. (2008). Genre - university textbook. Key words - motivation, (human) behaviour, Maslow, needs.

Text 2: Reference - b, Herlihy, J., Gleeson, K., & Turner, S. (2010). Genre - abstract of a journal article. Key words - human behaviour, asylum, assumptions.

Text 3: Reference - a, Black, J., Hashimzade, N., & Myles, G. D. (2009). Genre - subject-specific dictionary entry. Key words - behavioural economics, decisions.

Text 4: Reference - c, Hothersall, S. J. (2008). Genre - review. Key words - interrelationships, macro / micro, group behaviour, community, individual.

3 Explain that a limited number of key words express the topic of a text , and that they are usually content words rather than general or academic words. Elicit key words from Text 1 with the whole class, asking students to justify their selected words. If students suggest non-key words, ask the class why they are not key words (they express an example or detail rather than main ideas).

Answer

The word *behaviour* links all four texts.

TASK 4 Identifying purpose in texts

1 This task enables students to understand types of purpose of academic texts. Ask students to work through the activity individually before comparing answers. Ask students to say which words are more associated with subjectivity (*evaluate, claim*).

> **Answers**
> 1 define 2 exemplify 3 evaluate 4 explain
> 5 outline 6 describe 7 claim 8 state

2 Explain that this activity examines the purpose of the four texts they have just read. Remind students that this investigation of purpose completes the 'genre, audience, purpose' idea introduced in Task 1.

> **Answers**
> Text 1: b Text 2: c Text 3: a Text 4: d

3 Present or elicit possible evaluative questions to ask, e.g. *Does the text achieve its purpose?*, *Is the information clearly presented?*, *Is there sufficient information to support the text purpose?* Ask students to refer back to the purposes given in 2 to ensure that these are met for each text, e.g. *Does Text 2 (the journal abstract) clearly express the conclusion of the journal article?*; *Does Text 4 (the review) offer sufficient evaluation?*

TASK 5 Identifying perspective in texts

1 This task introduces a core aspect of academic texts: perspective. Explain that perspective refers to a way of looking at something, and is associated with objectivity. An academic text normally has a number of perspectives (which could also be called *aspects* or *angles*) and the author selects these perspectives in order to organize and analyse their material.

> **Answers**
> 1 academic / theoretical 2 physiological 3 social
> 4 philosophical / theoretical

2 This activity makes students aware that perspectives may be explicitly stated, or more implicit, i.e. the reader has to work them out. The Academic Language box, below, introduces further examples.

> **Answers**
> 1 implicit 2 implicit 3 explicit 4 implicit

ACADEMIC LANGUAGE

Perspective Words and phrases expressing perspective

The Academic Language boxes in this course use examples from the texts in the module. Go through the explanation and examples and check the grammatical terms. Students should be familiar with terms such as *noun* and *adjective*, but may be less so with *adverbial*: this is a clause element rather than a word class (part of speech). Refer students to the Language Reference section on Expressing perspective, on page 204.

TASK 6 Understanding the language of perspective

1 This activity illustrates how even quite short text extracts can include a number of perspectives. Students can work individually or in groups. You could put students in groups of four and ask each student to search for perspectives in one of the four texts; they can then present their findings to the rest of the group. By the end of the activity students should realise how many perspectives can be covered, and how different examples of related language can be used to express these.

> **Sample answers**
> Language examples given in brackets.
> **Text 1**: behavioural (*when a behaviour occurs*); psychological (*the study of motivation*); physiological (*the fundamental physiological ones*); military (*danger, defence*); social (*social*); individual (*our own unique potential*)
> **Text 2**: political (*asylum, refugee, decision-makers, immigration*); legal (*legal definition, judgments, refugee, crucial area of law*); individual (*individuals*); economic (*refugee*); behavioural (*human behaviour*); geographical (*UK*); psychological (*psychological*); psychiatric (*psychiatric*); theoretical / academic (*empirical evidence*); interdisciplinary / academic (*cross-disciplinary research*)
> **Text 3**: individual (*individual behaviour*); behavioural (*behavioural*); economic (*economics, economic analysis, economic decisions*); psychological (*psychological insights*); theoretical / academic (*observation of anomalies, standard models*); human (*human*); social (*social*); cognitive (*cognitive*); emotional (*emotional biases*)
> **Text 4**: social / societal (*social milieu, social, the family within society, community, society, social life, social work*); individual (*individual, individual and society*); theoretical / academic (*theoretical frameworks*); psychological (*psychology*); behavioural (*group behaviour*); cultural (*the relevance of culture*); natural (*the natural environment*); religious (*the faith community*).

2 This activity should be very straightforward and quick. Extend it by substituting other perspectives using the same expressions, e.g. *from a medical perspective, ethically speaking*. Practise pronunciation through repetition and pairwork. Offer simple statements and ask students to supply appropriate perspective expressions to contextualize them, e.g. *This approach is likely to be expensive* becomes *As far as finance is concerned, this approach is likely to be expensive.*

3 This builds on the practice in 2. Students should create meaningful observations, as in the example. Encourage students to relate human behaviour to their own subject(s).

TASK 7 Using cover and Contents to navigate a textbook

1 This task builds on the elements of a text, and simulates navigating a whole textbook. Point out that naturally this navigational process is more realistic using an actual textbook; doing this is the aim of the final task of the module, Task 9. The questions are examples of the type of question which readers naturally ask when approaching a new book. Elicit further questions, e.g. *Will this textbook meet my needs?* Monitor and encourage students to provide fuller answers.

Answers

Audience: students of health science and related subjects (e.g. pharmacy, psychology); nurses

Topics: health & illness, behaviour, cognition and beliefs, social context, childhood, ageing, mind and body, pain, stress, promoting health, professional issues. Perspectives: medical, behavioural, cognitive, social, biological, psychological, professional

Limitations: specific conditions, causes of illness

2 By looking at the Contents page, students can quickly check some of their answers to 1. This activity also gives practice in searching through a Contents page for specific known items, and browsing a Contents page to see what is covered.

Sample answers

1 Audience profile: as 7.1, students of health science and related subjects (e.g. pharmacy, psychology); nurses

2 The headings provide a broad rationale for the more detailed coverage in the chapters within each part. They serve to organize the content and make it easier for readers to navigate the text and find what they want.

3 This activity practises searching through a Contents page for specific known items. Conduct brief feedback for students to say how they did the activity, e.g. finding key words, analysing concepts.

Answers

1 Glossary   2 References   3 Chapters 6–9 (Part 2)
4 Preface   5 Chapter 1

TASK 8 Navigating and analysing a textbook extract

1 Set a time limit for students to read Text 5. You could limit their reading to just the first paragraph, which should be sufficient to indicate which text it follows on from.

Answer

Text 1

2 Allow students sufficient time to finish reading Text 5. Check students have the correct answer to this activity, before dealing with closer meaning and language in following activities. Remind students of the importance of perspective: in this text the authors have selected three perspectives which are the basis of their analysis of motivation, and these perspectives are given their own headings in bold.

Answer

c

3 Explain that reading academic texts is not merely a passive process. Successful academic readers have a reason for reading, and have their own methods of recording what they read. This activity reflects this good practice. The example student annotations indicate the type of information being presented, to get students started.

Answers

1 Makes a claim / offers explanation: 5, 6, 8, 9
2 Introduces and defines a technical term: 4, 7, 10

4 Explain that by extracting and contextualizing these three technical terms, students have replicated one of the processes of academic reading. Emphasize that a key purpose in reading is to identify, extract, and note down key technical terms in order to extend knowledge. Point out that actually writing the definitions, rather than only identifying them, should help their understanding.

Answers

Instincts: patterns that are hard-wired or programmed to occur in response to internal or external events.

Primary drives: either deprivation or stimulation produce a need state in the organism, which in turn gives rise to a drive to satisfy that need.

Cognitive appraisals: judgements that people make about the situations they are in.

Each of these key terms relates directly to the appropriate sub-heading, i.e. instincts are genetic factors, primary drives are biological factors, and cognitive appraisals are cognitive factors.

TASK 9 Independent research – text navigation

1 Explain that there are a number of Checklists in the book: these are repeated together from page 209. The checklists are designed to be generic rather than specific, so they can be repeatedly used with different texts. This first checklist, A, invites students to reflect on their reading and how it has extended their knowledge and language.

2 and 3 Set up the independent study task and check that students know where to find whatever resources are available. Stress the importance of recording the publication details for each text they find, so that they can locate it again if required, and they can include this information if they use material from the text in their own work. Make time in the next class for students to present their findings, and make it clear that all students need to do this.

1B **Writing** Academic writing

TASK 1 Critical thinking – evaluating academic writing ability

1 and 2 Students evaluate their own ability in academic writing through a series of questions which are presented as 'can do' statements. Some students may be too self-critical or not critical enough. In such cases you could volunteer your own view of their ability, and ask them to rethink, but avoid too much intervention as the aim of the task is to self-assess. 2 encourages students to illustrate their ability through example; they can also include any teacher feedback on previous tasks.

TASK 2 Understanding the purpose of writing

1 and 2 This task presents four examples of student writing tasks. Check the written genre first, then ask students to complete the rest of the table. If students have not done the Reading module, briefly explain the concepts of genre, audience, and purpose. As with many student writing tasks such as essays, the audience is typically the tutor or examiner.

Sample answers

Task 1: Genre – summary. Audience – academics within the discipline. Purpose – to present the main points of a presentation to a wider audience. No. of words – 800 (max). Comments – Most of the audience did not see the presentation.

Task 2: Genre – timed / exam essay. Audience – the assessing tutor(s). Purpose – to establish whether the student can meet the required standard for a formal assessment. No, of words – not specified, but students must write two essays in two hours. Comments – Two discussion questions leading to timed essays.

Task 3: Genre – research essay. Audience – the assessing tutor(s). Purpose – to provide a 'vehicle' for students to demonstrate that they have carried out research in their discipline; to establish whether the student can present it in an appropriate argument. No. of words – 2,000. Comments – A longer essay with time for reading and research; students have to decide their own essay title.

Task 4: Genre – research report. Audience – internal tutors, external examiners, other scientific staff. Purpose – to summarize a research project (and possibly add interpretation and recommendations). No. of words – unknown, as specified in Writing Guidelines. Comments – Writing guidelines are given on the website, e.g. re presentation, structure, style, typical errors, etc. - these should be closely followed.

TASK 3 Reflecting on your own writing process

1 Start by eliciting how students write, and write stages in the process on the board. Students may come up with some of the points given in this activity, or have further points. This shows that different people may adopt different processes in writing. When checking the answers, it should also become apparent that some stages could be done in more than one writing phase.

Sample answers

write the body of the text	while-writing
generate ideas	pre-writing
read good examples of similar texts written by other students / academics	pre-writing
logically organize your ideas	pre-writing / while-writing
write the introduction to the text	while-writing
narrow down the topic to a clear focus	pre-writing
decide on which perspectives to include	pre-writing
critically read what you have written to check the logic, and rewrite as necessary	post-writing
work with other students and discuss your ideas	pre-writing / while-writing
delete any points that are not relevant	pre-writing / while-writing
search for sources - research the topic to find supporting evidence and examples	pre-writing
critically evaluate the chosen sources	pre-writing

2 Elicit further stages or ask students to note these down. Encourage personal responses, and accept unusual answers which may work for some students, e.g. *go for a walk to reflect on the order of the text*.

Sample answers

come up with a topic of particular interest	*pre-writing*
prepare a preliminary question to answer or a working title	*pre-writing*
work out your main argument	*pre-writing*
delete some of the more peripheral ideas and add any new ones	*pre-writing / while-writing*
reach a conclusion or an answer to your question	*pre-writing / while-writing*
prepare a list of useful sources and possible citations with references	*pre-writing*
plan the text at paragraph level, including topic sentences	*pre-writing / while- writing*
check the text for language accuracy, and rewrite as necessary	*post-writing*

3 This activity applies the stages to a specific writing task. The stages need to reflect the research which goes in to the text. Students should see that longer written tasks like this are likely to have repeated stages in the process.

Sample answers
Most likely to be repeated:
- work with other students and discuss your ideas
- critically evaluate the chosen sources
- critically read what you have written to check the logic, and rewrite as necessary
- check the text for language accuracy, and rewrite as necessary

4 The final activity in the task personalizes the process, allowing students to describe and explain their writing process to others. Conduct a feedback stage and write any additional stages on the board. Encourage students to note these down and try them out. Give a strict time limit of 1 minute in order to concentrate their thoughts and productivity. Students can then exchange and comment on each other's processes.

TASK 4 Identifying features in an introduction

1 This task elicits what students may already know in terms of the features an introduction typically contains. If possible, bring in some examples of introductions – from previous student essays or other sources.

Sample answers
Essential: b, c, g, h
Optional: a, d, e, f, i (conclusion is stated in deductive style, not in inductive style)

2 Ask students to read the four thesis statements carefully, and do the activity. Then ask which thesis statements follow a more objective, detached style (2 and 3), and which are more subjective (1 and 4).

Answers
g and h (and i, optional)

TASK 5 Analysing an introduction

1 This task presents the first of three sample introductions to student essays. Go through the essay title and elicit the main points which students should include when answering: a presentation of motivating factors in apparently selfless human behaviour; a justification of why these are important; exemplification and evidence as support for the argument.

Answer
Sentence 8: *This essay aims to examine altruistic behaviour from an evolutionary perspective, leading to three possible motivating factors, which are then evaluated.*

2 Students can work either individually or collaboratively. Students need to work out the function of each sentence in this activity. If they are having difficulty, do one or more sentences as a whole-class activity. Optionally, ask students to evaluate the introduction in anticipation for Task 7. Note down any evaluative questions they ask, to refer to in Task 7.

Answers
1 a 2 b 3 d 4 b 5 e 6 e 7 c 8 g and h
Not included: f, i

3 This activity requires students to work out the purpose of the introduction as a whole. It is expressed from the viewpoint of the reader, so the term 'audience' is used. Allow students time to work alone first before eliciting and negotiating the final class sentence. Keep a record of it so that it can be modified later in the class or course.

Sample answer
By the end of the introduction the audience of the text should *be clear about the topic, focus, and aims of the text, the reason for writing it, and have an idea about how the text is organized.*

ACADEMIC LANGUAGE

Noun phrases (1) Expressing information concisely using noun phrases

Start by eliciting what students know about noun phrases. Explain that these are where most information is conveyed in academic texts. They tend to be quite dense and complex. Go through the material in the box, and refer students to the corresponding Language Reference section on page 206. The key point is that a large amount of information can be expressed in a noun phrase. There are further Academic Language boxes on noun phrases later in the course.

TASK 6 Using noun phrases

1 Go through the example, and elicit the key changes. First, students need to identify the head noun. Often a verb from a longer sentence or clause is used as the head, as in this example, *assess → assessment*. Stress that not all the elements in the phrase need to be changed, e.g. the phrase *human behaviour* is best kept the same.

Sample answers

1 predictable individual <u>behaviour</u> in a variety of global contexts ...
2 recent psychological <u>research</u> into altruistic behaviour ...
3 individual psychological and financial <u>benefits</u> ...
4 further <u>studies</u> into human behaviour during stress ...
5 people's <u>actions</u> that are motivated by self-gain ...
6 employee's / employee behavioural <u>changes</u> related to workplace tensions ...

2 Explain that the noun phrases created can function in different ways in a sentence, typically as Subject or Object. Students should notice that the example uses the same noun phrase as the example in 1, showing how a sentence can be reduced to a single noun phrase, which in turn can be used as the subject (or object) in a new sentence which contains further information.

Sample answers

1 These factors led to predictable individual <u>behaviour</u> in a variety of global contexts.
2 Recent psychological <u>research</u> into altruistic behaviour suggests that while people act selflessly they do have an expectation of receiving something back in return.
3 Acting selflessly can bring individual psychological and financial <u>benefits</u>.
4 Further <u>studies</u> into human behaviour during stress are needed.
5 In order to determine the limitations of altruistic behaviour, we observed people's <u>actions</u> that are motivated by self-gain.
6 We found that the main cause of lower productivity were employee's behavioural <u>changes</u> related to workplace tensions.

3 This activity extends 2 into students' disciplines. Optionally, put students from similar disciplines into groups to write sentences collaboratively. As a checking activity, ask students to present their sentences to other students for critical feedback on language and content.

TASK 7 Evaluating essay introductions

1 and 2 Go over Checklist B, which is repeated alongside the other Checklists on page 209. Explain that they should evaluate each introduction A–C in turn in relation to the given essay title and plan. Encourage students to make notes while they evaluate; suggest that they can do this by using a simple grid with the criteria in six rows and the essay introductions in three columns. Monitor the activity and once they have all selected their most effective introduction, ask them to compare.

Answer

- Introduction A is the most effective introduction – relevant to essay question and logically organized, but quite long.
- Introduction B opens with two eye-catching rhetorical questions which are not always appropriate for an academic text, and no rationale is given.
- Introduction C contains some irrelevant content and the ideas do not always flow logically from one to the next.
- Neither B nor C define the key term *altruistic*, nor do either of their thesis statements indicate the organization of the essay.

3 In groups or individually, students suggest specific improvements for one of the two introductions from 2. Improvements should arise from the criteria in Checklist B, e.g. *x* is not relevant to the essay title, so it should be cut. Conduct whole-class feedback, inviting critical analysis of the suggested improvements.

Sample answers

Introduction B could be improved by: more focus – generalized comments are related to essay question but do not lead to an answer; style more academic - converting rhetorical questions to statements, e.g. *Possible reasons why altruism is important are* ...; provide rationale; add definition of key term *altruism*; add comment on citations - provide evidence (citations), then say why relevant; thesis statement should add something new and specific to that essay.

Introduction C could be improved by: improving flow by making clearer connections between ideas in sentences, e.g. by introducing new topics clearly ; simple linking language would help achieve this, e.g. *A further factor is* ...; add rationale saying why question is important / interesting; improve relevance by focusing on question set, not a different (though related) question.

TASK 8 Planning, writing, and evaluating an introduction

1–4 The title can be answered from general knowledge and ideas rather than specific research, so the focus is on planning the essay and writing the introduction. An important part of the writing process is self-evaluation (using Checklist B) and peer evaluation. Emphasize that students have much to learn from each other and this process involves giving and receiving feedback in a secure environment.

TASK 9 Independent research – introduction techniques

1–3 This task aims to promote independence and personalization through a guided search. Use library services or online resources such as Google Scholar. Ask students to write down introduction features to use themselves and their action plan, then evaluate.

1C Listening Lectures (1)

TASK 1 Predicting the content of a lecture

1 and 2 Explain that this task reflects the reality of listening to a lecture – normally students have some ideas or expectations about the content before listening. The first activity invites students to present and evaluate their experiences of lectures, which may vary significantly. The lecture title is given in 2; accept all predictions as none can be wrong.

TASK 2 Navigating a lecture: understanding the introduction

1 and 2 ▶1.1 This task brings in typical features of a lecture, including basic details of the lecture and lecturer, plus rationale and aims. In many cases, visual information can be presented more quickly, and is appropriate for lecture details (title, etc.) and denser material such as a bibliography.

> **Answers**
> 1 The five features are best presented both orally and visually.
> 2 1 Lecture title and topic: O/V   2 Lecturer biodata: O/V
>   3 Limitations: O   4 Rationale and aims of the lecture: O/V   5 Interaction with audience: O/V

3 This activity can be done while watching for a second time. Explain that students can re-use lecture Checklist C in this course / in their studies.

> **Answers**
> Lecture title: Making the most of higher education in English-speaking countries
> Lecturer: Dr Kathleen Quinlan
> Comments: American, with experience in several English-speaking countries
> Discipline: Education
> Topic / main focus: Education / international students studying for degrees in English
> Rationale & aims: Exploring assumptions in such contexts, and answering the questions *What is university learning? How can you make the most of that educational experience? What do you want to get out of a university education?*
> Limitations: Restricted to English-speaking countries; does not cover differences between these
> Key terms & definitions: None
> Supporting information: Slides

TASK 3 Using navigational language to aid listening

1 and 2 This task introduces slides as visual aids to understanding content. Some lecturers put up their slides on the university LMS (Learning Management System) for students to access, so it is a useful skill to link these visuals with how the lecturer uses them.

> **Sample answers**
> 1 1 Slide 1 uses a visual image as a metaphor – this can help understand abstract concepts.
>   2 Slide 2 shows a pile of rocks representing learning as an increase in knowledge (quantitative), and some close-up details of trees to illustrate looking at the same thing in different ways (qualitative).
> 2 1 a   2 b

ACADEMIC LANGUAGE

Signposting (1) Guiding the audience

Students have already listened to signposting language used by the lecturer. This Academic Language box explains the main reasons for using such language and presents several examples from the lecture in this unit. The lecturer style varies, with a mixture of personal and inclusive style (*I, we*) and more 'detached' style (*This lecture*).

TASK 4 Navigating a lecture

1 and 2 This task extends the range of signposting language, and links this with the function and main point for each sentence. In 1, students can see that such language is interactive and inclusive (*we, your, let's*), and in 2, they should be able to match this with the given functions. Allow students to work together if necessary.

> **Answers**
> 1 g First we need to …   2 a So your first reflection question is …   3 d Now let's take a look at …   4 b On the right hand side, you'll see …   5 f … he came up with five …   6 e So I could give you an example of …   7 c Another way of looking at things is …

3 and 4 ▶1.2 These activities focus on the delivery and the main points. Invite students to comment on the lecturer's delivery and how this contributes to their understanding: explain that students can learn from all presenters and lecturers in order to inform their own presentations. Check students' notes on the lecturer's main points before whole-class checking. Stress the importance of note-taking: it helps understanding while listening, and serves as a record of the lecturer's material.

> **Sample answers**
> 3 1 Lecturer's accent and pronunciation - clear, American accent
>   2 Type of delivery - some use of notes, not scripted in great detail, fairly fast delivery

3 Use of visuals - PowerPoint slides used; these add useful detail

4 Lecturer's questions and interaction with the audience - audience are given tasks to do while listening; limited audience interaction

5 Other - some personal anecdotes, but these are relevant to the points she is making rather than digressions

4 1 A concept, e.g. *transportation* or *learning*, means different things to different people.

2 Students reflect on how they know they've learnt something.

3 Research shows you can learn in two different ways: quantitative and qualitative.

4 By looking at things from a different perspective you can change the way you understand things.

5 1 quantitative - accumulated knowledge; 2 quantitative - memorizing; 3 quantitative - acquiring facts to apply; 4 qualitative - connecting new knowledge to the world around you; 5 qualitative - interpreting and understanding reality in a different way

6 Giving an illustration of a quantitative outlook (learning vocabulary)

7 Giving an illustration of a qualitative outlook; showing the change from a quantitative to a qualitative outlook

5 ▶1.3 The final lecture extract briefly concludes the lecture, which gives students the opportunity to look back over the parts of the lecture they have seen and evaluate these. Where students say they have difficulties, encourage them to use new strategies to help overcome these. Note-taking is an excellent area of improvement for most students.

Sample answers

Kathleen Quinlan sums up her lecture briefly but effectively. She:
- signals using a sentence stem (*So that brings me to the end of the talk.*)
- reviews the main questions covered
- rounds off by referring back to an earlier metaphor (*So you've started down an important path, ... whatever those might be around the bend.*)
- reminds students of the relevance of the lecture to the real world.

TASK 5 Note-taking (1) - evaluating different techniques

1 The final task moves the focus of evaluation from the lecture itself to note-taking. Often, students do not take sufficient notes. Point out that although listening can be challenging, taking notes while listening can help focus on the main points in the listening text. Stress that the only way to achieve proficiency in listening and note-taking is through practice.

1D Speaking Student discussions

TASK 1 Evaluating your discussion and seminar skills

1 and 2 This module introduces student discussions, using material based on the lecture. The first task acknowledges that people can learn in different ways, and asks students to evaluate different aspects of their discussion skills relating to such things as speaking style and interaction. The issue of culture and stereotypes may emerge, e.g. the perception that people from some cultures are better listeners / speakers than those from others. This task may show that the reality is more complex.

ACADEMIC LANGUAGE

Interaction (1) Checking and confirming

As with other Listening and Speaking Academic Language boxes, this one looks at functional / notional language. The Listening module (1C) linked signposting language with function and meaning; similarly, these examples link interactive language with function and meaning. Extend the language by eliciting further examples using the function word in the expression, e.g. *explain → Could you explain that, please?*

TASK 2 Individually preparing and discussing

1 and 2 Explain that the next two tasks contrast two approaches to preparing for a discussion. Monitor and make sure all students write notes on their responses. Remind students that the lecturer in 1C used examples to illustrate and support her points, and that students should do the same. Stress that they should also respond directly to the lecturer's slides. In the group discussion phase, check that students understand the guidelines, and set a time limit for the discussion. The student observer can choose to either participate or remain silent, and in either case should use the guidelines as points to evaluate the performance of the group. Allow time after the discussion for the student observer to offer whole-group feedback. Monitor during the discussion and give feedback if appropriate, including to individuals where necessary, e.g. on the need to contribute fully.

TASK 3 Collaboratively preparing and discussing

1 and 2 The method of preparation in this task contrasts with that in Task 2. Encourage a supportive atmosphere, and during the discussion phrase make sure students give their own responses to the lecturer's advice. Stress that they do not have to agree, and should feel able to question their lecturers. Ask students to select a different observer, following a similar procedure to the previous task.

TASK 4 Critical thinking – evaluating discussion skills

1–3 The final task allows students to reflect on the different approaches to conducting a discussion. Make sure students feel comfortable evaluating their own performance and the collaborative preparation process.

1E **Vocabulary** Flexibility

TASK 1 Recognizing word forms and how they are used

1 This activity uses examples from the unit to highlight the importance of choosing the correct word form for a particular context. Students should look at the sentences individually first, without checking in a dictionary, and make guesses where they are not certain.

Answers
1 credibility; reliance 2 security; common
3 analysis; behaviour

2 As students compare their answers in pairs and check in their dictionaries, they can briefly revise and check the terminology used to describe different word forms and also focus on dictionary skills. Make sure that students know how and where to find the different forms of a word; either as separate entries, or as 'run-ons' at the end of another entry. Ask them which clues in the sentence helped them to identify the correct word class.

Answers
1 credible - adjective; credibility - noun; rely - verb; reliant - adjective; reliance - noun
2 secure - adjective or verb; security - noun; commonly - adverb; common - adjective
3 analyse - verb; analysis - noun; behave - verb; behaviour - noun

3 Students should not try to paraphrase the complete sentences here, but just focus at phrase level. In some cases, it may be awkward to paraphrase exactly the same idea using the alternative forms, so they could just show how the word might be used in a similar context. During feedback, ask why the writers chose the phrasing and words forms they did, i.e. because in most cases it is the most concise way to express the idea.

Sample answers
1 which involves **relying on** assumptions ... (*involving* + *relying* on would sound awkward); which is **reliant on** assumptions ...
2 people who put themselves in a less **secure** position for ...; occur too **commonly** to ignore
3 an approach to **analysing** economic situations; insights into the way individuals **behave** to ...

TASK 2 Using different word forms to express perspective

1 This task builds on the key vocabulary set introduced in module 1A (page 010) for describing perspective. Students complete as much of the table as they can individually, then work in pairs or small groups to compare and fill any gaps. Briefly check understanding during feedback, such as the difference between *finance* (about the practical process of managing money) and *economics* (looking at the wider economy). Ask students to suggest other key perspective adjectives relating to their own discipline area.

Answers

	Noun	Adjective	Adverb
1	finance	financial	financially
2	the economy / economics	*economic / economical*	*economically*
3	*history*	historical	*historically*
4	*geography*	geographical	*geographically*
5	science	*scientific*	*scientifically*
6	society	*social*	*socially*
7	*psychology*	*psychological*	psychologically
8	*medicine*	medical	*medically*
9	the law	*legal*	*legally*
10	*technology*	technological	*technologically*
11	language	*linguistic*	*linguistically*
12	culture	*cultural*	culturally
13	*behaviour*	behavioural	*behaviourally*
14	*theory*	theoretical	*theoretically*

2 This activity recaps some of the different phrases commonly used to express perspective (see Task 6, page 011) and provides more practice in how different words forms are used in context.

Answers
2 social 3 financial 4 the law

3 Ask students to pick out the perspective phrases used in 2 (*... speaking; the ... context; from a ... perspective; As far as ... is concerned; in ... terms*) and direct them back to the perspective phrases in 1A (Task 6 page 011). Encourage them to try out a variety of different ways to rephrase the examples and ask which ones work better than others. Note that many of these phrases can also appear in different positions in the sentence.

Sample answers
1 In a historical context; From a historical perspective; In historical terms
2 a child's immediate environment, socially speaking, is family and home
3 Financially speaking; In terms of finance; In financial terms;
4 Legally (speaking); From a legal perspective; In legal terms

UNIT 2 **Sustainability**

ACADEMIC FOCUS: DISCURSIVE TEXTS – PRESENTING AN ARGUMENT

INTRODUCTION

Unit 2 aims to develop students' ability to identify and understand the presentation of an argument within the theme of Sustainability. This theme runs through all the modules, with topics including energy, transport, and urban planning providing a range of different perspectives, stances, and arguments for students to explore. Academic discourse is not simply about presenting objective 'facts', but also involves adopting a stance and presenting an argument to persuade others of your position. The goal of the unit is for students to be able to recognize a writer's stance, the arguments and supporting evidence they put forward, and to construct an argument of their own based on ideas drawn from sources.

2A Reading develops students' abilities to identify main points in a text, ignoring details such as examples and references at first reading. This is an important skill when faced with a lot of reading as part of an academic course, and with long, potentially daunting texts. Students read a fairly long discursive text, in which the main points of the writer's argument have been highlighted. They then look again at the text to identify which arguments reflect the writer's own stance and which present alternative perspectives. Finally, they identify the type of supporting evidence given, thus giving them a full picture of how an argumentative text might be structured.

2B Writing focuses on developing and expressing an argument in the main body of discursive essay, thereby building on the work on introductions in module 1B, The module presents three short OUP texts to provide input, leading to a writing task in which students produce a main body paragraph setting out an argument, supported by evidence in the form of citations. The module introduces the use of citation and referencing conventions in writing, a key skill for students in EAP that is developed throughout the book.

2C Listening aims to encourage students to critically evaluate lecture content rather than simply noting down and memorizing lists of points, another crucial skill that is developed throughout the book. Students watch four extracts from the second authentic lecture of the course on the topic of sustainable cities. During the first two extracts from the introduction, students establish the topic of the lecture, by focusing on key terms and signposting language. The second two extracts develop specific arguments which students then discuss and evaluate.

2D Speaking again encourages students to develop an argument, this time as part of a discussion activity, following on from the topic of sustainable cities in the listening module, and using new input from reading sources. The aim of the module is for students to put forward a logical argument, supported by evidence as part of a seminar discussion. Discussion techniques, such as interrupting where necessary and linking to others' contributions help students to develop their ability to participate in an academic discussion.

2E Vocabulary focuses on accuracy and avoiding potential ambiguity caused by minor language errors. It concentrates especially on the prepositions typically used after key academic nouns, adjectives, and verbs.

DISCUSSION

1 This task introduces the topic of Sustainability, encouraging students to think about how the concept comes into many aspects of modern life and academic study. Write the words *sustainable* and *unsustainable* on the board. Ask students to work in small groups to note down characteristics relating to these words. You could suggest an example to get them started. Collect feedback, with explanations if necessary, and write the suggestions on the board.

Sample answers
Avoiding / creating waste; conserving / using up limited resources; efficient / inefficient (use of resources); limiting / causing environmental damage; recycling / consumerism; long-term / short-term solutions

2 Using the suggestions in 1, agree a definition of *sustainability* as a class. Then in their groups again, students discuss the topics. Ask students to take turns keeping brief notes of their discussions so they can report back later.

Suggested definition
Sustainability = the use of natural resources in a way that does not harm the environment and can be continued in the long term

3 The final task brings in the ideas of perspective and stance; how different people may view the same topic from different perspectives and how this may affect their stance. Ask each group to report two contrasting views of <u>one</u> of the topics they discussed in 2. If you have time, this could lead to a class discussion about why issues of sustainability might provoke such contrasting views. Encourage students to give specific examples to illustrate their points, if possible from their own experience, e.g. *In China, we have a big problem with pollution from traffic and from industry. We know we have to control this, but at the same time, we want to enjoy all the benefits that economic development brings.*

2A Reading Argumentative texts

TASK 1 Establishing a purpose for reading

1 This activity introduces the concept of selective reading; prioritizing what is most relevant to read and only reading for the level of detail necessary for your purpose. Students new to EAP may be used to reading texts in the language classroom word by word from start to finish. Whilst they may naturally use selective reading techniques when reading in their native language, they may need to be encouraged to transfer this to English texts. Students look at the flow chart and questions individually or in pairs before discussing the issues that arise as a whole class.

Sample answers
1 The main topic can be found in the title or subheadings and the introduction (or abstract if there is one).
2 Selective reading is very important when students have a lot to read in a limited time.

2 This activity follows on from using book covers and titles to navigate texts (in module 1A) and focuses on predicting content from first impressions – an important skill for students when researching a topic and selecting what to read. Make sure at this stage that all students understand what *wind energy* is.

Sample answer
How the wind energy industry has developed in past years and something surprising or unusual about this development (students can suggest what this might be).

3 This is a discussion activity which encourages students to activate existing knowledge and vocabulary about the topic, so they can link the new ideas in the text to what they already know.

TASK 2 Understanding the topic of a text

1 This task helps students establish the basic topic of the text. Point out the glossary explaining the unusual adjective *splashy* if students don't notice it. Note: the text describes wind power as 'the splashiest success story', i.e. it has been talked about a lot in the media, but it does not say that the development of the industry is 'successful.'

Sample answers
1 a
2 **Energy potential** is the amount of energy that could *possibly* be generated by wind power in a particular area.
Installed capacity is the amount of energy that is *actually* being produced using wind power in an area.

2 This is a relatively long reading text, so this task aims to help students break it down in a more manageable way. It highlights the typical organization of a text within paragraphs, i.e. **topic sentence** + explanation of main point(s) + details (examples and evidence)

Answers
1 b   2 c   3 a

3 In doing this task, refer students back to the flow chart in Task 1. Ask when you might want to read a text, focusing only on the topic and the main points and not the details (i.e. to decide whether it is relevant to your studies).

Answers
a **bold**
b **bold** & normal
c grey

TASK 3 Identifying the main points and stages in a text

1 This task uses the structure of the text established in Task 2 to identify the specific main points and stages in the writer's argument. Emphasize to students that they do not need to read all the grey details in the text in order to complete the table.

Sample answers

Para	Stage in the argument	Main point
1	Describes the background and identifies an issue / question.	The development of the wind energy industry worldwide is uneven. Why?
2	Puts forward one perspective on the situation.	*Technological innovations* mainly influence the growth of the wind energy industry.
3	Puts forward *another / an alternative perspective* on the situation.	*Economic issues* mainly influence the growth of the wind energy industry.
4	Critiques these two perspectives.	These views *cannot fully explain* why the development of wind energy is so uneven in different parts of the world.
5	Puts forward *the writer's stance / perspective.*	*The main influence on the development of the wind industry has been social / environmental movements.*

2 This short task further emphasizes the idea that students do not need to understand (and look up) every word in a text in order to understand the main points.

Answers

Paragraph 2: Words to do with mechanics / engineering / technology

Paragraph 3: Words to do with business / economics

TASK 4 Recognizing the writer's stance

1–3 Two key concepts, **perspective** and **stance** are easily confused, especially as the word *perspective* is commonly used with a range of meanings (as in this text). In terms of academic writing, perspective is mainly objective and refers to a way of viewing a topic. In this text, you can view the development of the wind energy industry from a *technological perspective* (= how the development of technology has affected it), *a market / economic perspective* (= how economic factors have affected its development) and *a political / social perspective* (= how social / political / environmental movements affect it). **Stance** is a more subjective concept and refers to the writer's belief, opinion, or judgement about a topic, or their main argument. In this case, the writer's stance is to do with which of these factors (or perspectives) has had the most significant effect on the development of the wind energy industry. Although he mentions arguments put forward by others (with different stances), he believes, based on evidence, that the effect of social / environmental movements has been more significant than the other factors, and this is what he will go on to argue for in the text that follows.

Answers

1 b

2 Paragraph 5, last sentence: This book argues that the global development of the wind energy industry cannot be understood without examining the interactions of environmental activists and organizations with governments, energy sector actors, various institutions, and the general public over the last four decades.

3 Writers often establish other common arguments (alternative stances) in order to critique them before putting forward their own stance.

TASK 5 Recognizing citations in a text

1 This task draws students' attention to the use of citations in the text, in preparation for more detailed work on citations and referencing conventions in module 5B. Students should be able to identify which of these people and groups refer to a specific publication and which to a general group, without looking back at the text.

Answers

Specific published text (S): CNN, 2001; Johnson and Jacubsson, 2000; Paul Gipe; Redlinger, Anderson, and Morthorst, 2002; the International Energy Agency; Heymann, 1998; Lauber, 2005.

General group (G): wind power advocates, energy professionals.

2 As students have already analysed the structure of the text, ask them to identify which paragraphs match these three topics, then simply scan for the references.

Answers

1 CNN, 2001

2 Heymann 1998, Johnson and Jacubsson 2000, wind power advocates, Paul Gipe

3 Redlinger, Anderson, and Morthorst 2002, Lauber 2005, energy professionals, the International Energy Agency

3 This activity highlights a style of citation that will be picked up again in the writing module. Students new to academic texts may find these long lists of references in brackets rather confusing and distracting, so this task is aimed at demystifying them and explaining their purpose.

Sample answer

The references provide examples of studies which support the point made in grey.

Noun phrases (2) Using nouns to present alternative arguments

This box illustrates some of the variety of ways that different sides in an argument can be presented in a discursive text. After students have read through the examples, ask them how these sentence openings might be used together with references, like those highlighted in Task 5. Get them to look back at the text if necessary to find these openings, which are often followed by a more specific reference (or references) at the end of the sentence or in a following sentence. With students new to EAP, emphasize the importance of using these two together, i.e. plural nouns to refer to general groups + specific references to provide evidence / support.

TASK 6 Presenting alternative arguments

1 and 2 Much of this vocabulary should be familiar to students; these tasks encourage them to think about the meaning (by identifying near synonyms in 1) and to use the words creatively and flexibly to generate different nouns phrases. These activities could be done individually, in pairs, or as a whole class on the board. Encourage students to experiment with different patterns and discuss which ones work and which sound awkward, rather than focusing on a small set of 'correct' answers. Refer students back to the Academic Language box, especially the use of plural (rather than singular) nouns in this context to refer to a group (*supporters, critics, opponents*, etc.).

Sample answers

1   activist / advocate; critic / opponent; expert / professional; movement / supporter; research / studies

2   opponents of air travel; alternative energy experts; research into climate change; the environmental movement; advocates of public transport; population trends; supporters of recycling; waste experts (many other combinations possible)

3 Students may not be able to use the exact noun phrases they created in 2 here; they may need to adapt them to fit the contexts. Encourage them to use a variety of reporting verbs.

Sample answers

1   Supporters of recycling point out that recycling campaigns are …

2   Research into public transport usage has found that areas with restrictions …

3   Waste experts argue that many consumer goods …

4   Recent research into climate change suggests that global weather patterns …

5   Opponents of air travel maintain that greenhouse gas emissions …

TASK 7 Identifying supporting evidence in a text

1 Students now turn to look at the role of the grey sections of the text in giving supporting evidence.

Sample answers

a   Paragraph 1: Recent studies show the United Kingdom has the strongest, most dependable, and most convenient onshore winds, as well as the highest offshore wind potential (CNN, 2001). However, the United Kingdom ranked sixth in Europe in installed wind power capacity at the beginning of 2008 …

b   Paragraph 2: Wind turbines now provide commercial bulk power in California, Hawaii, … (Gipe, 1995)

c   Paragraph 3: A 2008 report of the International Energy Agency exemplifies this approach: The group of countries with the highest effectiveness … used feed-in tariffs (FITs) to encourage wind power deployment.

2 This task highlights different types of support that can be used in a text; statistics, research findings and specific examples, or more general arguments. Students also need to distinguish between support from other sources and the writer's own evidence. Point out that not all of these types of support are used in this text.

Answers

a   statistics from CNN and AWEA in grey text in paragraph 1; studies mentioned followed by references, in paragraphs 2 and 3; statistics from the IEA in paragraph 3

b   none

c   Paul Gipe in paragraph 2; the IEA in paragraph 3

d   throughout, but especially paragraphs 4 and 5

3 This discussion activity aims to focus on the role of evidence in a longer text. Points to draw out in feedback might include:
- Evidence from sources makes an argument stronger and more credible
- Evidence from published academic sources is typically more convincing and credible than general arguments from non-specific sources (e.g. *opponents argue* … with no follow-up reference) or non-academic sources (e.g. CNN = news media)
- Statistics / research findings may be given more weight in some disciplines (e.g. sciences), but expert academic argument is also a relevant source of support
- Reading and understanding detailed evidence (the grey text) isn't necessary to understand the basic points, but may help to understand in more depth
- In-text references can be followed up to learn more about specific points of interest in a text. An important tool in research is following chains of references from one source to another, especially from a secondary source to a primary source.

2B **Writing** Discursive essays

TASK 1 Presenting an argument at paragraph level

1 and 2 This task gives students two examples of main body paragraphs from discursive texts which demonstrate how an academic argument can be set out with a main point, supporting points, and evidence (as they also saw in the text in module 2A). The two texts are from different sources and demonstrate two quite different academic styles. It is important to emphasize that both are legitimate styles and neither is better than the other.

Sample answers

1 **Text 1**
The main point: congestion charging schemes can be successful in reducing traffic congestion.

Supporting points: as well as reducing city centre traffic, they increase public transport use; existing schemes (London) could be successfully adopted elsewhere (New York).

Evidence: figures from the London congestion tax system (from Transport for London, 2004); projections about how a similar scheme could affect traffic in New York (from Zupan & Perrotta, 2003).

Text 2
The main point: changing consumer behaviour is an important strategy for curbing greenhouse gas emissions & oil use.

Supporting points: America is important in influencing other countries on this issue; consumers need to be educated and motivated to change their behaviour for 'the greater public good'.

Evidence: quotation from politician John McCain - a non-academic source with no specific reference.

Note: although it is a non-academic source, the quote from John McCain supports the argument and provides evidence about public attitudes on this topic, so it is a legitimate source to quote in the introduction.

2 Topic: both texts are about strategies for reducing road traffic / congestion / pollution

Perspectives & stances: Text 1 takes a fairly narrow, practical perspective, looking at the effectiveness of congestion charge schemes - the stance is not strongly expressed, but the text implies the authors' approval for this approach. Text 2 takes a wider social / political perspective and takes a clear stance that favours changing people's attitudes and behaviour.

Source: Text 1 is from a journal article; specialist audience (researchers); likely to contain specific details and analysis in order to make detailed comparisons of different policies. Text 2 is from an academic book; audience of academics and students interested in the problem from a range of disciplines; its purpose is to propose solutions and persuade.

Use of citation: Text 2 includes specific references - to a primary data source (Transport for London) and another academic study (Zupan & Perrotta). Text 1 only uses a quotation from a politician (John McCain) to demonstrate that this is an approach with mainstream political support.

TASK 2 Critical thinking - generating and organizing ideas

1 Ask what students notice in the essay title about the source of the quotation (the same as Text 2), its style (discursive, persuasive, emotive), and its stance (it suggests there is a problem that urgently needs to be addressed, but doesn't offer a solution here). In discussing the link between the essay title and the texts, point out that Sperling & Gordon take a macro view of the issue, while Timilsina & Dulal tackle it at a more micro level. Also look at the actual essay task (*Discuss the effectiveness of …*) and elicit which solutions the two texts mention.

2 Students here focus on translating specific points from reading texts into arguments they might use in an essay. This involves summarizing and paraphrasing the key ideas already discussed in Task 1 and Task 2.1 above, so they should try to complete the sentences without looking back at the original texts if possible.

Sample answers

Text 1: One strategy for reducing *car usage and its effects that has already proved effective is to introduce congestion charging schemes which discourage people from driving into city centres* (Timilsina & Dulal, 2011).

Text 2: Strategies to reduce our dependence on fossil fuels for transport will only be effective if *there is a shift in the attitudes and behaviour of consumers, that is ordinary road users* (Sperling & Gordon, 2009).

3 and 4 In these tasks, encourage students to use specific examples from their own experience, e.g. schemes tried in their own countries. Set a time limit for each stage - brainstorming, then organizing by perspective. Students don't need to find something for every prompt, but should generate a variety of ideas.

5 This task asks students to consider possible stances. Emphasize that there is not a simple answer here; *yes, there are effective solutions* or *no, matters will only get worse*. Their stance is more likely to involve: *yes, … but; yes, … if; no, … unless*. Stance is often influenced by which perspective seems the most important, e.g. the economic, political, social, etc. Encourage groups to write down more than one possible stance, even if they don't agree with them all.

6 This is a reflective task to allow students to think about their own reaction to the topic and to consider how they might go about answering the question, based on the input and ideas generated so far. These are still initial ideas and students should not attempt to draw up a detailed essay plan at this stage. You may choose not to ask for feedback on this task, just to give students time to think and process the ideas for themselves.

TASK 3 Analysing and evaluating a main body paragraph

1 This follows on from the features of an introduction looked at in module 1B. As before, main body paragraphs will vary a lot, so the sample answers are a guide only.

> **Sample answers**
>
> Essential: a, e (if necessary & not defined before), f, h
>
> Optional: c, d, g (but expected in most essays), i (but usual), j
>
> Not relevant: b (comes in the introduction)

2 and 3 This paragraph is intended as a generally good model paragraph, demonstrating some of the features in 1. One point of discussion is whether it is necessary to define and explain the terms *electric cars* and *hybrids*, as the student does here. Students often include lots of definitions as they are relatively simple and take up space, when the terms could be seen as common knowledge to the average educated reader, and certainly to a subject specialist. Emphasize the balance needed between defining technical terms, but assuming general knowledge.

> **Sample answers**
>
> 2 • technological (solutions) perspective
> • a, c / d, e, f, g, h, j
> • the writer is wary about the issues surrounding these technologies
> • a discussion of problems and issues with green vehicles (e.g. cost, infrastructure, continued congestion)
>
> 3 1 Yes, the main argument is clear in the opening sentence: progress in vehicle technology to solve environmental problems.
> 2 Each point flows fairly logically into the next:
> Main point: huge progress has undoubtedly been made in vehicle technology.
> • manufacturers are making more efficient cars
> • evidence that consumers are switching to these cars 'demand for hybrids has increased'.
> Explanation: specific type of vehicle technology = electric cars 'Perhaps the most prominent development has been …'
> • description of electric cars & why they are effective 'which produce almost zero emissions'
> • description of hybrids
> • why hybrids are a popular choice.
> Evidence: effectiveness of electric & hybrid cars in reducing emissions, indicated by evidence from a study.
> Link to next paragraph - reservations and problems with this technology.
> 3 Electric cars and hybrids both explained (but is this necessary?); SUVs not defined / explained.
> 4 Yes. The citation from Sperling & Gordon supports the trend; the citation from the study (Cruickshank & Kendall) supports the effectiveness of electric/hybrid cars in reducing emissions.
> 5 Evaluation acknowledging progress in vehicle technology at the start: 'huge progress has undoubtedly been made'; evaluation of research 'the adoption of electric and hybrid cars can significantly reduce …'; writer's stance, i.e. they have reservations about this

approach, is expressed in the final sentence linking to the next paragraph: 'However, whilst progress in vehicle technology seems promising, there are still a number of issues and problems to consider around so-called 'green' vehicles.'

ACADEMIC LANGUAGE

Citations (1) Incorporating references

This box introduces the basic conventions involved in giving references in an academic text. There is more detail and practice with citations and referencing in Unit 5. Most of the texts in the book use author-date conventions, and this is the focus here. However, it is important to recognize that different systems are used in different disciplines (and different institutions, publications, etc.) and to emphasize that students will need to check which conventions they need to use. This is an opportunity to ask which conventions students have already seen. Check that students have understood the basic principles with a few questions:
- What is the difference between a citation and a reference? (*citation = information from a source; reference = details of the source*)
- When do you include a reference in an academic text? (*when you use any ideas or information from a source - book, article, online, etc. - in your own writing*)
- What are the two parts of a reference in an academic text? (*1 in-text reference, 2 full reference details in bibliography / reference list*)
- What different types of referencing system are there? (*author-date, numerical system - various forms exist*)
- What information appears in the text? (*author-date: name of author(s) + date of publication - NOT initials, more than 3 authors can be shortened to first author's name + et al.*)
- What appears in the bibliography or reference list? (*full details including: (all) author's name(s) and initial(s), date, title of book / article + journal, other publication details*)

TASK 4 Incorporating citation in an essay

1 and 2 The sample student paragraph includes two examples of clear, correct citation and in-text references. Once identified, ask students how the two examples in the paragraph differ, referring them back to the Academic Language box. The first gives the authors' names first with the in-text reference (date + page number) followed by a reporting verb, the second gives the in-text reference at the end of the sentence, as an example of one such study. The first gives a page number because it refers to a specific idea in the source text; the second doesn't as it refers to the study as a whole.

> **Answer**
>
> Two sentences contain citations as below. The remainder express the student's own ideas.
>
> **As Sperling and Gordon (2009, p.151) point out**, even in the United States, the market for large, 'gas-guzzling' SUVs has been shrinking, and demand for hybrids has increased.

Studies have shown that the adoption of electric and hybrid cars can significantly reduce atmospheric emissions and, after the initial investment, they could be comparable in cost terms in the future **(Cruickshank and Kendall, 2012)**.

3 Ask students to quickly read Text 3 and identify the main point; i.e. car usage can be influenced by the urban environment and lifestyles. Ask whether this point came up in their group discussions in Task 2, in response to the prompt *urban planning*.

4 This activity introduces the concepts of paraphrase (expressing a specific idea from a source using different language) and summary (expressing a more general idea from across a source).

Answers

1 a a: paraphrase of sentence 1
  b b: summary of ideas in several sentences
  c a / b: mainly paraphrase of sentence 2 (includes some ideas from next sentences)
  d a / b: mainly paraphrase of sentence 2 (includes some ideas from next sentences)
  e a: paraphrase of final sentence
2 a b b b c a d b e b

5 Ask students what they would need to add to the sentences in **4** to use them as citations in an essay, i.e. correct in-text references. Encourage students to use a variety of referencing styles (reference before/after the citation, different reporting verbs).

Sample answers

b As Sperling and Gordon (2009, p.161) point out, most Americans drive to work ...

c In the US, increased suburbanization and urban sprawl mean that ... (Sperling and Gordon, 2009).

d Sperling and Gordon (2009) explain how poor urban planning often means that ...

e Americans have struggled to reduce ... (Gordon and Sperling, 2009).

TASK 5 Writing a body paragraph of a discursive essay

1 This is an opportunity for students to review the information generated throughout the module, and revise the ideas they discussed and noted down in Task 2. Emphasize that academic study involves developing and sometimes revising your ideas in the light of new information.

2 For this writing task, students could just make use of the source texts in the module or you could ask them to research other sources on the topic. If they are going to do their own research, it might be best to restrict them to only one or two extra sources.

3 Emphasize that academic writing is often a process of drafting and redrafting. Peer evaluation activities like this should be seen as an opportunity to improve on a first draft.

2C Listening Lectures (2)

TASK 1 Critical thinking - evaluating an argument

1 This task introduces the topic of sustainable cities and encourages students to think critically about a statement put forward by the lecturer. This statement, intentionally presented out of context, is intended to provoke debate. Encourage groups to draw out both support for the statement and criticisms, giving specific examples wherever possible. Monitor discussions and challenge students to explain and defend their positions, rather than just settling for vague *I agree / disagree* comments.

2 and 3 These tasks aim to activate some of the vocabulary students may already be familiar with around the topic. You could start off by noting down some of the key vocabulary that came up in group discussions and putting this on the board for students to add to.

Sample answers

demographic, growth, change, inequality, population, poverty, resources, slums, urban, urbanization, waste

TASK 2 Establishing the topic of a lecture from the introduction

1 ▶2.1 In this first short extract, the lecturer sets the scene for the main topic of sustainable cities, by looking at the more general context of world population growth.

Answer

population growth

2–4 ▶2.2 This extract continues the theme of population growth, using a graph to illustrate how the world's population has grown over the past centuries. However, the lecturer starts to link this to the main topic of the lecture, using clear signposts (as highlighted in the transcript which students will focus on later in Task 3).

Answer

2 Sustainable cities. Repeated focus on sustainable cities, sustainability, urban areas.
4 To set the scene and capture the audience's attention in an engaging way.

ACADEMIC LANGUAGE

Signposting (2) Focusing on the main theme
Students have already encountered signposting language in Unit 1C (page 019). This academic language box focuses attention on phrases used specifically to highlight the main theme of a lecture. Ask students which key verbs are used in the examples here (*look at, concerned with, focus on, concentrate on*).

TASK 3 Recognizing signposting language

1 and 2 ▶2.3 This task extends the range of signposting language and shows how it is used by four different lecturers. Tell students that they are going to watch very short extracts from four different lectures, by different lecturers, and on different topics. Stress that they should not try to understand the full context of the lecture, but just focus on the signposting language to identify the main focus stated in each clip. Show the extracts twice so that students can focus on the topic first and then the exact language second time around. Note that all of these lectures will appear later in the course.

Answers

1 Extract a: the UN Security Council
Extract b: the international UN human rights mechanisms, the charter-based bodies
Extract c: community ecology
Extract d: population distribution and access to resources

2 Extract a: For (the) purposes of this lecture, I'm going to be concentrating on ...
Extract b: I'm not going to look at ... as a whole ... I'm going to focus narrowly on ...
Extract c: So today we are going to focus this lecture on ...
Extract d: But really what we're concerned with today is ...

3 Students look back at the transcripts of the first two extracts to identify other signposting expressions (highlighted in transcripts on page 225).

TASK 4 Listening critically

1 As an introduction, you could write on the board *school of thought, movement, -ist / -ism* and ask students what they understand by these terms in an academic context. Many will be familiar with the concept of movements in areas such as Art (e.g. the Impressionists / Impressionism), explain that they occur across academic disciplines and describe a particular approach to a field. When they have completed the task, get brief class feedback to check that they have a broad understanding of all the terms to help with the next listening extract.

2 ▶2.4 Explain that students should focus on understanding the general concept of New Urbanism rather than making detailed notes here. They should just note down a few words and phrases as an aide memoire for the following discussion.

3 The aim of this task is not for students to repeat what they have heard or written down as notes, but to react to it critically. That is not to say that the discussion won't involve some clarification of particular points, but they should then focus on their own reactions to the concepts. Students can discuss the questions either in groups or as a whole class, depending on class size and time available.

4 and 5 These activities prepare students for the longer extract and following oral summary task. Write *criticism /*

criticize / critique on the board and elicit what students understand by the three words. Explain that *criticize* and *criticism* can be used in two senses; in an everyday context they usually refer to giving negative comments about something or someone, but in an academic context, they refer to giving an assessment of the good and bad points of something. *Critique*, as a noun and a verb, is only used in an academic context of assessment, which may focus on the negatives, but based on evidence and academic argument, rather than personal opinion. Check that students have grasped the concept (*too*) *Utopian* and the basic meanings of the groups of words in a–c before listening to the final extract.

6 It may not be immediately clear from the pictures which set of words, a or b, match which development, as there is clearly a lot of overlap in the features of the two. The answer here could be left open until after watching the extract. Students should, however, be able to identify that c refers to critiques of New Urbanism.

Answers

Seaside: b Celebration: a Critiques: c

7 and 8 ▶2.5 Students will need to make more detailed notes about this extract in order to prepare the oral summary in 8. As students will need to understand the whole extract for the summary task whichever group they are in, do not allocate A and B groups until after students have watched and compared their notes. Depending on time and numbers, the oral summaries can be delivered informally by one student nominated per group or as a more planned group presentation divided between group members.

TASK 5 Critical thinking – evaluating an argument

1 and 2 This discussion task again focuses on students' reactions to and critical evaluation of the content of the lecture, not just repeating the ideas they have already covered in their oral summaries in Task 4.8. Read out the quotation from the end of the lecture extract and elicit which aspect of sustainable development the lecture is highlighting (i.e. the social aspect). The discussion prompts guide students from recapping what they have heard in the lecture towards their own experiences and perspectives on the topic, but they do not have to follow them in a strict order.

2D Speaking Seminars (1)

TASK 1 Developing an argument

This module continues the topic of urban living from module 2C Listening. The aim is for students to develop an argument step by step, starting with their initial reaction to a topic, but then building on that with information from sources.

1 Read the discussion question as a class and tell students to write down their first reaction, i.e. the most important factor that makes a city liveable. They should not spend too long considering their choice or worrying about wording; they will develop their argument further through the following activities.

2 Students read their respective texts and consider how (or whether) it relates to their answer in 1. As they summarize to their partner, ensure that students don't just read each other's texts. Emphasize that a summary does not need to include all the details, such as the places on the top 10 list.

3 and 4 These activities encourage students to develop their initial ideas into a more academic style. Explain that spoken academic discourse is less formal and structured than writing, but should still use appropriate vocabulary and avoid vague or potentially ambiguous language (e.g. *a low crime rate* is more specific than *safe*). Explain that students may want to alter and develop their arguments based on their reading.

5 Students should present just their main point in one or two sentences as concisely as possible at this stage. They will have the chance to add supporting points, evidence, and examples in later tasks. Note and group on the board the different points that students come up with.

TASK 2 Supporting an argument with evidence

1 ◀))2.6 Students listen to three students taking part in a seminar discussion on the same topic. Explain that they will take notes in the first two columns only. These notes can be checked in pairs or as a whole class.

Sample answers

	Main argument	Support
A	*Transport is a key factor.*	Traffic congestion affects: - people's everyday lives (travelling to work or school) - business efficiency (adds to delivery time, fuel costs) - people's health and the environment (greenhouse gases) The London congestion charge has reduced traffic and pollution
B	Economic factors override everything else.	*The cities at the top of the list in Text 1 can afford to spend money on urban planning because they don't have to deal with so much poverty and crime.*
C	Crime is an important factor.	None

2 Students classify the type of evidence they noted for each student in the Support column into these four types, either individually, in pairs, or as a whole class. Encourage them to give specific examples in each case. There may be some overlap between 3 and 4.

Answers

A 2 evidence from other sources in this unit: London Congestion Charge (Text 2 page 029), but not explicitly referenced

3 examples from their own general knowledge: increase in transport costs due to longer delivery time; effect of greenhouse gases

4 examples from their own experience: own experience with congestion in London

B 1 ideas from the texts in Task 1: Bluestone et al. (distribution of income), Global Liveability survey

2 evidence from other sources in this unit : Dr Howard's lecture (New Urbanist towns)

3 examples from their own general knowledge: information about the situation in Zimbabwe

C none

3 Encourage students to think about which student's arguments sounded most convincing and why. Clearly Student C contributed very little. Students A and B offered slightly different types of evidence; A offered more from their general knowledge, B more from the sources in the unit, with references. Students should argue why they think one or the other is more effective.

ACADEMIC LANGUAGE

Interaction (2) Interrupting and linking

Ask students how effective they think the discussion in Task 2 was in terms of turn-taking and how the students linked to each other's ideas. Turn to the transcript of the discussion on page 226 to find the examples in context.

TASK 3 Introducing your argument and linking to others' ideas

1 In this activity, students need to first consider how the pairs of ideas relate to each other, i.e. does the second argument add to the first or does it offer an opposing argument? Encourage them to use different expressions from the Academic Language box to link the ideas, making any adjustments necessary at the start of the second sentence.

Sample answers

a / b Yes, I completely agree (that's important for some people), but …

c / d I think that's a really important point. …

e / f Yes, of course we need to consider waste and consumption, but …

2 Here students need to think beyond the mechanics of the linking expressions and add their own personal comments and reactions. For example, a student reads out sentence d, then adds *Yes, exactly, I think that's really important here. If you live in a rural village in Africa, for example, you're probably more worried about issues such as food and health than you are about traffic congestion, say.*

TASK 4 Participating in a seminar discussion

1 This is the main productive task of the module. Students have had plenty of input on the topic, and opportunities to discuss their ideas at each stage. Now they need to express these ideas using evidence and examples as support, as well as trying to manage the flow of a group discussion. Read through the guidelines as a class before dividing students into groups, ideally of four or five. Explain that one member of each group will take brief notes during the discussion, in order to summarize at the end, but the note-taker should still take part in the discussion. Give students a time limit of 10–15 minutes to conduct the discussion. Monitor but do not interrupt, instead allowing students to work through any difficulties themselves. Note any general points for feedback later.

2 To round off the topic, give each group a couple of minutes to recap and agree on the main points from their discussion, referring back to the notes taken. Ask each group to present their summary to the class, through a nominated group member or as a joint effort. You could ask the class to vote on the single most important factor that makes a city liveable, or maybe a top 5.

TASK 5 Reflecting on performance in a seminar

1 To start this final reflection task, you could offer two or three of your own observations about the effectiveness of the group discussions that you noted down. These should be general points rather than directed at particular students and include both positives and points for improvement. Give students a few minutes to work through the guidelines and evaluate their own contribution to the discussion. Encourage them to think about positive aspects as well as areas for improvement.

2E Vocabulary Accuracy

TASK 1 Choosing prepositions in noun phrases

As noun phrases are especially important in academic writing, understanding the prepositions that link the elements of a noun phrase together is also key for students to improve the accuracy of their writing.

1 Students should try to note down their ideas about the prepositions following these common academic nouns before they look in a dictionary. Note that more than one may be possible in some cases, an issue that will be addressed in 3.

> **Answers**
>
> debate on / about / over; interaction with / between; investment in / of; participation in; research into / on

2 Many of the gaps here can be filled with *of*, reflecting its frequency in academic noun phrases.

> **Answers**
>
> These are the prepositions used in the original sentences.
> 1 emergence *of*
> 2 accounts *of*; growth *of*; research *on*
> 3 quality *of*; level *of*; participation *in*
> 4 interaction *between*; adoption *of*; supply *of*; deregulation *of*

3 and 4 Elicit the difference between the usage of *investment in* and *investment of* (exemplified in the rubric). If students are struggling to explain the general category following these noun + preposition combinations, encourage them to suggest further examples. Note that while the difference in usage between *attitude of / to* is very clear, the difference between *evidence for / of* is more subtle (see note below). You may be able to elicit this difference or you may need to explain it. *Relevance* and *role* both follow a common pattern.

> **Sample answers**
>
> 3 1 attitude + to + the thing or group that people have an opinion about
> 2 evidence + for + the argument, theory, etc. you want to prove
> 3 evidence + of + something that exists or is true (**Note**: The difference in usage here is fairly subtle and in many cases they are interchangeable. The preposition *for*, though, suggests evidence that proves or supports a particular argument, theory, or position (*evidence for* vs *evidence against*). You would not normally use *evidence for* + a negative concept (~~evidence for bias / corruption~~). *Evidence of* is more neutral and simply suggests the existence (or not) of some evidence).
> 4 relevance of + something + to someone / something e.g. the relevance of art to everyday life
> the role of + someone / something + in something e.g. the role of women in the workplace

TASK 2 Identifying adjective / verb + preposition combinations

1 and 2 Here students need to think about the grammar (adjective or verb) that best fits the meaning, context, and choice of preposition.

> **Answers**
>
> 1 1 responding   5 incorporate
> 2 participated   6 ignorant
> 3 appropriate   7 benefitted
> 4 oriented   8 capable

UNIT 3 Creativity

ACADEMIC FOCUS: SUMMARIZING TEXTS

INTRODUCTION

Unit 3 focuses on summaries, whether that is a synopsis of a written text, such as the abstract of a journal article or the conclusion of an essay, or an oral summary of a lecture or a reading text. Throughout the unit, students explore the theme of creativity and innovation from a variety of different and sometimes unexpected angles, challenging them to consider and develop their own stance based on input.

3A Reading introduces the genre of academic journal articles, an important part of students' reading and research, especially at postgraduate level. Students learn how to navigate journal articles and become familiar with the different sections and features they might encounter. There is a particular focus on abstracts which students need to use in order to select what is most relevant to read and to maximize the time they have available.

3B Writing follows on from the work on introductions (1B) and body paragraphs (2B), with a focus on conclusions, as students build up to writing a complete essay in module 4B. Too often conclusions in student essays are simple summaries of the main points but draw no real conclusions and do not adequately address the thesis in the introduction. The activities in the module focus on linking the ideas and arguments throughout an essay (coherence) and considers ways to do this effectively through language (cohesion). It also looks at some of the features of conclusions that raise them above the level of a basic summary, such as comment and evaluation, mention of implications, applications, or further research.

3C Listening exposes students to more detailed technical content, encourages them to pick out main themes, and considers techniques for inferring the meaning of unknown vocabulary. Students also experiment with different note-taking techniques to find what works best for them and what is most appropriate for different content.

3D Speaking integrates reading and speaking skills as students work with a longer text to analyse, summarize, and finally discuss. The text, which follows on from the topic in the Listening module, puts forward an unusual and slightly controversial stance for students to react to. Throughout the module, students focus on how to introduce citations from sources in a spoken context.

3E Vocabulary explores how many words in English have both general, everyday senses and more specialized academic and subject-specific senses. The aim of this module is raise students' awareness of these different senses and also how they sometimes differ grammatically. More specialized senses of a word typically appear towards the end of an entry in a learner's dictionary, so students should be encouraged to read to the end of an entry rather than just settling on the first one or two senses which may not quite fit in the context.

DISCUSSION

1 The Discussion activity aims to encourage students to think about the unit theme, Creativity, and how this is important in academic study and research; not just in the Arts, but in areas such as Business, Education, Science, and Engineering, where we might more commonly refer to it as *innovation*. Start off the topic by putting the words *creativity* and *innovation* on the board, then underneath, *artist* and *inventor*. Elicit which type of person is typically associated with which quality, i.e. *artist – creativity, inventor – innovation*. Ask students to explain the difference between *creativity* and *innovation*, i.e. both are to do with seeing the world in new and different ways, but creativity is usually associated with artistic contexts and innovation with practical, scientific, or business contexts.

As students work in groups to read the quotation and discuss the questions, monitor and check they have understood some of the key words, e.g. *eccentricity, fickle*. If students are struggling to come up with examples, suggest the image of the 'mad scientist' from films such as *Frankenstein*, or artists portrayed as eccentric (e.g. Van Gogh). Contrast this with the positive image of new technology pioneers (e.g. Bill Gates, Steve Jobs) in the media.

2 Encourage students to think about a wide range of disciplines here; almost any area of academic study requires creativity / innovation in some form.

3A Reading Journal articles (1)

This module introduces the genre of academic journal articles. The rationale contains some key concepts for students to understand which may be worth spending some time on in class. To establish the difference between **primary** and **secondary** sources, write up *Einstein E = mc²* on the board and ask students where they could read about Einstein's famous theory. Write suggestions up under two columns with Einstein's original 1905 article in an academic journal (in German) on one side and other suggestions – physics textbooks, Wikipedia, etc. – on the other. Elicit which are primary and which are secondary sources and briefly discuss as a class the advantages and disadvantages of reading each type of source. Emphasize that although much research appears first in journal articles, they are not the only type of primary source (books such as monographs can also be primary sources, as well as data published in reports) and not all journals report on primary research (they can be discussion or review articles).

TASK 1 Understanding academic journal articles

1 The extent of discussion in response to this question will depend on the background of your students. Pre-university and undergraduate students may have very little experience of journals, whereas students undertaking postgraduate study may have mixed experiences that are interesting to share as a class.

2 Again, the amount of support and input from the teacher here will depend on students' backgrounds. If only a few students in the class have experience of journals, you could do this activity in groups instead of pairs, with one more experienced student per group. If students are struggling with terms such as *peer-reviewed* and *abstract*, refer them to the Glossary on page 199. Emphasize that there are not black-and-white answers here, but points for discussion.

Sample answers

a Yes – journal articles typically focus on a more specific area – a single issue or piece of research.

b They tend to be more formal (and technical) in style than some other genres, such as textbooks, because they're for an expert audience of peers, but style varies across disciplines and individual authors.

c Although they often report on primary research, journal articles can also discuss an issue or review other research.

d Yes, the reason why journal articles are considered to be reliable sources is because they have been peer-reviewed (read and checked by other academics in the field) before they are published.

e Yes, they can be written by one person or a team.

f Often they are more up-to-date, because they can generally be published more quickly than a book, but not in all cases.

g Yes, most academic journals are now available in print and online.

h There is no fixed length for a journal article but 4,000–7,000 words is the average length.

i Most journal articles start with an abstract.

j No, but some journals will specify a format and in some disciplines, there are common formats for journal articles.

TASK 2 Navigating journal articles

1 This task aims to introduce students to the format of journal articles and help them to navigate around an article to find the information that is most relevant to them. Note that some of the information a–i could appear in more than one section of the articles.

If you have internet access in the classroom, you could access one or both of the online articles used in the module using an academic search engine or library portal. The abstracts are free for anyone to access, but you will only be able to click through to the full text, contents page and other sections if you have paid for access, for example via a university system.

Sample answers

	Article 1	Article 2
a	1	1
b	1, 2	1, 2
c	3, 4	3
d	3, 4	3
e	5	4
f	5	5, 9
g	6	5, 6
h	6	6
i	9	11

2 This activity returns to the idea of selective reading identified in module 2A. You might want to point out as part of the discussion that most academics don't read journal articles in order, but skip to the sections they are most interested in, depending on their purpose for reading.

Answers
1 abstract
2 conclusion
3 references

3 This activity takes a brief look at some of the extra information sometimes included in a journal article. If you have online access, all of these examples are from article 2 and can easily be clicked on from the Contents list to check the answers. You could ask students when (if ever) they might want to access these sections; footnotes and appendices will probably be the most useful, especially for a student needing to understand an article in depth.

Answers
1 D 2 A 3 C 4 B

TASK 3 Identifying general features of abstracts

1 and 2 These activities give students a general feel for the features and form of an abstract before they look at the two examples in more detail. Encourage students to use the titles and source information here rather than reading the complete texts.

Sample answers
1 **Text 1**: *Applied Linguistics*, Linguistics / Business, one author (Holmes), 173 words
   Text 2: *Journal of Economic Geography*, Economics / Geography, a team of authors (Crescenzi, Rodríguez-Pose, and Storper), 134 words
2 An abstract is the text at the beginning of an academic article which summarizes the whole article, usually about 200 words; abstracts are also available and searchable separately. You can use an abstract to get a quick overview of the contents of a journal article, in order to decide whether it is relevant and whether it is worth reading or bookmarking to read later.

TASK 4 Describing aims

1 These expressions are already bolded in the texts, so students don't need to spend time searching for them. They should pick out instead which style(s) each of the writers chooses. Stress that these choices are often down to the style of the individual writer, although one or the other may be more common in particular disciplines.

Sample answers
1 Text 1: uses style b only
   Text 2: uses a mix of both styles, a and b

2 This task focuses on the variety of different forms and verbs used to express aims. During feedback, ask about the differences between the verbs used in the examples.

Sample answers
2 1 *In this article, we examine* the role …
  2 *This paper investigates* possible …
  3 *This paper discusses* the findings …
  4 *In this paper, I study how* …
  5 *… it will focus on* some new developments …
  6 *In this essay, it is suggested that* the decision-making process …

TASK 5 Identifying the features and structure of abstracts

1–3 Students should concentrate on picking out the features and generic language used in the abstracts rather than the details of these specific topics (especially the more specialist terminology in Text 2). Explain that not all of the features a–e appear in both abstracts.

Sample answers
1 a **Text 1**: *There is a long research tradition associating humour with creativity* …
  Text 2: None
  b **Text 1**: *this paper analyses ordinary everyday workplace interaction in a range of New Zealand white collar organizations in order to* …
  Text 2: *This article analyses the geography of innovation in China and India.*

c **Text 1**: *this paper analyses ordinary everyday workplace interaction ...* **Text 2**: *Using a tailor-made panel database for regions in these two countries, we show that ...*
d **Text 1**: *The analysis provides evidence that humour not only contributes to ...; The analysis suggests that the first category is pervasive and examples abound throughout our data set ...*

Text 2: *we show that both countries exhibit ...* (the remainder of this abstract is dedicated to explaining the findings)
e **Text 1**: *... the effective use of workplace humour to generate new ideas and stimulate intellectual progress is strongly associated with what has been labelled 'transformational' leadership.*
Text 2: Doesn't explicitly include conclusions, although implications can be inferred from the way the findings are described.

TASK 6 Using abstracts for writing and research

1 and 2 These activities give students practical examples to work through the process of deciding what to read and what not to read – selective reading. Answers throughout may vary, but students should be encouraged to explain their reasoning at each stage. As topics b and d are most clearly linked to the texts, students should select one of these to work with in 2.

Sample answers

1	Article 1	Article 2
a	✓ / ?	✓ / ?
b	✗	✓✓
c	?	✓
d	✓✓	✗

3 This discussion encourages students to think about researching and recording details of references in a very practical way. It is a common error to forget to record references accurately until it's too late and then waste a lot of time tracking the details down for a bibliography. All of these techniques (apart from 1) are valid and will depend on the learner's individual learning style and their studies.

Sample answers

2, 4, 5 All useful techniques.
1 This is insufficient information to include in a bibliography.
3 This can be very helpful, but remind students that they need to make sure they print out the title page of the article that usually includes all the reference details.
6 Reference management software will usually be more relevant to PhD students.

TASK 7 Independent research – exploring journal abstracts

1–4 This task encourages students to explore how the ideas introduced in the module relate to their own discipline. These activities are best set as homework and, because they only involve viewing abstracts, students don't require any special access. If students have access to a university library portal, this is a good opportunity for them to become familiar with it; otherwise, just direct them to a search engine such as Google Scholar. By working through the tasks, students start to get a feel for:
- the format of journal abstracts / articles in their own discipline
- how to select, use, and refine search terms
- some of the key journals in their own discipline.

Encourage students to keep notes (e.g. on abstract length and language used to describe aims) and report back on their findings in the next class. If you have students from different disciplines, they can compare how what they found was similar or varied, either as a whole class or in groups. Collate the findings of the class (e.g. average abstract length, most common language to describe aims).

3B Writing Essay conclusions

TASK 1 Identifying features of a conclusion

1 This task uses a generally good model of a student conclusion to help identify some typical features of essay conclusions. Start by focusing on the essay title. Check that students are clear about the key terms *learning disabilities* and *dyslexia*. Ask students what possible stances you could adopt in response to the task, i.e. agree with the statement (there is a link), disagree with the statement (there is no link), or agree but with reservations. Students read quickly to establish the writer's stance.

Sample answer
There is a clear link between learning disabilities and increased creativity, but the reasons for the link are not yet understood.

2 Point out that some sentences include two of the features and some features are not exemplified in this conclusion. As part of feedback, elicit which of the features will appear in most conclusions and which are optional – a and b will always appear, plus some form of comment / evaluation and one or more of the other features.

Sample answers
a 1 b 1, 2 c 1, 2 d 3 e 3 f 4 g none

TASK 2 Using minimizing language

1 and 2 For each example that students identify, they should describe the type of language used (modal, tentative verb, or adverb) and explain the reason for the hedging language by identifying what criticism the writer is trying to avoid (e.g. overgeneralization).

Sample answers

1 **Text 1**: but *may* also stimulate intellectual activity; The analysis *suggests* that the first category is pervasive; and *tends to* characterize some communities of practice more than others
  Text 2: *seem to* produce strong backwash effects

3 Encourage students to try out a variety of language in this activity. Collect a list of possible hedging expressions on the board as part of feedback.

Sample answers

1 The application of stricter visa controls *could potentially* have knock-on effects in both the business and education sectors.
2 With general acceptance that recorded cases *may only* be the 'tip of the iceberg', more thorough risk assessment is needed.
3 The recent research on dyslexic students *suggests* that they *tend to* be more creative than the rest of the population.
4 Less developed countries *can sometimes* place the blame for their slow growth rates on outside factors such as colonial legacies and free trade.
5 Children from wealthier, well-connected backgrounds are *generally* at *somewhat of* an advantage in the careers market.
6 *It seems that in many cases*, economic, social, and technological developments *may* have resulted in greater inequalities between different income groups in the world.

TASK 3 Ensuring coherence throughout an essay

1 In this task, students look at the introduction and an outline plan for an essay which they will use in 2 to match to one of two conclusions to form a coherent whole. Read the essay title as a class and elicit the

meaning of the phrase *ideas are currency*. As students read the introduction and outline, they focus on finding and explaining the terms highlighted. The aim of this task is for students to establish the topic and the main points. Use feedback on the key terms to elicit a summary of the planned essay, the main points, and how they are linked together logically. Ask:
- *What is the writer's approach to the question?* (focus on creativity in education and training, and innovation in the workplace)
- *What is the writer's stance?* (Western countries are falling behind in the global economy)

2 Having established the main points of the essay, and the focus and logic of the writer's arguments, students now look at two alternative conclusions to identify which one best fits to form a coherent whole.

Answers

B clearly matches the introduction and outline as it:
- recaps the thesis statement
- summarizes the points mentioned in the outline
- maintains the same focus (emerging economies, education, and innovation).

A doesn't achieve the above and brings up new points that haven't been mentioned in the introduction or main body.

3 If students are unsure which conclusion fits best, this activity should help to identify exactly why B is better than A.

Answers

Conclusion A: a recaps topic, but not thesis statement
Conclusion B: a, b, c (ref to Brahmbhatt & Hu), f/g it leaves the question open about possible implications for the future

4 It is worth pointing out here that as well as lacking coherence with the rest of the essay, Conclusion A also lacks hedging language which makes it feel overly confident and open to criticism.

Answers

It *seems that* these shifts are due *largely* to changing ideas about ...; *It remains to be seen how* ...

TASK 4 Understanding coherence and cohesion

1 and 2 These tasks recap the twin ideas of coherence (linking ideas) and cohesion (linking through language) that both affect the flow of an essay.

Answers

1 *coherence* – ideas – meaning – language – *cohesion*
2 knowledge economy: *knowledge flow, knowledge bases*
  emerging economies: *emerging economies, BRIC nations*
  education: *education*
  innovation: *new ideas, innovations, innovation in the workplace*

TASK 5 Writing a coherent conclusion

1 This is the main productive task of the unit. It follows the same format as Task 3, with an introduction and outline plan given for students to add a conclusion. It uses a different topic, but linked to the overall theme of creativity. This time students work in groups to go through the same initial steps of establishing the task and then understanding the introduction and plan.

2 If students are to carry out this writing task as homework, point out the evaluation criteria in Task 6.1 that they can use to check and edit their first draft before bringing it to the next class. Explain that the conclusion does not necessarily have to include all the points mentioned in the Checklist; points 3 and 5 are optional.

> **Sample conclusion** (152 words)
> It is becoming clear that in an information age, the role of education is increasingly to teach students the creative and critical thinking skills they need to select and process information effectively. This essay has put forward a variety of classroom activities that can be applied to good effect in encouraging these skills. The challenge, however, may come in changing the traditional teacher-student relationship to allow such free flow of ideas in a classroom with more emphasis on student participation. As studies into international students have shown, students from cultures where there is traditionally a greater distance between teacher and student already tend to find it difficult to adapt to the more interactive nature of Western academic culture. Changing the attitude and behaviour of both teachers and students in these cultures will undoubtedly take time and new ways of accommodating ideas about critical thinking alongside cultural norms may need to be found.

TASK 6 Critical thinking – evaluating a conclusion

1 and 2 Again, students are encouraged to review their own writing in a systematic way and to think about editing their first drafts. Peer evaluation can be very helpful for students to see what others are writing. Much may go unsaid as students notice but don't necessarily comment on interesting points (both positive and negative) in their peers' work. You may choose to pair students up with different partners each time this type of activity comes up, so that they see a range of different styles, approaches, and abilities. Alternatively, students could form regular study groups of four to six, who always review each other's work. The advantage of study groups is that students build up trust, can comment on progress, and if they carry out the Research Project (Units 7–12), they become familiar with each other's topics.

3C Listening Lectures (3)

TASK 1 Preparing for a lecture

1 Give students a few minutes to read the slide and questions, and maybe discuss in pairs, before giving feedback as a group. If necessary, explain that *Faster, Higher, Stronger* is the Olympic motto. The aim of this activity is to activate students' general knowledge, so encourage them to give any examples that might link sport and biomaterials.

2 Ensure that students have understood the meanings of these key terms that will appear in the lecture and encourage them to generate some more possible key words of their own. They will check their predictions in Task 2.1.

TASK 2 Establishing key themes in an introduction

1 ▶3.1 Whilst the lecturer in this extract is lively and engaging, the content is fairly dense, with a lot of potentially new terms. Divide students into A and B pairs so that each student focuses on noting down key words related to one of the two headings only. Don't give feedback on answers at this stage.

> **Sample answers**
> People and disciplines involved in materials science:
> scientists, engineers, chemists, physicists, mathematicians, biologists, biochemists, computer scientists, design technologists
> Words / phrases related to materials:
> structure, composition, properties, atomic structure, carbon fibre, fibres, mechanical strength, electrical properties, optical properties

2 and 3 Students compare their notes in groups of four (two As and two Bs) or as a whole class. Students may be keen to watch again because they didn't get everything down. Explain that they don't need to understand all the details in this section to get an overview of the topic. Discuss to what degree the topic matched their predictions from Task 1 and agree as a class a definition of materials science.

> **Sample answer**
> 3 Materials science is an interdisciplinary subject that is concerned with *the structure and composition of materials and how we can control their properties.*

4 and 5 ▶3.2 With a lighter note-taking load and less technical input, students can focus on the general points in this extract for discussion either in groups or as a whole class. Encourage students to explain and justify their choice in 5.

TASK 3 Inferring the meaning of unknown vocabulary

1 Ask students what sort of vocabulary in the lecture extracts was new to them and how they guessed the meanings. Feed back and ask which of these techniques students noticed and which they prefer.

Answers

1 a & b (bio & nano)
2 e
3 a (tiny – nano)
4 d
5 c & d (plates & springs)

2 Ensure that students don't use dictionaries for this task; they should be able to work out approximate meanings from the context in the transcript. Stress that they don't need to come up with precise definitions, the focus here is on decoding techniques.

Sample answers

1 massive structures - examples (*bridges, cars, nuclear reactors*)
2 biochemist - word parts
3 atomic structure - words parts / definition (*controlling the atomic structure, so arranging atoms in a material and adding new atoms of maybe a different material*)
4 nano-wires - word parts / synonyms (*very tiny little wires*)
5 double amputee - visual cue (*picture on slide*)
6 biomechanical engineering - word parts / definition / examples

TASK 4 Note-taking (2) – using different techniques

1 and 2 ⏯3.3 Students have already tried out several different note-taking techniques; using a checklist or 'free' notes (1C) and using headings (2C). In this task, students experiment further with different note-taking techniques. Divide students into groups of three, allocating each student as A, B, or C and direct them to the instructions on page 219. A and B students are given a specific style of note-taking (headings and key words, or a timeline with pictures or diagrams), whilst C is free to use whichever style they prefer. The activity will work better if students don't compare what they are going to do at this point. Before they watch the extract, read the questions in 2 so they are clear about both the style of

notes they should use and the aim of the note-taking, i.e. to answer the questions. Don't give feedback on the answers to the questions at this point.

3 and 4 Students compare notes in their A, B, C groups and discuss which style was most effective before they compile a short written description, combining the answers to the two prompt questions in 2. They could then either read out their descriptions or exchange them with another group to read. Feed back and discuss as a class which note-taking techniques were most effective for recording the information, and perhaps more importantly, for enabling them to complete the writing task. Stress that there is no right and wrong way to take notes, what works best will differ according to an individual's learning style, the topic and content of the lecture, and also the aim of the notes.

TASK 5 Critical thinking – developing your stance

1 This is an opportunity for students to think critically about what they have seen, to ask critical questions, and to develop their own stance. Start by asking what the overall stance of the lecturer was to high-tech materials in sport, i.e. generally positive. Students use the prompt questions to discuss and explain their own response.

2 The most obvious examples here might be new developments in science and medicine, but students might also come up with new theories and approaches in business, economics, or education that have proved controversial. These could be recent developments or drawn from history.

3D Speaking Seminars (2)

TASK 1 Reading in preparation for a seminar discussion

1 This module continues the topic from the listening module about (unfair) advantage in sport. Students start by noting down their initial reaction to the topic of drugs in sport, quickly in a single sentence. This will enable them to see how (or if) their stance changes through the module as they read about and discuss the topic.

2 Set a time limit of 3–5 minutes to read the text quickly to understand the general topic and identify the writer's stance. They should not worry about understanding the details at this point, as they will have time to go back and examine the text in more detail at the next stage. Feed back on just the main topic and the writer's stance.

Answer

The writer is sceptical about banning drugs in sport. He does not argue *for* the use of drugs in sport, but he does point out flaws in the arguments traditionally used to support banning drugs in sport.

3 Before students do this task, point out the superscript numbers throughout the text and ask what they are for. Point out the note about footnotes and ask what kind of information students would expect to find in the footnotes, i.e. reference information. Students need to understand for this task that the text is firmly backed up by proper references to sources, even though they are not shown here. Refer back to the different styles of in-text referencing mentioned in module 2B (page 032).

Read through the instructions and emphasize that students should make notes not just about the text itself (textual information), but also their reactions to what they read (personalized information).

4 and 5 As students compare their own notes to the sample, emphasize that everyone's notes will be different and they should find their own preferred style of making notes on a text. Feed back on students' preferred techniques to share best practice.

Sample answers

4 *Cooper points out flaws in some of the traditional arguments put forward for banning drugs in sport.*
Cooper suggests that the idea of banning drugs in sport may not be as logical as it first seems.
I think that the writer here raises some interesting questions about the reasons for banning drugs in sport.

ACADEMIC LANGUAGE

Citations (2) Referring to sources in a discussion

Explain that as well as referencing sources in writing, it is also important to make it clear where your ideas, evidence, examples, data, etc. come from, as part of an academic discussion. Explain that detailed references aren't necessary (other participants can ask you if they want to know more), but students should still acknowledge the source of outside information, for example, using the writer's name as in the examples here. Ask students to report orally the writer of Text 1's stance (as they did in Task 1.2) in a single sentence using one of the structures from the box. Collect different versions using a variety of structures and verbs. Encourage straightforward reports and interpretations.

TASK 2 Summarizing ideas from written sources

1 This task mimics a typical academic seminar activity, in which students report on reading by summarizing a text they have prepared, to lead into a more general discussion (in Task 3). Divide students into groups of four if possible, allocating them to A, B, C, and observer roles. Emphasize that each student should focus on summarizing only the aspect of the text which they have been allocated, not the whole text. Point out that in preparing their summary, students should not write and attempt to learn a 'script' and they will not be able to use the original text or their notes when they present. While students prepare, make sure that observers are clear about their role.

2 and 3 Monitor groups as they present their summaries and note any general points that you might want to add, after students have conducted their own group feedback with the observers.

TASK 3 Participating in a seminar discussion

1 Through the previous tasks, students should now be familiar with the arguments presented in the text, so explain that their discussion should move the debate on by focusing on their own comments and reactions to the topic. Remind them that they should try to use support from the text or from the lecture in module 3C where relevant (e.g. reference to the concept of *technological doping* mentioned at the end of Text 1, and the use of materials to improve performance mentioned in the lecture), as well as examples and arguments from their own experience. Allow around 10 minutes for the discussion. Monitor and intervene if you hear an example of unreferenced ideas from a source (*Sorry, where's that example from? Who put forward that argument?*).

TASK 4 Critical thinking – evaluating performance

1 and 2 These reflective tasks encourage students to think about their performance and what was most useful to them in preparing for the discussion. Students can work through the questions either individually, in pairs, groups, or as a whole class.

3 This final question invites students to consider the concept of stance and how their own stance can (and arguably *should*) be affected and develop as they read and discuss new information on a topic. Refer students back to the sentence they wrote in Task 1.1 about their reaction to the topic of drugs in sport, for comparison.

3E **Vocabulary** Identifying senses

TASK 1 Identifying general and specialized senses

1 Students should be familiar with all of these words and be able to quickly come up with simple definitions and examples, in preparation for the next activity.

Sample answers

These are from the *Oxford Advanced Learner's Dictionary*; students' definitions can be much simpler.

concentration the ability to direct all your effort and attention on one thing, without thinking of other things. *This book requires a great deal of concentration.*

OR a lot of something in one place. *A concentration of industry in the north of the country*

---

corridor a long narrow passage in a building, with doors that open into rooms on either side. *His room is along the corridor.*

corruption dishonest or illegal behaviour, especially of people in authority. *The new district attorney has promised to fight police corruption.*

majority the largest part of a group of people or things. *The majority of people interviewed prefer TV to radio.*

metre a unit for measuring length; a hundred centimetres. *The table is two metres long.*

stress (*noun*) pressure or worry caused by the problems in somebody's life. *Things can easily go wrong when people are under stress.*

2 and 3 The aim of this activity is to highlight the phenomenon of words with both general and specialized uses, not to focus on these specific vocabulary items. Emphasize that students shouldn't get caught up trying to understand the exact meaning of these sentences or the highlighted words. Encourage them to make guesses based on the context or other language clues in the sentences and come up with very general definitions (*It's a type of …*). If you have students from the relevant disciplines, you could briefly go through the correct definitions of the specialized senses (below).

Answers

2 1 Law   2 Ecology   3 Computer Science
  4 Literature   5 Engineering   6 Chemistry

3 Definitions are from the *Oxford Advanced Learner's Dictionary* or *Oxford Dictionary of English*

majority: Law: the age at which you are legally considered to be an adult
corridor: Ecology / Geography: a long narrow strip of land that follows the course of an important road or river
corruption: Computing: the process by which a computer database or program becomes debased by alteration or the introduction of errors
metre: Literature / Poetry: the arrangement of strong and weak stresses in lines of poetry that produces the rhythm
stress: Engineering / Physics: pressure put on something that can damage it or make it lose its shape
concentration: Chemistry / Science: the amount of a substance in a liquid or in another substance

TASK 2 Understanding grammatical differences in usage

1 Use the dictionary entry to demonstrate how general and more specialized uses of a word can differ not just in meaning, but also in terms of grammatical features and therefore usage. In the example here, the more general sense of the word is uncountable, whereas the more specialized sense can be used as a countable noun and so can take a plural form.

2 and 3 Again, students should initially make general guesses about the meaning of any words that are not familiar, then focus more specifically on the grammatical differences between the pairs. As an extension, you could then ask students to suggest which disciplines the phrases could be from. In many cases they are academic senses used across several disciplines. As homework, students could note down three to five words from their own disciplines that have general and specialized senses. In groups, they then take turns to explain their words, giving examples and explain any differences in usage.

Sample answers

2 and 3 Definitions are from the *Oxford Advanced Learner's Dictionary*

1 a the production of something, especially electricity, heat, etc. - uncountable noun
  b all the people who were born at about the same time - countable noun

2 a an object or a work of art put in a public place, for example a museum, so that people can see it - noun
  b to show clearly that you have or feel a particular feeling, quality, or ability - verb

3 a the way that somebody behaves, especially towards other people - uncountable noun
  b the way a person, an animal, a plant, a chemical, etc. behaves or functions in a particular situation - countable noun

4 a action rather than ideas; in reality - uncountable noun
  b a way of doing something that is the usual or expected way in a particular organization or situation - countable noun

5 a an idea or a belief that is based on various pieces of evidence which are not always true - noun
  b to build or make something such as a road, building or machine - verb

6 a a way of achieving or doing something - plural noun
  b the value found by adding together all the numbers in a group, and dividing the total by the number of numbers - countable noun (usually singular)

UNIT 4 Information

ACADEMIC FOCUS: COMPARING, CONTRASTING, AND EVALUATING

INTRODUCTION

Unit 4 aims to develop students' skills in comparing, contrasting, and evaluating texts. The unit covers a range of text types including textbook extracts in the reading and writing modules and poster presentations in the listening and speaking modules. There is a focus on identifying and extracting key meanings from texts, including main points and the authors' stance; students use this information in productive output including written summaries and spoken presentations. All the modules develop students' critical thinking and evaluation following given criteria.

4A Reading focuses on academic textbooks, looking at subjectivity and objectivity in language and concepts. Students learn to read text extracts for key information including publication information, main points, and the authors' stance. Having identified this information in two texts, students are able to use it first to summarize each text and then to compare, contrast, and evaluate the two texts. This comparison can reveal differences in how and why authors select the information in their text. In doing these tasks, students practise an authentic academic reading process. The module also looks at lexical cohesion: how the meaning in a text is connected through repetition, synonyms, and rephrasing of words.

4B Writing consolidates the writing work done in Unit 1 (essay introductions), Unit 2 (incorporating citation in a body paragraph), and Unit 3 (essay conclusions). Students build on these skills to plan, structure, write, and evaluate a comparison essay, reflecting the academic focus of the unit. The writing module gives students practice in selecting material from source texts to incorporate into their essay, and focuses on a range of comparative and evaluative language. Students also work out the most appropriate structure for their essay, which they write following a carefully planned structure.

4C Listening introduces poster presentations, which are becoming popular in a wide range of academic (and commercial) settings. Students critically evaluate different aspects of the poster presentation event, including the poster itself and the question and answer phase. These skills should build students' confidence in actively participating in such events. The tasks are interactive and communicative, and aim to reflect the processes involved in poster presentation events.

4D Speaking continues with poster presentations, and guides students through the process of selecting a topic, researching and preparing relevant material, practising the spoken phase of the presentation, and anticipating audience questions. This preparation process leads to the presentations themselves, which reflects the collaborative and interactive nature of poster presentation events.

4E Vocabulary looks at ways that students can create variety in their writing and avoid repeating key words frequently in a text by using synonyms and antonyms. It also investigates where synonyms can be easily substituted and where there are subtle differences in meaning and usage that need to be considered.

DISCUSSION

1 and 2 The Discussion aims to relate the unit theme of Information to students' experiences. Ask students to work in the same groups for the whole discussion. Activity 1 explores concepts, presented in a mind-map, e.g. 'managing information' and 'information systems'. Ask each group to explain all the possible concepts, inviting contributions from all members of the group. Activity 2 focuses on further vocabulary related to the theme. You could elicit affixes (prefixes and suffixes) and write these up for students to try to use with the word 'information'. Further examples include: *misinform, informative, informatics, information theory, information science, information superhighway*; and the blends (parts of two words combined) *infotainment* (information + entertainment) and *infomercial* (information + commercial). Make sure students explain the concepts they come up with. Use vocabulary reference resources (e.g. online dictionaries) as necessary.

3 and 4 These activities personalize the concept of 'information', i.e. they relate it to individual students. 'Information' may initially be seen as a broad, general concept, but the questions should lead to a recognition of how students engage with information – dealing with it, organizing it, remembering it. Optionally, ask further questions, e.g. *What are the most effective ways for universities to present information to students?* The final activity invites students to identify and explain the kind of information related to their discipline. You can add further concepts, e.g. currency: *How current / up-to-date is the information? How does the type of information change over time? What do students need to do with the information? What are the most effective ways of selecting and remembering information?*

4A Reading Textbooks (1)

TASK 1 Critical thinking – evaluating objectivity in texts

1 and 2 Check the terms 'objectivity' and 'subjectivity' by giving examples, e.g. '*The earthquake struck at 0945 on a scale of 7.5*' (objective) and '*The effects of the earthquake are devastating*' (subjective). Also refer students to the Glossary on page 199. Explain that although academic arguments are to some extent based on objective facts, there is an enormous amount of subjectivity: interpretation, stance, evaluation, and argument itself are all subjective notions – they vary between different people. The first two activities focus on vocabulary, and students should realize that some items can be in either / both categories. Make sure students explain their choices, using examples as appropriate.

3 This activity enables students to relate the content of different genres to the two concepts of objectivity and subjectivity. The example illustrates that newspapers do far more than report facts: they tend to interpret and comment on the news. These themes are investigated more fully through the module. Time permitting, conduct whole-class feedback to share interesting ideas, e.g. *there are two main purposes of a university prospectus: to give information on which courses are available; and to promote the university. The latter purpose is clearly more associated with subjectivity – through techniques such as attractive photographs and carefully selected information.* As an extension, continue with these themes as a discussion relating to various perspectives, e.g. economic (the need for the university to attract students to cover its costs), ethical (how information can be presented through selection), and linguistic (the choice of language to promote the message).

TASK 2 Engaging with a text

1 and 2 This task offers a useful way into a textbook text: as we rarely approach a text 'cold', i.e. without any idea of its content, the task encourages students to activate their knowledge of and interest in the content before reading. The first two activities lead in to the text by building on the notion of 'journalist'. Ask any social science and arts students in the class to offer their ideas after those of any scientists – their views may differ.

Accept all responses to the statements in activity 2, and ask students to give reasons.

Sample answer

Journalist: flexible; good observer; able to report what they see / hear / read; works to deadlines and briefs; fits in with the style and aims of who they report for (e.g. a particular newspaper / TV company); good user of the language; possible knowledge of other languages; able to deal with a wide range of people; confident, and needs initiative and self-direction.

3 Give a time limit so that students only read the first section, *Proof*, at this stage. Remind students that they should also systematically check the publication details (source) of the text; this will inform their answer. Ask students to say why the other two choices are wrong: they are details but not the main point.

Answers

1 primarily (b) students of journalism (who are likely to want to become journalists); also (a) the general public (if they are interested in this topic).

2 (b)

3 (c)

4 In the final activity, students read the whole text. Stress that their main reason for reading is to work out the authors' stance, particularly in relation to the points in 2 which are extracts from the text. Ask students for feedback on how they reached their answers, e.g. the concluding sentences of some paragraphs (such as 3) are strong indicators of the authors' stance.

Sample answers

1 The authors strongly argue for this.

2 The authors agree with this.

3 The authors accept that newspaper reporters are widely accepted to interpret the news, but the authors express scepticism about it.

TASK 3 Identifying the main points in a text for a summary

1 Explain that the main purpose of this task is to organize the material based on the text in order to write a summary. Stress that it is better to write a summary from notes on the main points rather than directly from the text itself: a summary should use the writer's own language as far as possible, and not include details from the text. Reading and note-taking is good academic practice. Allow plenty of time for this task. For activity 1.1, ask students identify the sentences in the text which express the main point in each paragraph. For 1.2, encourage this language development work while students are doing the first activity so that they look up unknown words with a purpose in mind. As a guideline, explain that there will always be unknown words in a text, so students should focus on extracting the meaning and not get distracted by looking up every

unknown word. At this point, or later, spend some time on students' vocabulary recording techniques / books / resources. In the final stage, 1.3, students should use the sentences they have identified as a basis for writing their own paragraph summaries.

Sample answers

1.1

1 Information requires corroboration.

2 Charges against people must be proven.

3 Reporters should have a minimum of two reliable sources, or documented proof, for each news story.

4 Newspaper reporters increasingly are asked to interpret the news.

5 Interpretation too often leads to guesswork and subjectivity.

6 Where are the facts there?

7 Too frequently, reporters take their orders to explain causes and effects as license to take leave of the facts.

8 As usual in journalism, the solution is to include more facts.

9 The order to interpret, to analyse, to explain the news should be seen as an order to find more, not fewer, facts - to conduct that extra interview in search of a quote that might explain why, to read that extra document in search of a crucial explanation, to observe the scene more closely in search of a telling detail.

10 They should also be interested in nuances, concepts, and ideas, but they should be looking to translate these subtler thoughts into what is essentially the language of journalism - the language of facts.

1.3

1 Reporters need to corroborate and attribute facts in order to protect people's reputations.

2 Journalists need to 'prove' charges against people.

3 Reporters need to ensure that they have at least two reliable sources for a story, and when making a charge, they should interview the accused person.

4 Newspaper readers want newspaper reporters to interpret news stories.

5 Interpretation can be dangerous, as it can lead to guesswork and subjectivity.

6 If there are no facts, interpretations of the same event can be very different.

7 Reporters should not ignore facts.

8 Guesswork is problematic; instead, a reporter should include more facts.

9 Although it can be difficult to find facts, reporters need to try harder to do so.

10 Reporters need to notice detail and body language, but ultimately they need to communicate by reporting facts.

2 The second activity prepares students to write their summary in the next task. Put more proficient students with others who might be less so, to help them. Ask students to reach agreement on what the main points are before checking answers.

TASK 4 Summarizing a text

1 This task provides staging and guidelines on how to write a summary. Students have laid the foundations in Task 3. Explain that the student summary is brief and includes only the main point. Analysing the summary enables students to see how they can themselves build up their own summaries.

> **Answers**
> 1 c 2 b 3 d 4 a

2 and 3 Explain that when using notes to write a summary, a further selection process needs to take place. If you read out the ten main points in Task 3, it should become clear that the text is quite repetitive: part of its persuasive style is to break the main point of the whole text into a series of very closely related points, one per paragraph. Many of these can be grouped together. Monitor during the writing process, and encourage students to write shorter rather than longer summaries. You can write up the following evaluation criteria for a summary (taken from Oxford EAP B1+ page 069):

- Complete: it includes the main points of the text, but not supporting points, details, and examples
- Concise: it is as brief as possible
- Clear: it is easy to understand
- Creative: it uses some technical terms in the text but mainly the summary writer's original language.

After the peer-evaluation stage, read out or show the suggested summary below as an example of how a summary can be written using just 10% of the original word count (in this case about 470 words down to 44).

> **Sample answer**
> In their text on *Interpretation*, Lanson and Stephens (2008, p.192–3) argue that the growing trend in interpretation in news reporting is worrying, particularly when news reporters offer interpretation based on limited facts. They conclude by stating that facts are essential in news reporting.

> **ACADEMIC LANGUAGE**
>
> **Cohesion (1)** Using related words and synonyms in a text
>
> Explain that cohesion is a strong feature of all texts, and is achieved in different ways. Subsequent Academic Language boxes develop the concept, and there is further information and examples in the Language Reference section from page 201. This box looks at how words are repeated, and synonyms used, to carry essential meanings through the text.

TASK 5 Identifying cohesive words to confirm themes

1–4 This task focuses on sets of related words in Text 1 to illustrate part of the cohesion of the text. In the first activity students need to look at the essential meanings of the words, while in activity 2 they use the

notions of objectivity and subjectivity (from Task 1) to rank the words. Similarly, activity 3 requires students to categorize the words, and the final activity presents some more evaluative words. The task shows the richness of related words in a text, and should also help students build their vocabulary. As an extension, ask students to find a text in their own discipline and carry out a similar analysis.

> **Answers**
> 1 1 attribute 2 better 3 information
> 2 1 documented, attributed, unsupported, unfounded
>   2 reality, interpretation, speculation, guesswork
>   3 transcribe, report, interpret, comment
> 3 1 Words related to facts: *facts, information, sources, records, interview*
>   2 Words related to activities around facts: *corroboration, attribution / attributed, report, double-checked, transcribed, confirmation, investigate*
> 4 These words are essentially evaluative words related to facts and doing things with facts. Further examples from the texts could include: *documented proof, better, trustworthy, needed, of course, credibility.*

TASK 6 Extracting and noting down key information in texts

1–5 Explain that this task leads to the writing of another summary, based on careful notes taken on Text 2. To help students understand the key information in the two texts, this is presented in table form. Once this table is completed (at the end of activity 5), students can see how all this key information contributes to the meaning of the texts. For example, the place of publication informs the content. Give students a time limit of just a few minutes to complete the Text 1 column and rows 1–4 for Text 2. Check this information before students start reading Text 2. They can then complete the 'main topic and themes' row for Text 2. For activity 4, remind students of the purpose of the coloured text, as presented in the Academic Language box above. Activity 5 repeats the process of extracting further key information from a text, including the main point and the authors' stance. Remind students that authors' stance tends to become apparent throughout a text, but particularly later in a paragraph and the whole text.

As an extension, ask students to identify the perspectives in the texts:

Text 1: geographical, historical, cultural, political

Text 2: academic (research cited), sociological (trends in entertainment), geographical (tsunami), historical (recent developments), political (corruption, Wikileaks), research (epistemological)

Answers
1-3, 5

		Text 1	Text 2
1	Date of publication	2008	2011
2	Place of publication	USA / New York	Australia / Melbourne
3	Genre	textbook, professional handbook	university textbook
4	Audience	students of journalism, media analysts	university (?sixth form) students
5	Purpose	to present an argument	to present information on recent media trends, and present an argument
6	Main topic and themes	reporting, journalism, establishing facts	news publishing / broadcasting, journalism, information, entertainment media, e.g. TV, social media, e.g. Facebook; other themes include the fact/opinion balance in news media
7	Main point	facts are essential in reporting the news, despite pressure on journalists and reporters to interpret the news	news has shifted towards entertainment (infotainment)
8	Authors' stance	supportive of reporters who present facts	journalists have a key role to play in democracy, identifying malpractice, and connecting with their audience

4 The yellow words are related to new media & infotainment; the blue ones are related to traditional news media.

6 Students can work together on this summary, using information selected from the completed table. As with Task 4.2, encourage students to be concise and avoid repetition. About 60 words should be about right for the summaries, perhaps a little longer. Remind students to include the parts of the summary given in Task 4.1. They can also evaluate each other's summaries using the criteria in Task 4.3.

Sample answer
In their text 'The infotainment monster that ate the news industry', Bainbridge, Goc, and Tynan (2011, p.43–4) report how 'infotainment' (i.e. information and entertainment) has begun to sideline traditional media such as TV. They state that while current audiences do to some extent engage with news programmes, they access news through non-traditional outlets such as social media.

TASK 7 Comparing and evaluating information in two texts

1 and 2 This task reflects the process of academic writing, in which students have to compare, contrast, and evaluate material in multiple texts on the same topic. Stress that students should refer to the information in their completed tables plus their summaries of the two texts. Go through the evaluation criteria in Checklist F, and do a whole-class example for one criterion, e.g. the first (which is the most objective), to illustrate differences between the two texts.

Sample answer
Content and commonalities: Both texts make the point about the importance of facts in news reporting; Carl Bernstein is cited in both texts. The first text mentions only news reporting, while Text 2 gives examples of several more modern media technologies such as YouTube and Facebook. The stance of the two author groups varies: the Text 1 authors take the traditional view that the job of journalists and reporters is primarily to report facts, while the Text 2 authors accept that journalists have a role beyond this, and need to find ways of connecting with their audience.

TASK 8 Independent research – comparing sources

1 As with other independent research tasks, set this one up briefly in class and ask students to report back on their findings in a later, specified, class. Explain that the main purpose is to find, compare, and evaluate source texts in their discipline. The whole task can be done either individually or in small groups within the same or similar disciplines. The second activity can be done either outside the classroom, or in a subsequent lesson.

You could also broaden the discussion by asking students to relate the principles of objectivity and interpretation discussed in the texts to academic contexts. Suggest questions such as *How far are various academic genres concerned with interpretation as opposed to the presentation of facts?*

4B Writing Comparison essays

TASK 1 Analysing an essay question

1 and 2 The first task in the module lays the groundwork for writing a comparison essay: understanding the question and working out relevant points to include. Activity 1 presents a typical essay title. Explain that there is usually a topic and a focus, and that the focus is essentially a limitation – students should limit their answer to the focus and avoid other areas of the topic. Having established the three parts, invite students to provide relevant material to support an answer to the essay title, either individually or in pairs / small groups, and finally as a whole-class activity. Accept any relevant ideas as they come up; these can be refined later. Students may wish to use points raised in the two reading texts in module 4A.

Answers

1 *Compare and contrast* - instruction
the presentation of information in two different types of media today - main topic
focusing on how effectively the information is communicated - limitation

3 This activity gives students the opportunity to evaluate the relevance of given items. Explain that a recurrent feedback point in student essays is the issue of relevance: many essays contain material that is irrelevant or only partially relevant to the essay title. Ask students to say why each item is relevant or not, e.g. the item *Historical overview of changing media – growth of internet and social media* could be useful, brief background information, but is not relevant enough to form a main point in an essay.

Answers

- Definition and discussion of what we mean by 'effective communication'
- Selection of media: TV broadcasting, and individually accessible media (blogs, social media)
- Major types of information presented: news / current affairs; public service info.; personal information

4 This activity focuses on the generation of ideas to include in an essay. Say that students can use a mind-map, as in the example, or another visual / linguistic representation of ideas. As with other activities in this task, students can work either individually or in pairs / small groups.

TASK 2 Writing a basic essay plan

1–3 In this task students build on themes they have considered for their essay, and group these into paragraphs. Emphasize the importance of cohesion and connection between the different themes. For example, students could first look at how non-news factual information (e.g. wildlife reports and documentaries) is presented in different media (e.g. TV, current affairs magazines). This material could be presented in one paragraph or two, depending on the essay structure, which is covered in more detail in Task 7. These themes could lead to the presentation of news in the same media. Evaluation can be either integrated throughout or blocked in a single paragraph at the end of the essay body. Monitor and give help as needed, before moving on to the evaluative stage (activity 2) which is based around Checklist G. Students can first evaluate their own structures, and then those of other students. During the redrafting stage, activity 3, check that students are making appropriate changes in response

to their notes from 2. As a variation, ask students to exchange structures so that they work on other students' essay plans.

TASK 3 Researching: selecting relevant material in a source text

1 Explain that students will read two short text extracts in this module, taken from the same sources as the Reading module (4A). Set a time limit, as the mechanics of this task should be familiar from the previous module.

Sample answers

Date and place of publication	2011, Melbourne
Context and relevance to essay task	Covers the topic of media & digital revolution, and presents relevant information on recent media trends through a relevant argument; certain media are mentioned, e.g. social media, which may be selected as one of the media types.
Main point(s)	that the recent digital revolution has resulted in a serious decline in TV viewing

2 The next stage of this task reflects the academic reading process by focusing on the selection of relevant information from the text to use in the written text. Stress that this should be purpose-driven rather than random, so that students select material to meet the needs of their plan.

Sample answers

Relevant information: newspaper circulation figures have declined; YouTube and Facebook have to some extent taken their place; the future of communications is 'user-led'.

3 In the final activity of the task, students practise the mechanics of writing sentence-based citations for their selected extracts. Monitor, focusing on accuracy and variety of structure. Emphasize that spelling the authors' names correctly, and getting the date and page numbers accurate, is an essential skill in order to avoid possible plagiarism.

Sample answers

Bainbridge, Goc, and Tynan (2011, p.45) report that the future of communications is 'user-led'.

It has been argued that YouTube and Facebook have to some extent taken the place of newspapers (Bainbridge, Goc, and Tynan, 2011).

The impact of the digital revolution on news viewing patterns suggests that newspapers are in terminal decline (Bainbridge, Goc, and Tynan, 2011).

YouTube and Facebook have to some extent taken the place of television.

Comparing and evaluating Using adjectives, adverbs, nouns, and verbs

The language of comparison and evaluation is complex, and is covered in several different Academic Language boxes together with two major sections in the Language Reference: Comparison and contrast, page 202, and Evaluation and stance, page 205. This box emphasizes the connection between comparison and evaluation – typically when things are compared, they are also evaluated. As many of the examples show, one single language structure is often both comparative and evaluative, e.g. *the most dramatic impact*. As there is a lot of information in this Academic Language box, you could ask students to study it before or after the class, together with the relevant Language Reference sections given above. The examples illustrate the wide range of choices available to the writer.

TASK 4 Comparing and evaluating ideas

1 This activity can be prepared individually, leading to a comparison in pairs / groups. Encourage students to analyse the media systematically, using the criteria given – they can also add their own criteria, e.g. cost, flexibility, interest. Students should naturally use examples of comparative and evaluative language; you can monitor and note down good / bad examples of such language use.

2 This activity continues with the notion of evaluating media, based on the ideas in Text 1. Go through the example, which illustrates critical thinking: the student has looked beyond the content of the text and found an important related point which is not mentioned. The example should encourage students to be critical of the text and the ideas in it, as they should be with any text.

Sample answers

1 Partly – although the text states that newspaper circulation figures have been declining, it doesn't mention online content, which is growing.

2 It is relevant, but limited and not well evaluated (see below).

3 Limited – the extract relies on one main source (Sorensen, 2007).

4 The writer does not appear to evaluate these citations effectively.

5 The text it does not mention that these newspapers' online content is expanding.

3 The final activity in the task sequence emphasizes the practice of evaluating citations, essentially answering the question *So what?* You could ask students to practise their sentences in pairs: based on the example they could say:

Student A: *Bainbridge, Goc, and Tynan (2011) report that newspaper circulation figures have declined as a result of the internet.*

Student B: *So what?*

Student A: *Well, they fail to mention that these newspapers' online content is expanding.*

TASK 5 Comparing specific points across multiple texts

1 Give a short time limit for this task as the text is short and students have been practising identifying the main point in a text. Time permitting, allow students to compare and evaluate each other's summary sentences.

Sample answer

Lanson and Stephens (2008, p.191) argue that news reporters should position facts above all other considerations, including their opinions, and resist pressure to do otherwise.

2 If they have done Unit 4A Reading, students should by now be familiar with extracting key information from a text, presenting this in tabular form, and reprocessing it for their own purpose. Make sure all students complete the table, and carry out a visual check where possible.

Sample answers

	Text 1	Text 2
1 Date of publication	2011	2008
2 Place of publication	Melbourne	New York
3 Genre	university textbook	textbook, professional handbook
4 Audience	university / older high-school students	students, journalists, media analysts
5 Purpose	to present information on recent media trends, and present an argument relating to the same topic	to present an argument (relating to the topic of reporting facts)
6 Main topic & themes	media & digital revolution	news reporting & facts and interpretation
7 Main point	that the recent digital revolution has resulted in a serious decline in TV viewing	that news reporters should position facts above all other considerations, including their opinions, and resist pressure to do otherwise
8 Specific media mentioned	newspaper, social media, television	blog, talk TV, news (implicitly newspapers)

3 Having looked at meaning, students now turn to the language of evaluation in the two texts. Explain that identifying evaluative language is a key skill in working out the authors' stance. From looking at the rich amount of evaluative language extracted from the texts, students can see how the authors' stance is demonstrated.

Sample answers

Evaluative language

Text 1: significant impact, dramatic impact, decline, phenomenon, dubious quality, trend, no one … / no one …, user-led, fundamental shift

Text 2: suspicious, solid fact, uncomfortable … predictions, speculations, attempts at mind reading, evasions, distortions, piecing together (positive connotation), voicing an opinion, struggle, urgent, not that much clearer, ultimately, facts do matter

Explanation of how the evaluative language demonstrates the authors' stance: This language helps express the authors' stance in relation to the specific media mentioned in each text. In Text 1, the authors appear to accept that the new media are bringing about a revolution, while in Text 2, the authors are suspicious of the new media and opinion-based media; they support the primacy of facts in news reporting.

4 The final activity in the task requires students to focus only on the essentials of the two texts: the main points and arguments. Ask students to cover the previous page to see how many of five evaluative questions in 4.2 they can recall. These questions should eventually become 'automatic' for students when approaching new texts.

Sample answer

Text 1 argues for the decline in TV; Text 2 emphasizes the production of news and the importance of facts rather than opinion which is associated with blogs, etc.

TASK 6 Focusing back on the essay question

1 This task echoes Task 1, using the same essay title. In this task students analyse the question more deeply, relating the four given statements to their understanding of the question. The first of these is clear, while the other three are probably good advice in most contexts.

Sample answers

1 Agree: the essay title explicitly states 'two different types'.

2 Agree: although no geographical perspective is explicitly stated in the title, this kind of essay title allows the student to limit their answer, e.g. geographically / historically / culturally.

3 Agree, depending on the context: academic essays require support, although at lower levels / ages this is less expected.

4 Agree: ultimately writers should develop their 'voice', which is related to their style and way of selecting and presenting their material.

TASK 7 Structuring an essay

1 and 2 This task extends the work done in Task 2 through the presentation of three possible essay structures. Check students' understanding of 'themes': these refer to student-selected themes such as those in Task 1.4, which are used as points for evaluation. After

doing the task, explain that structure 1 is a 'traditional' student essay structure, and is particularly common in mainland Europe. This structure 'blocks' the two media types selected, followed by two themes. The other two structures are more 'dynamic' and purposeful, being driven by a particular theme. In structures 2 and 3, the writer has more actively managed their response by selecting their themes and using these to drive their essay. The only difference between the two is that structure 2 evaluates both media types in each body paragraph using one theme (e.g. reliability, global reach, cost, flexibility, interest), while structure 3 reverses this, i.e. one media type and two themes per body paragraph.

Allow students sufficient time to revise and adapt their plan in the light of this analysis. Encourage them to work collaboratively. Conclude by saying that the more integrated approach of structures 2 and 3 more closely reflects academic argument; for the less experienced writer they might be harder to manage, but ultimately may be seen as more effective. As a further variation, students could include more themes in their essay, though comprehensiveness (including all the themes you can think of) may come at the expense of depth of coverage, given the word limit.

Answers

1 a present evaluation at the end of the essay: essay 1
 b integrate evaluation throughout the essay: essays 2 and 3

2 a have a 'theme-driven' focus: essays 2 and 3
 b offer a 'media types-driven' focus: essay 2

TASK 8 Planning and writing a comparison essay

1–3 This task is the culmination of the work done in the previous tasks. Writing a 1,000-word essay can take some students a lot of time, so it is a good idea to limit the time available by setting a deadline. Try some of the following techniques:

- Do some of the writing in class and some independently.
- Set specific writing activities in the class and monitor closely, e.g. writing the introduction.
- Practise writing fluency by giving students a very short amount of time, e.g. 2 minutes, and asking them to write as much as possible on an aspect of their essay – decide on the aspect first so that the 2 minutes are spent writing not thinking.
- Write one paragraph collaboratively, enabling more material to be added and more critical evaluation to take place.
- Give one week for the whole essay, with daily deadlines for students to show you what they have written in the previous 24 hours.

Techniques like these are designed to enable students to write more fluently. Monitor students at this stage so that they do not leave their writing to the last moment.

Encourage students to extend their range of language, and ask them to check their work using the suggested

Checklists on page 209. They can do this as they write and at the end of the process.

TASK 9 Critical thinking – peer review and feedback

1–3 The final task is reflective and evaluative. Explain that the purpose of such a task is to develop self-criticism and reflection which should lead to higher quality written work. Some students may be unwilling to evaluate / criticize peers, particularly when influenced by factors such as gender, perceived status, and personality. One way to break these down is to invite criticism of an anonymous piece of written work; this can be that of a past student with their permission. You could also present your own work for criticism. Encourage critical responses from small beginnings, e.g. by including an obvious spelling mistake, then work up to more 'higher level' evaluation based on the essay structure.

Finally, assess the essays and give written feedback. Ask students to keep this feedback to refer to throughout their EAP studies, so that they can monitor areas of weakness and improvement.

4C Listening
Presentations (1)

TASK 1 Identifying and explaining key components in a poster

1 The module starts with a task to make sure students understand the poster presented on page 067. Give a time limit for students to quickly look at the poster and match the five sections. Explain that the division into sections reflects a logical organization and makes it more accessible. A poster such as this is likely to be just one of many on display, and participants do not have much time available to read each poster.

Answers
```
a 4  b 1  c 2  d 3  e 5
```

2 and 3 These activities aim to enable understanding through a communicative activity. Students focus only on their chosen section, which uses time efficiently. Ask students to work individually during the preparation stage, although if necessary you and/ or other students could help less proficient students. During the explanation stage, encourage students to ask clarification questions to ensure understanding, and make sure they write brief notes when listening – these are needed in the next task.

TASK 2 Comparing a poster and a poster presentation

1 ▶4.1 This is a listening and note-taking task with the added dimension of the visual, i.e. the poster. Ask students to note down the points made by the presenters, and show the video extract once. Do a quick visual check. As with all note-taking activities, make sure all students write notes and do not accept that they may prefer to simply remember the information – they will quickly forget it (if they ever understood it) if they do not record it.

Sample answers
Section 1
Knowledge Transfer (KT):
- the exchange and dissemination of knowledge and information
- particularly associated with research universities
- increasingly being recognized as valuable activity
- at the heart of activities at universities (e.g. lecturers & professors are disseminating knowledge & information through their lectures and seminars, also disseminating to a wider audience, through their publications, which are reaching a global audience)

Publications:
- essentially global

Section 3
Open access journals
- free at the point of use: users, e.g. students / public don't pay
- users (e.g. university libraries) had to pay for journals in the traditional model
- important to maintain quality → content is peer-reviewed, i.e. other researchers, from the same subject area, review the work
- plagiarism detection is easier – using anti-plagiarism software

Section 2
Universities
- need to look at what they do with innovation
- the cycle starts: direct investment in educational research → the development of increased levels of research in universities & emergence of high-tech companies → an increase in economic competitiveness → economic growth → more money for investment

2 This activity links students' pre-listening task (Task 1) to the information in the poster presentation. This reflects the academic process of reading, understanding, and predicting before listening, and then comparing the two versions. As an extension / variation, ask students to identify extra information included in the presentation which is not given on the poster.

Answers to extension task
Section 1 extra information:
- KT is increasingly being recognized as valuable activity
- at the heart of activities at universities (e.g. lecturers & professors are disseminating knowledge & information through their lectures and seminars), also disseminating to a wider audience, through their publications, which are reaching a global audience

Section 3 extra information:
- users (e.g. university libraries) had to pay for journals in the traditional model

Section 2 extra information:
- universities need to look at what they do with innovation

3 ▶4.2 Students may already have noticed some of the presenters' evaluative material; this activity requires students to identify it using the transcript. (Alternatively, they can choose to read the transcript while listening.)

Answers (comparative and evaluative language in **bold**)

1 KT is **increasingly** being recognized as being **a valuable activity**, as I say particularly by researchers and developers in universities.

2 And **increasingly** publications are reaching a **truly global** audience.

3 Yes, **in the past** publications tended to be more restricted in their reach, whereas nowadays they're **essentially global** – in terms of their access but also in terms of their authors, the researchers who write for them.

4 **This contrasts with** the more traditional model, which is on a payment basis – journals were published in print form only, **which can be expensive**, and you had to pay.

TASK 3 Listening to a question and answer stage

1 Section 5 of the poster presents two long quotations from different sources. Students can work either individually or collaboratively to work out exactly what they mean. If necessary, do one as a whole-class activity. Encourage students to use dictionaries to access the meanings of unknown words, e.g. *harnessing*.

Sample answers

The first quotation means: Britain needs more innovation, which is vital in increasing the country's wealth. It needs to invest in knowledge, and use knowledge in business and services.

The second quotation means: University research is very important in contributing to business innovation, although it shouldn't be too commercialized so as not to threaten company research.

2 ▶ 4.3 Explain that the question and answer phase of the poster presentation is the most important for many participants, as it gives them the opportunity to directly respond to material in the poster and seek further clarification from the creator of the material. Before listening, you could ask students to predict possible questions arising from the work they have done on the poster. Show the extract once and allow students time to write after each question. The answers below are in full sentences, but accept note form from students.

Answers

Question 1: What they're saying is that universities are expensive and they are a vital part of a country's knowledge base. And universities are also vital in coming up with innovation. As the quote says, innovation is essential to Britain's growth and economic development.

Question 2: I don't think they're saying we shouldn't have knowledge for its own sake, but that the country needs to invest more, and invest more wisely.

Question 3: Universities have a central part to play in research, and creating value and so on, but they should remember that they are universities, not companies. Perhaps it's best to leave companies to get on with more market-focused products, and allow universities to flourish in the more traditional areas of original thought and freer research.

3 and 4 ▶4.4 These activities invite students to predict, and then note down and compare, the presenters' answer to a speculative question. Conduct feedback before showing the extract to hear all the students' predicted answers.

Answers
- greater investment in digital publishing & open access publishing
- publishers are not going to give all their content away
- more open access publishing compared with more restricted, expensive publishing for those who can pay for it

TASK 4 Critical thinking – evaluating a poster presentation

1 and 2 Allow a short amount of time for students to evaluate the poster and the presentation. Checklist I provides a wide range of different criteria – including visuals, language, and questions – and you could divide these up among different students / groups to save time and provide more focus. Make sure that students come up with concrete suggestions for improvement, as suggested in the example.

4D Speaking
Presentations (2)

TASK 1 Critical thinking – selecting a topic

1 and 2 This task aims to enable students to decide what type of information can be effectively presented on a poster. Encourage students to sketch out language and visuals to help them decide. They can also add further topics. Go through one or two examples as a whole class, and elicit reasons why these would be effectively / ineffectively communicated via a poster. At the end of this comparison, ask students to select one topic to work with in this module.

You could invite students, especially those who seem to be strongly visual learners, to suggest ways of presenting analyses and arguments in visual forms.

Sample answer

2 It is important for a poster to have a reasonable balance between text and visuals; a very wordy, text-heavy poster is likely to be seen as unattractive and off-putting for many potential viewers. Therefore a visual dimension is highly desirable. Certain abstract concepts can be challenging to represent in partly visual form. Of the topics in 1.1, an argument for a specific approach could be difficult, as could a detailed analysis of works of literature (as in the Student's Book example). This is partly because arguments and analyses are associated with text - both written and spoken text - which tends to be dense and abstract.

TASK 2 Planning and researching a poster presentation

1 The first activity requires students to finalize their choice for a poster presentation. Encourage students to use the examples in Task 1 either to choose from or inspire them to find a new topic. Make sure it is suitably academic, like the examples given. Examples of non-academic topics might be: collecting wargame models (this is a hobby); celebrity culture (this is a possible topic but needs an academic approach, e.g. an analysis of celebrity culture using an existing theoretical approach); Asian architecture (this is too broad, so needs narrowing down and focusing, e.g. the pressures of globalization on traditional Chinese architecture). Students can form their own groups or you can assign them; probably a maximum of three is advisable to ensure full participation by all students. Ideally, both / all students in each group should agree on the topic, to maintain their interest. Go through the guidelines in class, or ask students to read them in advance independently. Work out how much of the planning is to be done in class, depending on the available time, and how much can be done independently. It might be advisable to use class time as 'workshop' or advisory time, using you and the available facilities as resources as required. A common danger is for students to put off starting work on the project until late in the process, resulting in rushing at the end. To help avoid this, set frequent (e.g. daily) deadlines for students to follow, and check their progress at these points.

2 The spoken stage needs some planning, but in a different way from the more rehearsed presentations covered in Units 7, 10, and 12. Give a time guide for the spoken phase of the presentation, e.g. 2 or 3 minutes (maximum 5). As point 5 of the Guidelines states, it is useful to prepare by anticipating certain questions arising from the material in the poster, but not all questions can be predicted. Students can think of and note down possible answers for the questions they can predict, but advise against rehearsing and memorizing such answers. Due to its interactive nature, the question and answer phase is characterized by interruptions and digressions. Monitor and give help during the whole planning stage as required.

ACADEMIC LANGUAGE

Asking questions about a poster Spatial expressions and question forms

Explain that this functional language is very useful when presenting from a visual such as a poster, and students should become familiar with it and practise it. They can do so in pairs, taking turns to ask about the poster on page 067. You can also model the functions for students to repeat, paying attention to rhythm, stress, and intonation. There is a lot of variety in the functional language and in the critical language, and students have a choice of how direct they want to be, e.g. *Why is this relevant?* (direct) vs *I'm not sure why this is relevant* (indirect).

As a practice activity, prepare some questions and distribute these to students in pairs. Examples of questions could be: *Why did you choose this topic? What did you learn during the preparation stage? How did you find your sources?* Questions such as these can be used to promote fluent responses: students ask and answer within a time limit, and try to limit hesitation, ums / ers, and repetition. In this way they should be better able to answer more critical questions after their poster presentation.

TASK 3 Viewing posters and preparing critical questions

1 and 2 This task needs to take place in an agreed subsequent lesson. If possible, use a large classroom or public space to display the posters. Optionally, invite other participants to attend, e.g. other students and/or teachers. Allow a fixed time for students to view the posters and prepare their questions, perhaps 5 minutes per poster. Before students arrive, prepare the space and bring suitable stationery, e.g. adhesive. It is also advisable to check that all students have completed their poster to avoid embarrassment.

TASK 4 Giving a poster presentation

1 and 2 The previous tasks in the module lead up to this task. Decide on how to manage the event; for example draw up a detailed timetable for each poster presentation and stick to it. Alternatively, allow a more relaxed atmosphere and let the presentations take place more organically. Depending on the class size, two or more presentations could take place simultaneously, but unless the class is very large, it is probably best to do them consecutively. Students value your feedback; try using a pro forma (e.g. a one-page document with criteria for each presentation and space for your notes). Give feedback either publically or only to each group. Public, i.e. whole-class, feedback can be presented more generally rather than naming specific groups.

TASK 5 Evaluating a poster presentation event

1–3 The final task continues with the evaluative nature of Tasks 3 and 4. It is important for groups to reflect on their process so that they can improve next time. Manage the group feedback so that all participants are able to contribute in a non-threatening atmosphere. Remind students of the value of peer feedback and evaluation.

4E Vocabulary Variety

TASK 1 Understanding how synonyms alter meaning

1 This is part of entry from the *Oxford Learner's Thesaurus* which provides not just lists of synonyms, but definitions, examples, and notes to help students distinguish between them. The aim of this task is to demonstrate how synonyms may have a similar meaning and can be directly substituted in certain contexts, but also how they can vary subtly in meaning and usage. Explain that the choice of synonym can depend on context and also on the perspective of the writer (see notes below).

Sample answers

1 *traditional* (*conventional* and *mainstream* would seem awkward as both YouTube & Facebook are quite usual or normal nowadays)

2 *conventional* or *mainstream* (*traditional medicines* would include things such as herbal remedies, i.e. those used before the development of Western, science-based medicine)

3 *traditional* (this suggests a cultural perspective in which a *traditional practice* is viewed as somewhat old-fashioned or not necessarily in line with modern ideas)

2 and 3 Students should discuss what they already know about these sets of words before they check any in a dictionary. Note that in a standard learner's dictionary, they may find that the definitions are almost identical, so they should look also at examples to get a feel for differences. Each pair should select one set to exemplify, which they can present to the class as part of feedback on the whole task. Identify where students have pinpointed the meaning and usage well and where there is a mismatch in terms of context or usage.

Sample answers

2 a **range** - many / several different types of a thing (emphasis on the number of things) - *a wide range of activities*
   choice - different things you can choose from - *the choice of treatment / method*
   diversity - many things that are very different from each other (emphasis on the differences) - *genetic / cultural / ethnic diversity*

 b **disclose** - to make something known (usu. sth to do with the speaker / writer) - *disclose personal information*
   uncover - to discover sth previously unknown (sth to do with sb else) - *uncover evidence about sth*
   leak - to make secret information public (journalism) - *leak documents to the press*

 c **analyst** - a person who studies a particular area and gives their opinion, esp. finance or business - *a financial analyst*
   critic - a person who expresses an opinion about a book, film, etc. - *a literary critic*
   commentator - a person who is involved in a particular area and gives their opinion, esp. on politics or society - *an influential commentator on US foreign policy*

 d **information** - things that you know, read, or find out about; a very general word - *For more detailed information, see ...*
   data - information that has been gathered to find out about sth, esp. as part of research - *research data*
   statistics - numerical information gathered about sth to perform calculations - *government statistics on homelessness*

TASK 2 Using antonyms to avoid negatives

1 and 2 Encourage students to consider antonyms that are not just direct opposites (*not relaxed → tense*, rather than the awkward *unrelaxed*) or even a single word (*not ... diverse → more limited*). As students rewrite the sentences, remind them that they may need to make changes. In feedback, share and discuss possible alternative antonyms and rewordings. Ask students which wordings sound better and explain that a single word with a negative meaning will sometimes be more elegant and concise than a negative construction. They are especially useful to construct more concise noun phrases as in 3 and 4, or to avoid double negatives such as in 4, which can be potentially confusing or ambiguous. As an extension, students select a piece of their own writing, such as the essay in 4B, and find four or five examples where they could substitute synonyms or antonyms to improve their style. They then present their 'before' and 'after' sentences, in pairs or groups, and explain how they made their choices. Encourage discussion about which changes are improvements and which are less successful.

Sample answers

1 ... in the news media is **vague / ambiguous**.
2 ... there was a **more limited / narrow** range of news media ...
3 ... on people's **irrational** fears.
4 ... who have / with a **conservative** approach to ...
5 ... he was clearly **tense** and **reluctant** to ...
6 ... which they condemn as **unreliable**.

UNIT 5 Patterns

ACADEMIC FOCUS: CITATION AND REFERENCING

INTRODUCTION

Unit 5 focuses on the important area of citation and referencing, a key skill in all academic contexts. Whilst referencing conventions can vary greatly depending on the system preferred in a particular discipline or institution, there are some key principles that apply across the board. Building on the general principles already introduced in previous units (see 2B and 3D), the aim of this unit is to familiarize students with some of the different functions, styles, and formats of citations and their associated referencing conventions in reading, writing, and speaking, connected through the theme of patterns; social, economic, and in nature. Students have plenty of opportunities to explore both the macro issues of why we use citation and the effect of different styles on the reader, as well as the detailed 'mechanics' of how to incorporate citations into their own work.

5A Reading looks in detail at citation and referencing conventions in the context of literature reviews, which by their nature tend to be densely referenced. This module explores the theme of socio-economic trends via extracts from the literature review sections of two journal articles; one about definitions of poverty across the EU and the other describing the changing role of women within the workforce across time. Students become familiar with a variety of different types, styles, and functions of citations.

5B Writing concentrates on the 'nitty gritty' of citing accurately and appropriately from sources, using correct referencing conventions and avoiding plagiarism. The module uses a selection of short extracts, both authentic source texts and students' reports, all around the theme of patterns in nature, followed by analysis, discussion, and practical writing activities to reinforce these key skills.

5C Listening examines the use of references to people and sources in the context of a lecture. The lecture extracts, on the theme of economic cycles, provide examples of spoken citations that give the historical background to a topic. The module also gives students further practice with different note-taking techniques.

5D Speaking gives students practice in working as part of a team and the specific communication skills involved in negotiating, allocating tasks, and reaching consensus. Students work in teams to plan a small-scale group research project which involves selecting a topic, dividing up research tasks, and then preparing and giving a group presentation. The key skills practised here can be transferred to a variety of teamwork situations that students are likely to encounter in their future studies.

5E Vocabulary highlights the way in which certain words typically appear in particular patterns and grammatical constructions. These patterns can catch students out at this level, as they tend to focus on expressing complex ideas and constructing more complex sentences. Highlighting these patterns and encouraging students to include them as part of a regular, systematic proofreading checklist can help to reduce errors in their writing.

DISCUSSION

1 This lead-in activity introduces some key concepts and vocabulary associated with the unit theme, Patterns. Students should suggest their own definitions, using examples to help distinguish between the terms.

> **Suggested definitions** (from *Oxford Advanced Learner's Dictionary*)
>
> **cycle**: a series of events repeated many times, always in the same order
>
> **distribution**: the way that something is shared or exists over a particular area or among a particular group of people
>
> **structure**: the way in which the parts of something are connected together, arranged, or organized
>
> **tendency**: a new custom that is starting to develop
>
> **trend**: a general direction in which a situation is changing or developing

2 This activity aims to demonstrate how trends occur in all areas of life and are relevant across disciplines. Set a time limit and encourage groups to come up with just one simple answer for each topic as in the example.

3 Read through the question and example here so that students are clear that they need to describe how a specific trend might occur across time or place. Encourage students to think about different perspectives and variables here, possibly coming up with more than one example in each category. So in the example given, place might also encompass life expectancy trends across urban and rural populations in the same country. Or students could extend the idea to take in other variables, such as income groups, or men vs women. As an extension, you could elicit examples of *cycles*, *distributions*, *structures*, or *tendencies* in the same topic areas.

5A Reading Journal articles (2)

TASK 1 Critical thinking – analysing and evaluating a definition

1 and 2 This task introduces the topic of the reading text in Task 2, definitions of poverty, via critical thinking activities. The task encourages students to ask critical questions about apparently straightforward information, such as definitions, to question their basis and appropriateness across different contexts. Ensure that students have adequately understood key terms in the definition, *household income, national median*. The discussion question in 2 should encourage students to raise critical questions of the *Surely that depends on …* type. Students from a non-EU background might benefit from some teacher input about the make-up of the EU and differences between EU member countries in terms of cost of living, standard of living, etc.

3 and 4 After feedback on 2, students go on to think about their own responses to the issue of how to define poverty. They should identify potential problems and factors to consider rather than trying to arrive at their own definition.

TASK 2 Identifying arguments from sources

1 Students follow the procedure established in previous units (a GAP analysis), to first identify what type of text they are going to read.

> **Answers**
>
> genre: academic journal article
>
> audience: academics / students in Sociology
>
> purpose of the text: to compare different ways that poverty is / can be measured across the EU
>
> date of publication: 2010

2 These questions encourage students to draw out the main points of the text and consider how they overlap with the suggestions they put forward in Task 1. As some of the concepts in the text may be difficult to grasp, encourage students to think of examples wherever possible and follow the pairwork with whole-class feedback to ensure that the basic points are clear before moving on to the next task.

> **Sample answers**
>
> Issues and problems raised:
> - measuring absolute vs relative poverty
> - the differences in standards of living between the richest and poorest member states make comparisons difficult
> - relative measures reflect wealth inequalities not necessarily poverty
> - low income doesn't take account of other factors (for example, how much government support is available for those on low incomes or the availability of free health care in one country but not another)

3 Point out that the references in the text have been highlighted to help students identify more easily who said what. The statements in this activity paraphrase the key arguments from the text. As some are easier to differentiate than others, encourage students to identify the most obvious ones first, leaving the trickier ones to last. Ask whether the citations (what these sources said) came before or after the in-text references, i.e. a mixture of both.

> **Answers**
> ```
> 1 e  2 d  3 a  4 b  5 c  6 f
> ```

4 This question aims to highlight how as academic readers and researchers, students can follow up references to other sources in a text to further explore aspects of a particular topic which they are interested in, for example, in order to write an essay on the topic.

a Townsend (1979), The European Commission (2004)

b Guio (2005), Förster (2005), Nolan & Whelan (2007)

c Fahey (2007), Brandolini, (2007), Kargas & Ritakallio (2007)

ACADEMIC LANGUAGE

Citations (3) Quotation, paraphrase, and summary

This is the first of two boxes on citation in this Module and builds on the overview of citation and referencing conventions in 2B (page 032). The aim of this box and the following task is for students to notice how academic writers use a variety of citation styles, depending on the function and type of citation. Students will do more work on the practical mechanics of using different citation styles in the writing module (5B). Ask students to suggest when writers might choose each of these styles and why.

TASK 3 Recognizing different types of citation

1 and 2 It is worth noting as students look back at Text 1 to identify examples of these citation styles that the distinction between paraphrase and summary is not always clear-cut, especially as students cannot refer to the original sources for comparison. Students can suggest reasons for the writers' choice of citation style as they feed back their answers to 1.

Sample answers

a **a short quotation**: Townsend's (1979) definition of poverty as 'exclusion from ordinary living patterns and activities due to lack of resources'.
Reason: see example

b **a long quotation**: … by the European Commission in the following terms: An absolute notion is considered less relevant for the EU for two basic reasons. [...] which tends to vary considerably across countries (European Commission, 2004).
Reason: a long quote from a key authoritative source (the European Commission) to establish the current situation

c **a paraphrase**: Förster (2005, p. 32) notes that the labelling of the relative income measure as 'at risk of poverty' reflects the tendency of governments to interpret it as an indicator of inequality in income distribution rather than as a measure of poverty as such.
Reason: explanation of a specific point

d **a summary**: Fahey (2007) argues for the development of an EU-wide measure alongside a nationally relative measure
Reason: a summary of a whole argument

e **a footnote**: 1. For a recent review of this evidence, see Nolan and Whelan (2007).
Reason: the reference is not directly relevant, but may be of interest to the reader

f **more than one reference**: … recent exercises of this sort include Brandolini (2007) and Kangas and Ritakallio (2007).
Reason: examples of several studies that give evidence for this point

3 These short extracts, all from texts on similar socio-economic topics, give further practice in identifying different citation styles. It is worth noting in feedback how c and d use a blend of summary /paraphrase and quotation to ensure that the quotes fit in with the flow of the text. Students will return to look at these examples again in Task 4 to consider the role of comment and evaluation in citation.

Sample answers

a a summary

b several references as evidence for a point

c a short quotation

d a paraphrase + short quotation

e a footnote

4 This task encourages students to think about the writing conventions associated with citation and referencing. It is important to stress that these conventions vary between referencing systems, even similar author-date systems (e.g. the Harvard System, APA, MLA, etc.). That is why this book doesn't give definitive guidelines on the exact form of referencing conventions. It must be up to students to check the exact conventions they are required to use, for example on an institution or department's website. If students are already studying within their host university, this might be an opportunity to search for such information on the university's website. The aim of this activity is to highlight the type of details that students might need to check and adhere to.

Sample answers

- A longer quotation (such as from the European Commission in Text 1) is indented and has space before and after.
- Where the source of a citation appears at the start of a sentence (and may be slightly separated from the actual citation), the full reference is repeated directly after to make it completely clear – see long European Commission quote in Text 1 and Alan Greenspan quote in 3c.
- Where a citation continues over more than one sentence (as in 3d), reference reminder language is used to make it clear that the ideas in the second sentence come from the same source – 'the Forum's report goes on to stress' – see more on reference reminder language in Unit 6B.
- Where the whole reference is shown in brackets, there is a comma between the name and the date (Greenspan, 2003).
- Where a page number is shown, there is a comma after the date, before the page number – Forster (2005, p.32).
- Where more than one reference is shown in brackets, they are separated by semi-colons (Sastry, 2004; Machado & Hill, 2005 …).
- et al. can be used where there are more than three authors of a single text – the names of all the authors are shown in the reference list though.

TASK 4 Differentiating between cited material and comment

1 and 2 Whilst it may be relatively easy for students to identify citations in a text by picking out in-text references, it is also important to understand how the writer is presenting the citation in relation to their argument(s) and stance. If students are struggling to pick out language showing the writers' evaluation and stance in the example, refer them to the alternative version for comparison.

> **Sample answers**
> 1 a An absolute notion is considered less relevant ...
>   b (European Commission, 2004)
>   c *relies heavily on* ('heavily' suggests maybe 'too much'), *purely relative* ('purely' suggests is doesn't take other possibilities into account), *has been justified by* (you only need to 'justify' something that can be criticized)
> 2 The alternative version has the evaluative language removed so presents a more neutral stance. Note the difference in connotation between 'justify' and 'explain'.

3 Students apply the ideas discussed in 1 and 2 to further examples. Stress that there are not always clear-cut answers here as evaluation can be subtle and open to interpretation by the reader. It is, of course, also more difficult to judge out of context like this, so students should offer and justify their own interpretations.

> **Sample answers**
> a *It is **important** to remember however ...* shows that the writer is pointing out what they consider to be an important limitation of something that has gone before.
> b Neutral
> c Fairly neutral - although choice of the reporting verb *warning* - suggests that this is a bit alarmist.
> d *but similarly **cautious*** - writer's comment making a comparison (to a previous citation) and evaluation; ***Appropriately***, - evaluative adverb shows writer's stance, i.e. there are solutions to the problem, it isn't as bad as Greenspan suggests.
> e Neutral

TASK 5 Identifying supporting evidence from sources

1 This task introduces a second text, which is slightly simpler and uses citation in a different way from Text 1. Students will compare the two texts in Task 6. Set a time limit to read the text and decide which of the points are mentioned. During feedback, ask students to identify the synonyms that are used to paraphrase the ideas from the source (e.g. *labour force – workforce*; *reductions in working hours – work shorter hours*). Students can improve their own paraphrasing skills by noticing how others paraphrase.

> **Answers**
> Points mentioned: 1, 2, 3, 5, 6, 7
> Points not in text: 4 & 8

2 and 3 With only three sets of in-text references in the text, students should be able to able to quickly identify which of the points in 1 they support. Ask students which of the statements in 1 they could have made fairly confidently *before* they read the text (i.e. which could be said to be common knowledge, even to a non-expert). The idea of what constitutes 'common knowledge' (and so does not need citation as support) is often a tricky one for students to grasp and is generally something they get a feel for through reading in their own subject area and noticing where authors use citation to support points and where they do not, as here.

> **Answers**
> 2 1 No citation
>   2 Bosch *et al.*, 1994
>   3 No citation
>   5 Blossfeld and Hakim, 1997; Rubery *et al.*, 1999; Blossfeld and Drobnič, 2001
>   6 & 7 Gershuny, 2000; Anxo *et al.*, 2002
> 3 b

ACADEMIC LANGUAGE

Citations (4) Focus on author or content

The second Academic Language box in the module looks at another aspect of citation style: focus and emphasis. Allow students time to read the box and check understanding: *Why would you put the name of the author at the start of a sentence before the citation? When would you show the reference only in brackets at the end?* You could use the following examples to elicit the difference in emphasis:
- *There was a fall in the overall number of immigrants to the UK in 2012 (Home Office, 2013).*
- *According to data collected by the Home Office (2013), there was a fall in the overall number of immigrants to the UK in 2012.*
- *The British Government claims that there was a fall in the overall number of immigrants to the UK in 2012 (Home Office, 2013).*

TASK 6 Understanding focus in citations

1 and 2 These activities prompt students to compare the use of citation across the two texts in this module. Emphasize that neither style is correct; they are just two different types of text that require different citation styles.

> **Sample answers**
> 1 Text 1: a & d
>   Text 2: b & c
> 2 Text 1 contains more citations, more quotations and paraphrase, and more focus on authors as it is presenting potentially controversial arguments and stances which need to be clearly attributed.

Text 2 contains fewer citations, mostly in the form of general summaries, with a focus on content rather than author, because it is presenting general background information, much of which is common knowledge and fairly uncontroversial.

TASK 7 Independent research – citation in your discipline

1 This is another opportunity for students to see how the ideas in the module relate to their own discipline. Note that to see more than the abstract in many online journals, it is generally necessary to be registered, so this task may depend on access. It is best set as homework, but you should advise students that they may need to log on to a university system to get access to the full text of journal articles, for example, in a university library. Students could revisit the articles they found in the independent research task in 3A (page 044).

2 Students report back either formally, one-by-one, or more informally sharing what they found in groups. Collate the findings of the class in terms of referencing systems and balance of citation styles. Ask students what conclusions can be drawn (if any). Are the findings consistent for each discipline area? What are the key differences between disciplines?

5B Writing Citation

TASK 1 Critical thinking – why do we reference sources?

1 The aim of this activity is to encourage students to think about why citation is important in academic writing. They could argue for any of the points in the list, although 1 and 3 are probably the least valid reasons. You could divide the list into reasons why academics generally use citations and why students use them (such as to show their tutor they have done some reading).

2 Explain that these extracts are all alternative versions of the same idea from the introduction to a student biology essay. They are not intended to be complete introductions (or even complete paragraphs), but express a single point. Students should focus on which is the clearest and most persuasive. Point out the glossary note about the use of *ibid* in the second extract if students haven't come across this convention before. As the task has been about citation, this is an obvious point of focus, but students could mention other features such as style, language, explanations, etc. as well. Some students may point out that extract 1 is clearly plagiarized; this will be picked up in Task 3.

3 Some students may have already mentioned the use of citation. This activity focuses on the specifics of how citations have been used, recapping the ideas from the Reading module.

TASK 2 Attributing citations

1 The aim of this discussion activity is to elicit students' existing ideas and beliefs about plagiarism. Depending on the class, this may be a subject that has already been tackled or it may be completely new. Students should read Text 1 to check their answers before feedback after 3.

2 and 3 Text 1 is taken from a handbook for undergraduate students. It is aimed at the biosciences so tends to focus on *research* and *scientists*, but the main points are valid across disciplines. It aims to provide a realistic perspective on plagiarism from an authoritative source and shows that it is not just an issue in an EFL / EAP context, but for all students. Students compare and discuss their answers to 1 in their groups after reading the text.

4 This discussion moves on from what constitutes plagiarism to the wider context; reasons for and consequences of plagiarism. This is an opportunity, especially for students new to EAP and from backgrounds with very different academic cultures (which may have different ideas around the ownership of ideas), to discuss what to expect in their target academic culture (e.g. in the UK). The answers to these questions may differ in your own context, so this may be an opportunity to search for any guidelines on plagiarism issued by your own institution or those which students hope to attend. These are often published on university websites.

Sample answers

Reasons for plagiarism:
- Not understanding the concept of attributing sources
- Not understanding how to use referencing conventions correctly
- Not keeping a track of reading and source details accurately
- Not understanding what counts as common knowledge and what needs to be attributed

Intentional plagiarism is where the student knows they are cheating.

Accidental plagiarism is where the student forgets to add a reference (because of poor note-keeping, etc.), wrongly assumes that something doesn't need a reference (i.e. it is common knowledge or a common phrase), or doesn't make their referencing clear enough.

Teachers and examiners can easily **spot plagiarism** because:
- they are generally familiar with the literature in their subject, so spot others' ideas / language
- plagiarized content generally doesn't match the student's writing style so stands out 'like a sore thumb' and can easily be cut and pasted into a search engine to check the source
- institutions now use software to spot plagiarism (such as TurnItIn).

Penalties for plagiarism (at UK institutions) can vary from the individual piece of work receiving an automatic 'fail' grade to the student being expelled from their course.

TASK 3 Avoiding plagiarism

1 and 2 This task returns to the short extracts in Task 1 and compares them to the original source text on which they are based. Students start by identifying any clear cases of language which has been copied directly from the source and not attributed using an in-text reference. They then move on to look at how ideas are attributed and more generally evaluate how appropriate and effective the citations are.

Sample answers

1 This is completely plagiarized. Much of the language is completely lifted from the original with no attribution.

2 Correct in-text references, good paraphrasing, and appropriate comment / explanation.

3 Mostly correct in-text references. Accurate and correctly attributed quotation (although no page number). The second sentence starts with 'They' to show that it's from the same source (could possibly add *ibid* at the end to be even clearer). However, the final two sentences are copied almost word-for-word from the original - without the use of quotes, this could also constitute plagiarism.

Citations (5) Introducing citations

This box illustrates some of the variety of different language used to introduce citations. It also highlights a range of different reporting verbs that students will practise using in the following task. Ask why ideas, arguments, or theories are typically reported in the present tense, even when the source was published in the past (i.e. because the ideas are likely still those of the author), while research findings tend to be reported in the past tense (i.e. because they were events that actually happened in the past). Explain that this is not a hard and fast rule, but a tendency worth looking out for in reading.

TASK 4 Varying reporting structures

1 Explain that students here are looking for the verb which best collocates with the highlighted noun. After feedback, ask whether the examples here follow the present / past tense rule suggested above (they don't all). Elicit suggestions why they might not (e.g. use of past tense to report historical contexts, such as Charles Darwin's ideas).

Answers

1 proposed   2 placing   3 developed   4 made
5 provides   6 gave   7 offers   8 presented

2 Whilst some of these reporting verbs can be followed by more than one structure, by a process of elimination, there is only one possible final set of combinations. In both activities 1 and 2, encourage students to check in a dictionary any answers they are uncertain or disagree about. Most learners' dictionaries show information about common collocations and typical following constructions in examples. For activity 1, look up the bolded nouns, for 2 look up the reporting verbs.

Answers

1 b   2 e   3 a (f also possible)   4 d   5 c   6 f

TASK 5 Citing accurately from sources

1 and 2 In this task, the process of students trying to explain what they have read to a partner orally should help them to generate appropriate synonyms to use in paraphrasing. It also helps them to work out together the meaning of any unknown vocabulary. The skill of explaining 'in your own words' can be a difficult one, especially with unfamiliar subject matter, but is essential if students are to incorporate citations into their writing in a way that fits in with their own voice. Students can choose to report on any aspect of the source texts and should try to use a range of different approaches – refer them back to the academic language boxes in the module.

TASK 6 Citing from secondary sources

1 This task revisits the concept of primary and secondary sources introduced in 3A. Text 6 is from the same source as Text 1 in this module, a student handbook. Students read the text and then explain the three concepts in their own words without looking back at the text.

Sample answers

A **primary source** reports directly on new research or presents new ideas.

Note: In the case of new research, this is often in the form of a journal article, but a book (such as a monograph) could also present new thinking, theories, etc. As Text 6 is from the field of biosciences, it assumes that primary sources will all be in the form of journal articles rather than books, but this is not always the case in other disciplines.

A **secondary source** reports ideas from another (primary) source. Textbooks aimed at students will invariably be secondary sources.

Misrepresentation is where ideas are changed in the process of reporting them. The writer reporting an idea (in a secondary source) may have misunderstood the original source, they may have explained it poorly, or may have just made an error in reporting. Sometimes a writer may only select certain information from a source that supports their point, so that their reader doesn't see the full picture without reading the primary source for themselves.

2 Look at the in-text reference in the example carefully as a class to establish how secondary sources are typically reported, i.e. primary source + date + *as cited / quoted in* + secondary source + date. Elicit the difference between *quoted* (for a direct quotation) and *cited* (for other forms of citation, e.g. paraphrase). The examples here are all from previous texts in the book, so may be familiar (1 – Text 1, 5A; 2 – Text 2, 5A; 3 – Text 2, 4A).

Answers

1 Fahey, 2007, as cited in Whelan & Maitre, 2010

2 Bosch *et al.*, 1994, as cited in Anxo *et al.*, 2007

3 Sorensen, 2007, as quoted in Bainbridge, Goc & Tynan, 2011

TASK 7 Identifying, recording, and using references in writing

1–3 This task looks at the practicalities of researching, recording, and using reading as a source for citations. Note that this process is not completely fixed, these are just guidelines and the order of some of the stages could easily be exchanged (e.g. 4 and 5, 8 and 9) and some stages left out (e.g. 1–3 may not be necessary if working on a set text or from a reading list).

Answers

2 d   5 b   8 c   10 a

5C Listening Lectures (4)

TASK 1 Critical thinking – activating real-world knowledge

1 Reading the introduction to the lecture and discussing the questions here helps students to familiarize themselves with the topic and activate their background knowledge. Inevitably, some students will be more aware of these issues than others, so by working in groups, they can pool knowledge.

2 If some of these words are unknown, allow students to check them in a dictionary. You might want to limit dictionary look-ups to three or four words to encourage students to work with existing knowledge (even if it is rather sketchy) and only look up words which none of the group have any ideas about.

Suggested categories
(others could be argued for)

negative economic events: *crash, crisis, depression, recession*

economic problems (effects of above): *deficit, inflation, turbulence, unemployment*

positives in an economy: *development, growth, recovery*

political attitudes / policies: *laissez-faire, orthodoxy, policy*

TASK 2 Making notes on a chronological sequence

1 ▶5.1 The aims of this task are two-fold, to illustrate how lecturers commonly put new ideas into a historical context, and to revisit the idea of using visual note-taking techniques, such as timelines (see also 3C). This lecture extract is from the second section of the lecture. Ask students to look back at the introduction and identify what the lecturer says the second part will be about – *... but **secondly**, put that in the context of the fact that the global economy, over the past 100–150 years, does seem to ...* Feed back to establish the correct order of events before going on to 2. You may want to use the transcript, in which the key events are highlighted, to check answers, but make sure that students don't keep the transcript open for the next activity, which should be based on their own notes.

Answers

1929	Wall Street Crash & Great Depression
1945	end of WWII
	establishment of World Bank / IMF
1945-1973	Golden Age of Capitalism & sustained economic growth
1979-2009	deregulation & 'capitalism unleashed'
2009	global recession

2 and 3 Students work in A, B, C groups in order to focus on just one section of the extract and two or three key events each. Encourage them to use the key phrases from their notes, but to try to explain and summarize in their own words. Give students a couple of minutes to prepare, using only their notes. Monitor as they work in their groups and collect examples of good synonyms and paraphrases that students used to feed back at the end.

TASK 3 Recognizing citations in a lecture

1 ▶5.2 This task returns to the academic focus of the module, citation. Students watch a second very short extract in which the lecturer briefly introduces Keynes and the backdrop against which he was working. During feedback, you may need to fill in some of the historical background for non-European students.

Sample answers

1 end of WWI (1918) to 1936

2 after WWI Britain and France were imposing huge reparations on Germany to pay them back for the damage caused during the war

3 Keynes argued that this was economically wrong and that the reparations would prevent the German economy from recovering and so cause social and political problems in that country – which, of course, it did.

2 and 3 ▶5.3 In this slightly longer extract, the lecturer makes a number of references to specific works by Keynes: two pamphlets and a book. Ensure that students understand what a *pamphlet* is before they watch (this is a medium that is no longer used in this context, but was a popular way of circulating new ideas at that time). Stress that students will not be able to note down all the details about each publication (e.g. the exact titles), but should make notes about the main events they relate to. This is an important point for efficient note-taking as it is generally possible to check such details later, so lecture notes should be points that help students to remember and understand the key ideas.

Sample answers

2
- *The Economic Consequences of the Peace* – end of WWI, demand for reparations from Germany
- another pamphlet (title & date not given) – Churchill's decision to go back to the Gold Standard
- *The General Theory of Employment, Interest & Money*, 1936 – the Great Depression

3 1 See above

2 The lecturer may give the reference details at the end of the lecture, otherwise, these sorts of details are easy to check if students are interested.

ACADEMIC LANGUAGE

Citations (6) References to people, works, and ideas

As students have already looked at the transcripts and reference details, this box focuses attention on the different ways in which the lecturer introduces references. Ask students where they previously saw the use of past tenses to report the ideas of historical figures, i.e. the Charles Darwin examples in 5B Task 4.1, page 079.

TASK 4 Recognizing different styles of spoken citation

1 Students should be able to quickly scan to identify the reporting verbs and references here. In feedback, ask which style each example matches from the Academic Language box.

Answers

N.B: reporting verbs shown in bold, Keynes' works underlined

Keynes warned against saying that was just old economic orthodoxy

so after the First World War when **Keynes wrote** his first famous pamphlet called *The Economic Consequences of the Peace*, where **he warned that** the peace agreement …

Keynes wrote another pamphlet **saying** the economic consequences of Mr Churchill, **warning that** again would …

Keynes warned that the world just doesn't work like that …

And then most famously in 1936 Keynes published his major work, *The General Theory of Employment, Interest & Money*, where **he basically said that** economies don't naturally return to equilibrium

that was the first thing **he said** which, which quite radical at the time,

Keynes warned that actually cutting the budget deficit

and **Keynes said** it, it must be government spending,

Keynes said that you can't force people to borrow

so he likened, **Keynes likened** having a low interest rate …

so **Keynes said** you must use fiscal policy …

2 ▶5.4 This final extract gives students the opportunity to see how a different lecturer uses citation in a similar historical context. If students have already watched the Dr David Howard lecture (about Sustainable Cities from 2C), you could ask them to quickly recap the topic before they watch.

Answers

1 Friedrich Engels and (Karl) Marx

2 Engels's book *The Condition of the Working Class in England in 1844*

3 Friedrich Engels, in the turn of the, the middle of the nineteenth century, **wrote about** the condition of the working class in England; but **Marx and Engels**, his co-worker, **noted** the great levels of poverty amongst many of the working class people; So **in his book, written in 1845 called** *The Condition of the Working Class in England in 1844*, **Friedrich Engels looked very closely at** city structures and **he noted that** 'in every great city …'

5D Speaking Teamwork

TASK 1 Critical thinking – the role of teamwork

1 Divide the class into A and B groups of four to six students per group. If the class carried out the group poster presentation in 4D, this could form the basis of the Group B discussion, otherwise students could comment on their individual experiences of teamwork. Explain that the group should decide who will take notes. Set a time limit for the discussion. Monitor and gently prompt any students who are not contributing to join in.

2 After ending the discussion time, give students a couple of minutes to decide on the main points to come out of their discussion and how they will present their summary. Depending on the size of the class, summaries could be presented to the whole class (with only two groups) or by pairing up groups. Remind students that the groups have discussed slightly different topics, so their summaries will have to make the topics discussed clear as well as the points raised. At the end, you might want to give a few points of feedback on how well students worked as a team for this task, in terms of managing the discussion and allocating tasks (i.e. note-takers and summary presenters).

TASK 2 Planning a group research project

1 and 2 ◀)) **5.5** Throughout this task, students listen to extracts from a student discussion which illustrate some of the features and potential pitfalls of teamwork. They will also go on to identify some of the key functional language in 3.1. The first extract establishes the task, which is the same as the one students will carry out in Task 3. In feedback, focus on why the other suggestions were rejected as these may be relevant to students' own choices in the later task.

Answers

1 Task: Research a person who *has been influential in their subject area*
Objective: Present a short *profile*
Possible subjects: 1 Schrödinger 2 *Marconi*
3 *Prof. Stephen Hawking*

2 Schrödinger was rejected because his field (quantum mechanics) was too obscure and difficult to explain to a general audience. Marconi was rejected because although he was a well-known name, he was involved

in a lot of different areas and so a simple profile would be difficult to compile.

3 ◀)) **5.6** The second extract focuses around deciding what to research and allocating tasks. Again the decisions in the extract are relevant to the following task. The discussion brings up the issue of using Wikipedia for research. The participants in the extract decide that it's OK to use to look up basic facts in this context, but they should be checked against another source. There are often strong views in academic circles about the use of Wikipedia and other online sources, so this may form a point of discussion as part of the feedback here. Some arguments for and against:

For
- we all use Wikipedia in our everyday lives; students will be familiar with it
- for many basic details, such as in this task, it is fairly reliable
- it often gives information in a form that's more accessible to students than academic sources
- it's freely available without the need for registration (the case for most academic journals)

Against
- information can be patchy in quality and reliability
- despite attempts to mediate content, it is open to bias and distortion
- it is for a general rather than an academic audience, so different standards apply

Answers

1 Basic biographical data, an overview of his most important work (but not details).

2 They will all research the same information but in different sources.

ACADEMIC LANGUAGE

Hedging (2) Reaching agreement

This box revisits the theme of hedging language (see also 3B page 045) and picks out both minimizing expressions which soften what the speaker says and maximizing language to emphasize important points. The examples encompass a range of language types which perform these functions. Don't get too bogged down in classifying different structures (modal verbs always do *x*), but instead encourage students to analyse how different language choices affect the impact of a comment. As you read through the examples, ask the following questions:
- Which modal verbs in suggestions are typically minimizing and which could be maximizing? (Minimizing – *might, could, may*; maximizing – *should, ought to, need to, have to, must*)
- What type of questions are generally used to raise problems – *wh-* or yes / no questions? (yes / no – in asking the question you are suggesting the answer, i.e. this is a problem)
- What is the effect of *I think* before the hypothetical, *it would be better*? (Minimizing (this is just my opinion) + maximizing)

TASK 3 Preparing and giving a group presentation

1 Students look at the transcripts of the student discussion to identify examples of maximizing and minimizing language. These have been highlighted in 5.5 and left for students to pick out in 5.6. Note that not all the language fits exactly into the categories in the academic language box, discuss the different ways that the students in the extract minimize and maximize their message.

> ### Sample answers
> 5.5 Minimizing: 1, 2, 4, 6, 7, 8
> Maximizing: 3, 5, 9, 10
>
> 5.6 **I guess** the basics **would** be date of birth and ...
> This is an academic profile, **isn't it**?
> So **I think** that **would** be relevant in this case.
> ... we **don't need** to go into lots of detail.
> We **just need to** outline his most important work.
> **It's important we don't** get bogged down ...
> **Perhaps** we **could** all just choose ...
> So it **might** be helpful starting point
> Anyway I **could** check the University website ...

2 This mimics the task already encountered in the previous listening extracts, so the structure, steps, and aims should be fairly clear. Groups of three to five students will allow enough room for discussion and negotiation, without any group members being left with not enough to do. Allow students enough space to make their own decisions (and mistakes), but monitor to give feedback at the end (either here or after the presentations) on how well the groups managed their discussion, used hedging language, and participated equally.

3 How students tackle this research task will depend on the time and resources available. You may want to set the research phase as homework, so that students go away to carry out the research. Alternatively, if students have online access in class, they could conduct the research collaboratively in class. If students are encouraged to select sufficiently well-known figures, finding enough general information for a profile shouldn't take a lot of time. Stress that they can allocate research tasks in any way they want, they don't have to follow the plan from the listening.

4 Again this stage can be carried out in class or as homework if students are able to meet up outside of class. Depending on group size, it might not be practical for all group members to present part of the profile (in a group of five this might be too disjointed). You could suggest that any non-presenting students could be responsible instead for preparing some visuals, so that everyone contributes. As the focus of this module is on teamwork rather than presentation skills, you might want to make the presentations relatively informal, perhaps with students sitting facing their audience, rather than standing at the front of the class. Any visuals could be simple (e.g. a printout of a picture of the figure).

Make the aims and expectations of this stage of the task clear to students.

5 With a small number of groups, presentations could be given to the whole class. With a larger class, groups could be paired to run simultaneously. Divide feedback into two stages. Feedback on the final presentation could be peer feedback, with evaluation and comments from the audience. Feedback on the effectiveness of the teamwork throughout the task might be a combination of groups evaluating their own performance and your own comments, noted whilst monitoring each stage. Possible headings for this evaluation might include:
- discussion and negotiation stage (making suggestions, raising problems, coming to compromises, asking for clarification, use of hedging language, participation / contribution)
- research stage (allocation of tasks, participation / contribution, clarity of notes and input)
- presentation stage (allocations of tasks, participation / contribution, feedback and support).

5E Vocabulary Lexical patterns

TASK 1 Recognizing verb + verb patterns

1 and 2 This task focuses on the verb forms (*-ing* or *to-*infinitive) that typically follow specific verbs. Students use both meaning and grammatical clues to match the sentence halves, then work in pairs to compare their answers. Explain that while students need to learn the forms that typically follow individual verbs, there are patterns which can help them to group sets of similar verbs. Point out that these typical patterns are often illustrated in the examples in a dictionary entry. If you have access to a corpus, these patterns are also interesting to explore by searching for the key verbs and sorting corpus lines to the right.

> ### Answers
> 1 g 2 d 3 f 4 c 5 a 6 e 7 b
> Group 1: 1, 3, 4, 5 - verb + particle (preposition / adverb) + *-ing*
> Group 2: 2, 6, 7 - verb + object (somebody) + to do

3 This activity encourages students to think about other members of these two groups, using a dictionary to check any patterns they are not sure about and to use the constructions productively.

> ### Answers
> benefit from, concentrate on, persist in + *-ing*
> invite, permit, persuade + sb + to do sth

TASK 2 Identifying and using clause patterns

1 and 2 This activity identifies another common type of pattern that is often highlighted in learner dictionary entries as + *that* or + *wh-* after a verb, an adjective, or a noun. Again, students use both meaning and grammatical clues to complete the sentences. Feed back and identify the key word + linking word combinations. You could set the examples to be written as homework or allocate different words to different students to exemplify.

Answers

1 argue that
2 anticipate how
3 uncertain whether
4 conclude that
5 reasons why
6 questionable whether
7 unaware that
8 establish how

TASK 3 Identifying repeated patterns to decode long sentences

1 Repeated patterns following a verb, as in the example (*focused on identifying ... and also on finding ...*), are sometimes known as **parallel structures** and can easily trip even advanced students up both when they are reading and when they are attempting to construct longer sentences in their own writing. Because the second structure may be quite separated from its 'partner' verb, a certain amount of backtracking may be needed to decode it. The sentences here are authentic examples taken from the same sources as the texts already used in 5B (about patterns in nature). The example follows a pattern highlighted in Task 1 (*focus on + -ing*), 1 and 2 reflect the type of pattern explored in Task 2 (*unclear if* and *suggest that*) and 3 introduces a different pattern (passive reporting verb + *to be* – similar examples include *thought to be, shown to be, found to be*, etc.).

Answers

1 It is **unclear if** the behavior is opportunistic – that is, **if** any individual will do it – or **if** the behavior is specific to a class of honey bee workers.

2 Data presented here **suggest that** males avoid heat shielding, **that** worker bees ... are most likely to heat-shield, and **that** the behavior is very sensitive to context.

3 The migratory orientation program **is considered to be** very important for the survival of individual birds and **to have** a strong impact on the evolution of migration routes.

UNIT 6 Responsibility

INTRODUCTION

Unit 6 The unit aims to enable students to select and use material from source texts effectively in their own writing and speaking. Summaries occur frequently in academic texts and need to include an appropriate amount of detail for their purpose. Students learn first how to analyse the structure of academic sources, and in particular reports, which are characterized by a conventional structure. This leads to a range of summarizing tasks so that students are able to write an appropriate summary for their purpose. Through the unit, students summarize and synthesize material from a range of written texts as well as two lecture extracts and a seminar discussion.

6A Reading aims to familiarize students with research reports by looking at a number of report abstracts. Such reports are particularly associated with science subjects, though most disciplines make use of reports with some variations. Students learn to understand the structure of research reports, and use the structure to find the information they need. The module also develops students' critical thinking skills by identifying assumptions in reports, particularly in the abstracts and conclusions. Objective language is covered, and students learn to identify sections in reports that are more subjective than others.

6B Writing enables students to write carefully constructed summaries of different lengths for different purposes. Students analyse and evaluate source texts and sample summaries, and practise referencing: in particular using reference reminder language which serves to make their reader clear about whose material in the text is whose. In the process, students repeatedly practise identifying main points in a text to use in their summaries. This leads to a more complex summary, which students construct using carefully selected material from the three texts in the module. Students should then be equipped to access and summarize a wide range of academic texts for their purpose.

6C Listening develops the academic focus of summarizing based on two lecture extracts on the same topic. Students learn to select the information they need from each source, and process this first into a written then a spoken summary. Having the two extracts also enables students to evaluate the lecture content, style, and delivery using given criteria such as pace of delivery. Students can then apply these listening and note-taking skills to other contexts and for other purposes.

6D Speaking gives students their third opportunity to participate in a seminar discussion. The particular focus of the module is careful preparation for the seminar by reading relevant source texts to use selectively in the seminar. This reflects the academic practice of approaching a seminar with relevant ideas rather than simply thinking up ideas in the seminar itself. Students also develop their critical skills through formulating critical questions to ask in response to points raised in the seminar. They can then apply these skills in future seminar settings.

6E Vocabulary addresses the key language concept of collocation. Whilst students may be familiar with common collocations from everyday language (*make a mistake, heavy traffic*, etc.), they need to become familiar with the particular collocations used in both general academic contexts and also within their own discipline. This module aims to raise awareness of these important patterns that will help students develop a fluent academic style.

DISCUSSION

1 and 2 The Discussion aims to bring out the unit theme of Responsibility in relation to a range of major issues. Explain that essentially there is a problem implicit in each issue, which leads to the question of whose responsibility it is to address. Try one as a whole-class example, perhaps selecting two or three students to demonstrate a sample response. Encourage students to ask critical questions, e.g. *Why is it their responsibility?*; *How would they manage to do this?* Ask questions yourself to stimulate further questions. If appropriate, you can also focus the discussion on what the students themselves expect to contribute in their lifetimes; alternatively simply add 'students' to the list of agents. Activity 2 shifts the focus to the formulation of policy; this process is likely to vary across contexts. Invite students to give examples of different countries / regions (e.g. *Switzerland, Scandinavia, South America*) where different agents may have particular opportunities to contribute to policy.

6A Reading Reports

TASK 1 Understanding the structure of a report

1 This task applies GAP (genre, audience, purpose), introduced in Unit 1, to a key primary source: a research report. As its name suggests, the genre is reporting something (i.e. research) which has been undertaken.

Sample answers

Main purposes: *to add to human knowledge; to inform; to persuade; to present an argument*

The main purpose of a report is not to explain – secondary sources such as textbooks are more suited to that purpose. Also, they are not concerned with entertaining.

2 and 3 This task builds on students' knowledge of reports. Start by eliciting what they know, e.g. that reports typically follow a conventional structure, moving from more objective reporting (i.e. the background and method to the research) to more subjective material including interpretation of the results – this key point is brought up in activity 6. Set a time limit of about 2–3 minutes for students to complete the six report sections and the 'Section heading' column before moving to the other section headings. Students can work together to state the purpose of these using their own words.

Sample answers

Section heading	Purpose of section
1 Abstract	to give an overview of the whole report including its conclusion
2 Introduction	to introduce the topic and context, brief background information and a rationale for the research
3 Literature review	to present an overview of relevant recent research in the field
4 Background	to give background information and a rationale for the research
5 Method	to describe how the research was carried out
6 Results	to summarize the findings of the research
7 Discussion	to interpret and evaluate the results and their significance
8 Recommendations	to make suggestions for further work in the area
9 Conclusion	to restate the main findings and discussion points
10 Appendix	to present any extra relevant material, such as raw data, which is not necessary / too long to include in the body of the report
11 References	to list the sources used in the report

4 This activity asks students to consider the role of summary in a report – they should see that summary is widespread. Remind students that summary will be examined in the Writing module.

Sample answers

Abstract – briefly summarizes the whole report

Literature review – summarizes (selectively) the main points in the relevant literature

Results – possibly summarize the main results (though all the results should be reported)

Conclusion – summarizes and restates the main findings and discussion points

5 Set a time limit to read the abstract. Explain that students will typically have to read many abstracts in a limited time. Elicit the purpose of abstracts: to summarize the main points (including the conclusion) of a report; and to give sufficient information about the report so that the reader can decide whether to read the full report, or not. Explain that abstracts can be structured in different ways, and so may not always follow the pattern below; however, like introductions, they tend to move from the general to the specific.

Answers
1 Background
2 Method
3 Results
4 Conclusion

6 This activity brings out the objective / subjective distinction, which may have come up earlier in the task. Stress the importance of realizing that not everything in a report is objective, e.g. the authors of the report may interpret the results in certain ways and draw particular conclusions, while some readers may disagree with these interpretations. Another aspect of subjectivity is selectivity – the writer of a literature review can give more prominence to particular literature at the expense of others.

Sample answers

- The Method and Results sections are objective, and should not include opinion of the writer / researcher.
- The Recommendations and Conclusion are more subjective, in that they are the appropriate place for offering interpretation (which is subjective) and ideas for future work in the field. The Discussion has significant elements of subjectivity because this is where the writer can pick up on different aspects of the research and the results: selectivity is subjective because different people can select different things. The Literature review can be selective in what is included (i.e. this is subjective).

ACADEMIC LANGUAGE

Style (2) Expressing objectivity

This language box builds on the last activity by presenting relevant language which reflects the writer's style. Point out that with *it* and *there* structures there is no referent, i.e. it does not refer to anything but is needed to fill the grammatical subject. Elicit further abstract nouns to use as subjects, e.g. *This / The study, research, process, procedure.* Point out that using objective language does not necessarily mean that the content is objective.

TASK 2 Identifying objective language in a text

1 Point out that the report extract is an authentic text, taken from the body of the report in Text 1. If necessary, remind students also to ensure subject–verb agreement for full accuracy. Note that in gap 4, the verb *compared* is not in the past tense, but in the present tense / passive voice; it 'shares' the same auxiliary *are* as *are presented* (gap 3). As an extension / independent study task, ask students to make their own gap-fill texts by finding a similar text in their discipline, gapping out the verbs, and exchanging texts with other student(s).

Answers

1	were examined	6	are
2	were examined	7	perform
3	are presented	8	are reported
4	compared	9	emerges
5	shows	10	reduce

2 Monitor during the pairwork discussion, and refer students to page 208 in the Language Reference section for further details on the use of the passive.

Sample answers

The choice of the active or the passive is determined by the subject of the verb, and whether it is 'doing' the action or 'having the action done to it'. For example, in gaps 1 and 2, the action of 'examining' is done by the authors of the text, not the subjects of the sentences (i.e. 'private vehicles' and 'the same scenarios'), therefore the verbs are in the passive (it is not necessary to state who did the action because it is obvious from the context). For similar reasons, gaps 3, 4, and 8 are in the passive. The verbs in

the remaining gaps are in the active because in each case the subject of the verb is 'doing' the action, i.e. in 5 Figure 1 actually shows the information stated; in 6 the emissions are lower; in 7 it was the electric vehicles which in fact performed well; in 9 the pattern emerged, and in 10 the type of vehicles stated reduced the emissions.

TASK 3 Comparing and contrasting report abstracts

1 Ask students to do this task without using dictionaries, to show that they can extract key information by using the information they can understand from a text, rather than always trying to find out what they do not understand. The *context* includes information such as where and when the research is taking place, and what it involves.

Sample answers

	Text 1	Text 2
Context	UK city council - adoption of low-emission vehicle fleet	*Global algae production for biodiesel as an alternative to petrodiesel production*
Aim	*To present a study of low-emission vehicle adoption in a UK city*	To present the results of a case study of algal biodiesel and evaluate its competitiveness
Conclusion	Low-emission vehicles achieved reduced air pollution and health benefits	*Algal biodiesel could replace petrodiesel entirely; it should be commercial by 2018*

2 and 3 These activities require students to assimilate the key information, so that they can answer the following questions without referring to the text: *What does the research involve? Where / when does it take place? What is the aim of the research? What is the main conclusion?* By the end of this task, students should realise that such information is normally presented in an abstract. Activity 3 invites students to evaluate how clearly it is presented in each abstract.

TASK 4 Using report structure to find information

1 and 2 This task enables students to replicate the process of using report abstracts and contents in order to work out what is in the full text. Try discussing the first point as a whole-class activity to stress that students should provide a brief reason for their choice – covered in activity 2.

Sample answers

- evidence and arguments for the development of algae diesel - *likely to be included, as this is the title and main aim of the article*
- points in support of other (i.e. non-algal) alternative energy technologies - *unlikely to be covered, as the aim of the article is to argue for algae as a potential replacement for diesel, and not to discuss a wide range of other alternative energy technologies*

- a comparison of different types of algae - *probably not relevant, though this topic might briefly come up*
- an analysis of the cost of algae biodiesel compared to conventional diesel - *highly likely to be discussed, as the reader would expect the relative costs of the two technologies (algae and diesel) to be covered*
- a comparison of carbon emissions by various types of fuel - *likely to be included, but with certain limitations as the main focus is algae and diesel*

3 Similar to Task 1, this activity uses short text extracts to mimic the process of quickly reading a text. This requires students to process this information and logically situate it in the appropriate section of the report.

Answers

1 Introduction: d

2 Background - Why use algae?: b

3 Method: e

4 Results & discussion: c

5 Conclusion: a

4 This activity demonstrates that while the conclusion ties in closely with the abstract, it can present new information, and may have some discrepancies, i.e. slightly different / contradictory information. Suggest to students that they should not therefore rely on the abstract alone for a citation in their text - they should read selected parts of the report / article, especially the conclusion.

Answers

The main pieces of background information are repeated in both texts, i.e.

- that algae has potential as a biofuel source
- that currently it is inefficient / uneconomic.

New information in the conclusion:

- 'several major advantages' of algae mentioned; also that it can be produced on a large scale.

Discrepancies between abstract and conclusion:

- the main finding that biodiesel will be competitive (cost-effective) is repeated, but the date is different (2018 in the abstract / 2020 in the conclusion)
- the finding that greenhouse gas emissions would be reduced is repeated, but the amount is different (by '~5%' in the abstract) / '4-5%' in the conclusion).

5 The final activity assists students in navigating a report, and assessing the importance of using abstracts, together with selected other parts of the text, to do so.

Sample answers

Reading the abstract and conclusion of a report gives a very useful overview of the whole report, and is particularly useful in deciding whether to use the text in your own writing / research.

TASK 5 Critical thinking – identifying assumptions in a text

1 Check students' understanding of *assumptions*: something that is accepted / included in the text as being true, but is not actually a proven fact. Simple *wh-?* questions contain assumptions, e.g. *What have you read in the past seven days?* assumes that I have read something, though in fact I may not. Like many academic texts, the abstracts in this module contain a number of assumptions, and the authors do not refer to these (some texts state, *we make the assumption that ...*). Note that the two statements (a) and (b) in isolation are neither assumptions nor research findings - it is in the context of the article that they take these forms.

Answers

a is an assumption

b is a finding based on the authors' research

2 This activity continues with the theme of assumptions. To check understanding, ask concept questions such as: *Does the text state that Coventry City Council views local carbon emission vehicles as desirable?* (No - this is assumed to be the case). Item 2 is neither an assumption nor a relevant point - it is not mentioned in the text.

Answers

The text makes assumptions 1 and 3, but not 2.

3 This question is possibly more challenging. If students are finding it hard, give the answers and explain that major investment in algae production technology must currently be in place for the arguments to work. Although items 2 and 3 are not mentioned, they are arguably relevant to the research.

Answers

Assumption 1 is made. Items 2 and 3 are not mentioned.

4 Explain that many assumptions are reasonable, and students now have the opportunity to evaluate whether the assumptions they have identified are acceptable in the context of the reports.

Sample answers

The answers depend on the person's stance: many scientists believe that vehicle emissions contribute to climate change, though this is not proven and many do not believe it; there is a growing body of evidence linking conventional vehicle emissions with ill health effects.

TASK 6 Asking critical questions about a text

1 Set a time limit of about 2–3 minutes to encourage faster reading. When checking the answers, invite critical evaluation of the abstract, e.g. *Is it helpful to omit the conclusion from the abstract?* (no); *Is the abstract clear?* (it could be clearer). As a result of these, students may decide they do not wish to read the whole report.

Writing Summaries

Answers

Context: international; aviation CO_2 emissions

Aim: to encourage global sectors to work together to reduce aviation CO_2 emissions

Conclusion: not explicitly stated

2 The second activity develops the idea of asking critical questions. By the end of it, students should see how an apparently straightforward abstract can raise as many questions as it answers. As an extension, ask a group of students to search for the article, and if available, read it to find out which questions, if any are answered in the text.

Answers

1 b 2 c 3 f 4 a 5 d 6 e

3 and 4 Monitor while students formulate their own critical questions. Put students into groups if they are finding the activity difficult, so that there is more help available.

TASK 7 Independent research - searching for reports

1 Having read four sample abstracts and done a range of reading and critical tasks, students should be in a position to respond to the given statements. Accept all answers and encourage justification, i.e. reasons why, as suggested below.

Sample answers

1 Agree: this is one of the main purposes of abstracts, although some abstracts are more helpful than others.

2 Partly agree: abstracts generally offer most of this information in brief, though the rationale may be implicit in the background information - it should be expanded on more in the introduction.

3 Possibly agree: you would need to read a number of Discussion sections to evaluate this statement. Many Discussion sections are likely to be angled in favour of the authors' thesis / hypothesis and may not be as balanced as possible.

4 Partly disagree: the Conclusion may be very brief and only re-state the main points, perhaps with one or two limitations / recommendations for future research. The interpretation may be in a dedicated section with that title, or be part of the Discussion section.

5 Disagree: this depends on the type of essay. Citing one or two reports in itself may not be sufficient; a fuller literature review may be necessary, depending on the aims and word count.

2 and 3 Give a deadline for this independent research project. If possible, allow time in a specified class for students to present and exchange information on their journal / report abstracts. Encourage students to make notes while reading, to serve as a record of their reading.

TASK 1 Identifying topic and main points of a text

1 This discussion phase serves to activate students' interest in the module topic of responsible food purchasing. Ask students to define the terms for themselves and/or give examples, e.g. 'locally-produced' may be relative to the size of the country in question. As with all academic discussions, ask for reasons, e.g. *I would be willing to pay 15% more for organic food if I had children as this should benefit their health due to the lack of pesticides and antibiotics used in the production.*

2 Students should by now have enough ideas to read the text quite quickly and efficiently. Draw students' attention to the source, to establish the genre: a journal article extract. Tell students not to focus on unknown language in this task.

Answers

- Topic: consumer preferences for local production
- Context: consumer willingness to buy a food product in the USA - Kentucky and Ohio
- The main point: consumers seem willing to pay for locally-produced food products

TASK 2 Preparing, writing, and evaluating a summary

1 This activity presents the essential stages in writing a summary – say that students will follow this procedure in this module. Ask students to justify why the two non-selected stages are inappropriate for a summary.

Answers

Stage: *b*

Inappropriate stages:
- Copy down sentences from the text to use in your summary - the summary should use the writer's own language as far as possible.
- Add your own evaluation of the material to complete the summary - this is inappropriate for a summary because it is adding material that is not in the original text.

2 Explain that the Checklist can be used whenever students are writing summaries. As an extension, ask students to apply it to summaries which they may already have read, e.g. in Unit 4A Task 4 on page 058.

Answers

The following terms relate mainly to content: 1 contextualized; 2 complete; 3 correct

The following terms relate mainly to language: 5 clear; 6 creative

Item 4, concise, relates both to language and content.

3 and 4 Remind students of the stages in writing a summary: Unit 4A looked at the process of identifying main points and the authors' stance and using these as the basis for writing a summary. If students ask for a word count guide, suggest 40–60 words: it is very difficult to include the main points in less than 40 words, but a longer summary, e.g. 100 words, is probably too inefficient for many purposes as it would take up too much space. Summaries and abstracts are examples of texts that can be harder to write shorter than longer.

> **Sample answer**
>
> Hu, Batte, Woods, and Ernst (2012) investigated consumer preferences for value-added food products in two states in the USA. They found that certain US consumers are willing to support and pay more for locally-produced and other 'value-added' food such as organic.

TASK 3 Analysing the structure of a text for a summary

1 and 2 This task applies the principles of text structure analysis, which was applied to abstracts in the Reading module, to a report introduction. Stress the importance of logic and coherence in the order. Ask students if they know what order such texts would have in their first language: there may be differences. Do not check the answers until students have read Text 2, which essentially is to confirm their order.

> **Sample answers**
> ```
> 1 c-b-a-e-d
> 2 1 c  2 b  3 a  4 e  5 d
> ```

TASK 4 Analysing and evaluating a student summary

1 and 2 Ask students to quickly read the student summary before checking the answers to both 1 and 2. If they ask about the significance of the coloured text, either ask them to speculate on why some text is blue, or say that this point is covered in activity 3 of this task.

> **Answers**
> ```
> 1 c  a  d  b
> ```
> 2 There is no statement to gain the reader's interest (item c in 3.1), because this is unnecessary in a summary.

3 Students now focus on the language of the summary. As with most academic texts, a significant amount of the text is made up of generic language, i.e. language which can be used in a wide range of contexts regardless of the topic and discipline. Point out that using such language may seem mechanical, but it is how skilled writers construct their texts; emphasize that students need to build up knowledge of a large amount of this type of generic language.

> **Sample answers**
>
> In their article *[topic of article]*, *[name(s) of author(s)]* present their research into *[area of research]*.
>
> *[name(s) of author(s)]* focus particularly on *[main focus]*, defined as *[definition]*.
>
> The authors note the *[key background information]*, but cite the limited research into *[statement of gap in the research]*.
>
> They propose *[their main proposal]*.
>
> Their research findings indicate that *[main findings]* particularly in terms of *[first detail of findings]* and *[second detail of findings]*.

4 In this activity students analyse the Text 2 authors' use of two different types of words: general descriptive words, and technical words. The answers should enable students to select appropriate language when writing their own texts including summaries.

> **Sample answers**
>
> 1 The author selects synonyms for all the items except technical terms, i.e. 'product'. In general, technical terms are not paraphrased and there are usually no synonyms available.
>
> seek out - *locate*
>
> paucity of research - *limited research*
>
> product - *product*
>
> perceived - *view*
>
> willingness to pay - *willingness to pay / which they are prepared to pay more for*
>
> attribute - *qualities*
>
> heterogeneity - *variations*
>
> 2 a - they are technical terms

5 Ask for feedback on the summary using Checklist J.

> **Sample answer**
>
> The summary is complete in that it contains all the main points of the original text. Also, it is correct, clear, and creative (it uses the student's own language where possible). Regarding conciseness, it could be shortened slightly, which is a point picked up on in Task 5.

TASK 5 Writing a shorter summary

1–3 This task is informed by students' analysis of the summary in Task 4, and takes them through the process of writing their own summary. Stress the importance of a rigorous approach: rather than trying to recall what the main points in the source text are and then putting these down in a summary, students should follow the suggested stages: make notes on the text (activity 1); write a summary (activity 2) for a research paper; and reprocess this into a shorter summary to use in a shorter text such as an essay (activity 3). In doing so, students should see how the most essential information in a text can be distilled down to about two sentences.

Sample answers

1 Paragraph 1: research on farmers' markets in the USA → shows they benefit diversity and help develop localization

Paragraph 2: new CSA model → potentially minimal impact, but influence of CSA farms on consumer buying habits needs further research

Paragraph 3: summary of research from 2002 on CSA farms in the USA → raises various questions for future research into regional impact of local food selling

2 Brown and Miller (2008) reviewed previous research into farmers' markets and Community Supported Agriculture (CSA) in the USA. They reported research by Gillespie et al. (2007), which shows that farmers' markets benefit diversity and help develop localization and the development of a localized food system. Brown and Miller go on to evaluate the new CSA model, concluding that it has so far had potentially minimal impact. They acknowledge that the influence of CSA farms on consumer buying habits needs further research. Finally, their summary of research from 2002 on CSA farms in the USA raises various questions for future research into regional impact of local food selling.

3 Brown and Miller (2008) reviewed previous research into farmers' markets and Community Supported Agriculture (CSA) in the USA. They found that farmers' markets benefit diversity and localization, and that the CSA model has had minimal impact, but needs further research.

4 Finally, students consider the purpose of the different types of summary. Explain that summaries are extremely frequent in academic texts of many kinds. Elicit examples, e.g. *textbooks summarize such things as theories, research, schools of thought, and arguments.* Students can use summaries in both their spoken and written work.

Sample answer

Longer summary: integrated into a literature review in a longer text (e.g. research essay, dissertation).

Shorter summary: integrated into a shorter written text - an essay or paper; or a spoken text - a presentation or seminar discussion.

ACADEMIC LANGUAGE

Citations (7) Reference reminder language

Stress the importance of clarity in writing: the reader should be clear whose material is whose in a text. Unfortunately, in both student and published writing, this is not always the case. A typical area of uncertainty is when a significant amount material is being cited (as with a summary) and a reference is given at the end. To make the source of the content clear, advise students to introduce the citation clearly, and for each new sentence of the citation include reference reminder language, and then end the citation with an in-text reference. Go through the various examples in the Academic Language box so that students have a range of language to use.

TASK 6 Referencing in summaries

1 In this task students can see how reference reminder language is used in an authentic text. Ask them if the cited material is clear – as a result of the careful use of such language the reader should be clear that this material is not the authors' (Brown and Miller) but that of the cited source (Gillespie *et al.*).

Answers

The first reference to the source in this extract is: *Gillespie et al.* (2007). This is followed by reference reminder language: *they …The authors found … In addition … (Gillespie et al., 2007) … The authors' final point is that …*

TASK 7 Incorporating summaries into a literature review

1–3 This task is both realistic and potentially demanding for students. Remind students that summaries are written for a purpose; with literature reviews, summaries need to be included and synthesized from a potentially large number of texts. Go through the answers to activity 1 carefully, stressing the need for the summary to suit its purpose, particularly in terms of the amount of detail that can be included. Students can then write their literature review extract (activity 2), working either individually or in pairs / small groups for support. In the evaluation phase (activity 3), encourage students to look at a number of different texts, and relate each one to the checklist criteria.

Sample answers

1 The rewritten student summary is clearly slightly shorter; it starts with the authors' names and gets to the point of their research. Certain material is deleted from the first summary: the reference to and definition of 'locavores'; and the detail of food market growth in the USA. These changes are partly to reduce the wordcount, and partly because they add an unnecessary amount of detail for the purpose of the new summary, i.e. to incorporate as part of a literature review.

2 **Consumer attitudes to buying local food**

A number of researchers have conducted studies related to consumer attitudes to buying local food. Hu, Batte, Woods, and Ernst (2012) found that consumers in the USA are willing to pay more for 'value-added' foods, such as locally-produced and organic. Further research by Thilmany, Bond, and Bond (2008) looked into the buying habits of consumers of locally-produced food, again in the USA. While they found strong growth of farmers' markets, there appeared to be limited research into what motivates consumers to locate and pay more for local food products. Thilmany, Bond, and Bond (2008) also propose a new concept of 'willingness to pay' (WTP). They report considerable variations in buyers' habits and attitudes (*ibid.*). Meanwhile, Brown and Miller (2008) reviewed previous research into farmers' markets and Community Supported Agriculture (CSA) in the USA. They found that farmers' markets benefit diversity and localization, and that the CSA model has had minimal impact, but needs further research.

TASK 8 Independent research – summarizing a longer text

1 and 2 The module concludes with a personalized task. Encourage students to work within their discipline or a related subject area. Independent learning can be done collaboratively, so students may wish to work together and compare with other student pairs / groups. Refer students back to Checklist J, so that these evaluative questions become habit-forming.

6C Listening Lectures (5)

TASK 1 Preparing to listen to lectures

1 Explain that this module continues with the academic focus of summarizing from texts. Students will watch two lecture extracts: on the same topic of the UN but by different lecturers at the University of Oxford. Students can prepare in either pairs or small groups; as it is likely that some students may know very little about the UN and others may know more, try to spread the latter group out among the groups. Ask students to note down the information to refer to later; it does not matter if they get some details wrong.

2 and 3 These activities further activate students' knowledge of the lecture topic by responding to visuals. Ask students to try to explain slide 1 in their pairs / groups, focusing particularly on how the different parts might be related. Ask students to briefly note down their predictions in the final activity.

TASK 2 Understanding a lecture introduction

1 and 2 ▶ **6.1** Remind students of the related tasks in the Writing module, where they analysed the introduction to a report. They can apply the same principles and process to a spoken text, i.e. the lecture introduction. Show the extract once and check students' answers. It should not be necessary to repeat the extract, but suggest that students watch / listen to it again independently while reading the on-screen transcript – this will help link the spoken to the written word. In activity 2, ask students to add the new details in note form to their notes from Task 1.

Answers

a The lecture will focus on the Human Rights Council (some of the changes that have occurred organizationally to the UN human rights), and the Universal Periodic Review (the innovation captured within the UPR).

b charter-based bodies and treaty-based bodies

c The lecture won't cover:
- when the Security Council acts taking note of human rights violations in a country
- the World Health Organization
- the nine core human rights treaties / treaty-based bodies
- the UN as a whole and how all of its activities everywhere should focus on human rights.

TASK 3 Summarizing a key concept from a lecture

1 and 2 ▶ **6.2** This task uses 'intuitive' questions to lead to the main points. Demonstrate this principle using a new concept, e.g. ASEAN. Write this up and elicit questions, e.g. *What is ASEAN? When was it founded? Where does it operate? How is it managed?* The same principle can be applied to any new concept / organization. In Task 1 students predicted what UPR might be, then heard the first lecturer mention it in Task 2. Students should now be clearly focused in watching Extract 2. After watching, check that all students have made effective notes. Stress again that without notes students will quickly forget the lecture content.

Sample answers

1 and 2
- **What is the UPR?** the fulfilment by each state of its human rights obligations and commitments, a cooperative mechanism based on an interactive dialogue
- **What are the objectives of the UPR?** to assess positive developments and challenges; to assess the fulfilment of each member state of the United Nations, in relation to its obligations and commitments in the field of human rights
- **How does the UPR system work?** offers technical assistance to states as required, looks at the human rights situation of all 193 members of the UN on an equal basis
- **When are UN member states reviewed?** every four years (48 states per year)
- **What does the UPR review for each state? / What (points) does the UPR contain?** all the human rights treaties that the state has ratified, any additional voluntary commitments

3 Before students write, elicit the main characteristics of a summary: see Checklist J for details. Encourage them to draft their summary first without referring to the lecture transcript. They can then read this to fill in any gaps and check accuracy. As with written summaries, students should use their own language as far as possible, though the technical terms (e.g. *UPR, member states, human rights*) will remain the same as in the original text.

Sample answer

The Universal Periodic Review (UPR) refers to the fulfilment by each state of its human rights obligations and commitments. It is a cooperative mechanism based on an interactive dialogue, and aims to assess positive developments and challenges, and the fulfilment of each member state of the United Nations in relation to its obligations and commitments in the field of human rights. The UPR system works by offering technical assistance to states as required, looking at the human rights situation of all 193 members of the UN on an equal basis. The UN member states are reviewed every four years, meaning that 48 states are reviewed per year. The UPR review covers all the human rights treaties that the state has ratified, plus any additional voluntary commitments. It is a cooperative system to enable UN member states to fulfil their human rights obligations by offering technical assistance to states as required.

4 and 5 ▶6.3 Students watch the final short extract in order to identify the lecturer's main points (expressed in her conclusion) and reprocess these into a short summary. If students write more than one sentence, or an extremely long sentence, ask them to edit it down to about 40 words by concisely combining the main points in their notes and missing out detail such as the name of the UN Secretary General.

Answers

4　1　The UN Secretary General, Ban Ki-moon, said that the Universal Periodic Review 'has great potential to promote and protect human rights in the darkest corners of the world'; it is enabling a global picture of human rights.
　　2　We can see where a state explicitly doesn't have commitment regarding human rights, i.e. where it actively rejects UPR recommendations.
　　3　We see every four years how the state has lived up to its commitments on human rights.

Sample answer

5　The UPR has great potential to promote and protect human rights in the darkest corners of the world because it reports regularly on all UN member states; the results of the UPR show which states are not committed to specific human rights.

TASK 4 Understanding the main points of a lecture section

1 ▶6.4 Students should now be 'tuned in' to the topic of the UN, so you could start by asking them to fill in as much as they know about the points given. Ask students to say what kind of information is likely to be included in 'basic facts' (e.g. *number of members, year of foundation*). Their listening will then be well-focused. Mention that later (in Task 5) students will have the opportunity to compare and evaluate the two lectures / lecture styles. Show the extract once before checking answers.

Sample answers

Basic facts about the UN
- made up of 193 member states
- nearly every state in the world is a member
- it is a more valid organization than the League of Nations (its predecessor) because USA and Soviet Union were not members.

The role / purpose of the UN
- It is an inter-governmental organization (not a world government) – it can only do what its members allow it to do
- member states bear the responsibility for failures to act (e.g. in Bosnia and Herzegovina or Rwanda in the 1990s)
- it lacks true autonomy
- to maintain international peace and security

The make-up of the UN
- The UN consists not only of the Security Council but a wider family of bodies (he mentions the General Assembly, the World Court, etc.)

The aim of the lecture
- to focus on the Security Council and discuss collective security, i.e. that all members join forces to protect any one of its members from the unlawful use of force by any or any one or several states.

---

2 To encourage fluency in writing, allow students a fixed time to write their summary. Stress the importance of using the notes they took in 1; if they write the summary straight afterwards, they can also use their memory to add information, but point out that they will have forgotten most of this within a day – hence the importance of note-taking while listening.

Sample answers

Background information on the UN: facts, history, type of organization

The UN is made up of 193 member states; indeed nearly every state in the world is a member. It is a more valid organization than the League of Nations (its predecessor) because the USA and Soviet Union were not members. The UN consists not only of the Security Council but a wider family of bodies such as the General Assembly, the World Court.

Purpose, responsibilities, and limitations of the UN

The UN is an inter-governmental organization, rather than a world government. It lacks true autonomy and is only able to do what its members allow it to do. Its member states bear the responsibility for failures to act, such as in Bosnia and Herzegovina or Rwanda in the 1990s. Its main aim is to maintain international peace and security.

The aim of the lecture

The lecture aims to focus on the Security Council and discuss collective security, i.e. that all members join forces to protect any one of its members from the unlawful use of force by any or any one or several states.

3–5 ▶6.5, 6.6 These activities go into more detail in the lecture. To fully explain the lecturer's quotation in activity 3, students need to understand the background to the statement: essentially the authority of the UN rests with the member states rather than itself. In activity 4, students focus only on their selected aspects of the UN; this should enable them to focus closely on the detail related to this while ignoring the rest of the material. Quickly check students' notes before the explanation stage in activity 5. Ask students to look at the transcript only after they have attempted to present their summary.

Sample answers

3　The UN has no separate authority; the UN is not itself responsible, but its member states are.

4　**Peacekeeping**
　　UN Charter: not in the UN Charter, falls between Chapter 6 of the Charter (specific measures) and Chapter 7 (enforcement measures) → Chapter 6½

　　Definition: UN operations in which international personnel, military and civilian, are deployed with the consent of the parties and under UN command, to help control and resolve an actual or potential international or internal conflict

> Purpose: to suspend the conflict & gain time to allow the parties to resolve the conflict, i.e. to create space for diplomacy to work; peacekeeping is not = peace enforcement
>
> Operations & cost: an innovation, established in 1956 in the Middle East (Suez) - or 1948; from 1948 to 1987: 13 UN peacekeeping operations; since 1987: 53 new operations (four times as many in the past 25 years); this year alone (2011) 15 active UN peacekeeping operations, at a cost of US$7bn
>
> Responsibilities: peacekeeping, ensuring the delivery of humanitarian aid, organizing and observing elections, demobilizing armed forces, training police, verifying compliance with human rights agreements, etc. (= complex peace operations)
>
> International security: preventative diplomacy; peacemaking (= bringing hostile parties to an agreement); post-conflict peace building (= efforts to strengthen and solidify peace to avoid a relapse into conflict)

TASK 5 Comparing information from two lectures

1–3 This task brings together material from the two lectures, relying particularly on students' notes to achieve the tasks. Students will already have considered the points introduced in Task 1, so the first activity formalizes their thoughts. Make sure they provide the source for each piece of information. Activities 2 and 3 give students the opportunity to collaborate on the writing and evaluation of summaries.

4 and 5 Explain that in the final activities, students can reflect on their learning and the effectiveness of the delivery of information in the lectures. This is useful as students are likely to be exposed to a wide range of lecture styles and they can exchange ideas on how best to approach different lectures. Collate good points and pieces of advice for all students to use.

6D Speaking Seminars (3)

TASK 1 Reading to prepare for a seminar

1–4 This task gives students practice in the important activity of preparing for a seminar. In academic settings, students are normally expected to prepare for a seminar by reading suggested texts and/or gaining information from lectures. All students read Text 1. This text is quite challenging and you may wish to establish the topic, feed in some vocabulary, and elicit or give some examples so that students are clear about the context before they go on to pick out the main points of the text. If you think it's necessary, ask your students to read the text quickly and answer the following question: *What or who does the text talk about protecting?* Check students' notes while reading and after reading. It is more effective to actually write notes rather than go through a text with a highlighting pen because making notes demonstrates understanding and processing of the information in

the text. Help with any unknown language and/or ask students to use dictionaries. Following the first text, ask students to suggest specific recent examples or situations where the UN has been called on to protect citizens of a member state.

With the other two texts monitor to check that students are taking sufficient notes. Stress that they will need such notes to present their text effectively. Say that the student who is listening can either interrupt to ask clarification questions, or wait until the mini-presentation is finished before doing so. There is no need to write the summary in this task – the focus is on spoken summaries.

Sample answers
2 and 3

Text 1 Main points in note form, with evaluation in **bold**:
- *The Responsibility to Protect* introduced in a 2001 report by the International Commission on Intervention and State Sovereignty (ICISS)
- Adopted by the UN General Assembly at the 2005 World Summit
- 'A **revolution** ... **in international affairs**' (Lindberg, 2005)
- The report **broadens international responsibility** to protect to encompass both the responsibility to react to humanitarian crises and the responsibility to prevent such crises, plus the 'responsibility to rebuild' failed and tyrannical states
- This **reframed the debate** away from state intervention towards international responsibility for protecting endangered peoples
- A **new international political consensus emerged**, supporting what the ICISS report calls 'intervention for human protection purposes' (ICISS 2001: xiii).

Text 2 Main points in note form, with evaluation in bold:
- **Non-governmental organizations contribute to human security**:
  - as a source of early warning about conflicts;
  - providing relief operations in conflict / natural disaster;
  - supporting government / UN-sponsored peacebuilding.
- NGOs **play a central role in promoting sustainable development**, e.g. International Committee of the Red Cross (ICRC), its authority based on Geneva Conventions to protect & provide for war & violence victims
- Other NGOs include:
  - *Médecins Sans Frontières* (emergency medical assistance);
  - Save the Children (protection of children);
  - Amnesty International (human rights).

Text 3 Main points in note form, with evaluation in **bold**:
- The UN history of peacekeeping is **a 'failure', with little hope of change**
- Two solutions are: use contract labour to add to UN peacekeepers; contract labour to use force against human rights abusers
- Military contractors (i.e. private) are already used in conflict
- UN law should permit their use
- There are problems, but their use could provide great benefits
- Opponents to this idea may say the UN Charter does not allow it; but international criminal tribunals are widespread yet not in the Charter

- Political will needs to progress in this matter
- Using private companies under strict conditions may improve current peacekeeping results.

TASK 2 Preparing a logical argument for a seminar

1 and 2 Explain that the topic of the seminar is based on the unit theme of Responsibility, with a focus on which agent should have primary responsibility for international problems such as those stated. This develops and extends the unit Discussion on page 087 following the students' reading in this module. Say how much time students to have to prepare (e.g. 15 minutes), and decide whether students should do this individually (which helps ensure all students participate) or in pairs / groups (which encourages communication and discussion). Alternatively, the preparation stage can be done independently – as is likely to happen with academic seminars. If a student does not prepare properly, they are likely to have insufficient ideas, which in itself is a useful learning point. Depending on resources available, students can search for further information on some of the agents given in 1. Encourage students to anticipate weaknesses and difficulties in their arguments and selected agents; they can then think of responses to these, e.g. *NGOs may have much less money than national governments → NGOs are smaller and more able to adapt quickly and reach the people who matter, while governments may not be able to reach them so easily and efficiently.*

ACADEMIC LANGUAGE

Asking critical questions Questioning the logic of a contribution

Point out that the language presented here is to some degree indirect and 'polite'. In general, participants in an academic seminar avoid excessively direct, very informal, or confrontational language (e.g. *'You're wrong' / 'That's just ridiculous'*); the latter is more typical of informal conversations - which may themselves be on the same topic, but in a different context. However, the function of the language is clearly critical: the speaker is questioning and pointing out weaknesses. Stress the importance of such a critical approach, just as with written texts, students need to approach the content of spoken arguments critically. Practise the language as a whole class or in pairs.

TASK 3 Asking questions about a contribution

1 and 2 ◀))**6.7** Play the extract once or twice, pausing after each speaker as necessary. Students may also benefit from reading the transcript. Elicit one or two sample critical questions to encourage further questions, e.g. in response to speaker 2: *You're raising the question of accountability, but what about the people that NGOs serve? Aren't they naturally accountable to these people?* Conduct whole-class feedback to enable students to hear a wide range of questions, which they can themselves evaluate.

TASK 4 Conducting a seminar discussion

1 The final task brings together all the preparation into a seminar discussion. Remind students to base their arguments on their prepared points in Task 2, but to also respond to the arguments of other participants in the seminar – stress that a seminar involves the exchange of ideas rather than the delivery of a series of monologue arguments. Check understanding of the Guidelines and set the parameters: the timing, any particular rules (e.g. ensuring that each participant must make at least two contributions); finally stress the importance of reaching a resolution within the timeframe.

TASK 5 Summarizing the main points of a discussion

1 and 2 Allow students about 10 minutes to write their summaries; alternatively they can write them up after the class for the next lesson. In addition to reading other groups' summaries, you could give students the opportunity to question the students in that group, for example to determine why they reached their particular resolution.

6E Vocabulary Collocation

TASK 1 Recognizing collocations in a text

1 The aim of this activity is to demonstrate how students can notice collocations in their reading. This short extract is from Text 1 in the Speaking module (page 100) which students have already encountered, so they can focus on just the language rather than the content. Each of the words highlighted are common academic vocabulary that students might use in their own writing. Using the example, explain that each word might occur with more than one collocate; which could be an adjective, verb, noun, or preposition.

Answers

responsibility + **rests**; responsibility + **for** (doing sth)
form + the basis; the basis + **of** sth
generate + consensus; **international** / **political** + consensus

2 Students work first individually and then in small groups to suggest other collocations that might be used with these four key words. Encourage students to check any they are not sure about in a dictionary, where they may be shown in an example or a collocations box. If you have any specialist collocations dictionaries available, these could provide a further reference resource. Ensure they stay focused on the specific sense of each word as used in the text.

TASK 2 Identifying academic and discipline-specific collocations

1 and 2 Students don't need to identify the exact discipline in each case, but instead a general subject area, either quite wide or more narrow. In feedback, explain that whilst some collocations may be common across several academic disciplines (*strong correlation*, *adverse impact*, etc.), others are much more subject-specific. For example, *high diversity* is only found in the earth sciences (ecology, biology, etc.) to refer to the mix of species of plants or animals. In other contexts, more normal collocations would be *great / wide diversity*. Stress that students should to pay attention to those which are either general transferable academic collocations or relevant to their own discipline.

Sample answers

	Collocation(s)	Type	Field / discipline
1	a strong correlation between the two variables	1 adjective + noun (strong correlation) 2 noun + preposition (correlation between)	statistical analysis / academic research
2	women were asserting their rights as citizens	verb + noun (assert one's rights)	Law, Social Sciences
3	infection is acquired through human contact	1 verb + noun (acquire an infection) 2 adj + noun (human contact)	mainly Medicine
4	an adverse impact on the individual	1 adj + noun (adverse impact) 2 noun + preposition (impact on)	general academic
5	issues of corporate responsibility	1 noun + preposition (issue of) 2 adj + noun (corporate responsibility)	general, Business
6	statistical analyses were performed	1 adj + noun (statistical analysis) 2 verb + noun (perform an analysis)	statistical analysis, academic research
7	the high species diversity found in the tropics	adj + noun + noun (high species diversity)	Ecology
8	creating a complex network of social contacts	1 verb + noun (create a network) 2 adj + noun (complex network) 3 noun + preposition (network of) 4 adj + noun (social contacts)	Social Sciences

3 and 4 This diagram shows one possible way of recording collocations. Again start by identifying which are general and transferable, so worth learning, and those which are more discipline-specific. Encourage students to select one or two word forms for each of the target words to build similar diagrams, either individually, in pairs, or in small groups. If they are struggling for ideas, suggest particular relations, e.g. *adjective + noun*.

Sample collocations

adjective (major, new, serious, great, etc.) + **challenge**

verb (pose, face, present, overcome, etc.) + **challenge**

adjective (empirical, little, strong, convincing, etc.) + **evidence**

verb (provide, find, present, etc.) + **evidence**

evidence + verb (shows, suggests, supports, indicates, etc.)

evidence + preposition (of, for, from, against) + sth

apparent + noun (effect, difference, contradiction, lack of, etc.)

adverb (readily, immediately, increasingly, etc.) + **apparent**

conduct + noun (study, research, interview, analysis, survey, etc.)

5 In this simple research task, students investigate collocations for themselves by using an academic search engine as a basic corpus. This task could be carried out in class or as homework, either using a publically available search engine, such as Google Scholar, or a university library search. By searching for an individual search term, a list of entries will come up with the search term highlighted for each entry. Students need not understand the full context or click through to the articles listed, but simply look at the direct surrounding context, scrolling down and noting different patterns and combinations. Where an unusual collocation comes up, they could check the wider context (i.e. the specific discipline or subject area). Encourage them again to look for commonly recurring patterns or for combinations that are relevant to their own studies. For example, by searching for *evidence*, they will likely come across a number of examples for *evidence-based*, a very common academic term. If set as homework, students should report back on and compare their findings in the following class.

Alternatively, this task would also be very effective using one of the publically available academic corpora such as the *British Academic Written English Corpus* (BAWE); available via https://the.sketchengine.co.uk/open/

UNIT 7 Data

INTRODUCTION

Unit 7 The second half of the book puts more focus on academic research and this unit starts by looking at research data. As well as describing data accurately, students need to be able to interpret and comment on data. As readers, they need to recognize that the presentation of data is not always as entirely objective as it seems, but may be interpreted in a way that supports a particular argument or stance.

7A Reading aims to highlight how even apparently straightforward expository texts are not completely neutral and objective, but are influenced by the writer's perspective and stance. Students read texts from two different sources which take different perspectives on the same topic; crime statistics. They analyse these to see how comment and evaluation are integrated into description in academic texts. They also work further on improving their reading speed.

7B Writing focuses on the text that accompanies visual data, such as graphs and charts, sometimes known as data commentary. Some students, such as those with an IELTS background, may be familiar with describing data. Data, however, is not typically considered in isolation, but presented within a longer text and linked to the arguments and wider context of the topic. This module encourages students to think about how interpretation and evaluation is incorporated into data commentary.

7C Listening encourages students to ask critical questions about what they hear. In this module, they listen to a presentation. The aim of the activities in the module is to give students practice in understanding visual data in a presentation, but also to encourage them to evaluate the presentation.

7D Speaking gives students an opportunity to present a set of data of their own choice, in the form of a graph, chart, etc. The aim of the module is to encourage students to balance clear description with elements of interpretation and evaluation. The module culminates in short individual presentations, giving students confidence in presenting within a clearly defined task.

7E Vocabulary is the first of the shorter vocabulary activities in the second half of the book which primarily aim to raise awareness and offer practice on topics that relate to the unit. In many academic contexts, such as when describing and explaining data, it is important to specify exactly what you are referring to avoid ambiguity or confusion. These activities focus students' attention on different areas where they need to be specific and on the type of language to do this.

Research Project (1) Through the second half of the book, students are guided through the steps needed to plan, research, and write an extended research project. The aim of the project is for students to investigate a topic of their choice in their own subject area. The Research Project boxes in each unit give guidance and questions for consideration that can be used as a self-study guide or in class. The first box introduces the task and guides students through the process of choosing an initial topic and getting started on research.

DISCUSSION

1 This Discussion aims to explore what students already know about research and research methodology, and to establish some key vocabulary that will appear in following units. Students start by pooling existing knowledge about these research methods.

2 Write the words *quantitative – quantity* and *qualitative – quality* on the board. Establish clearly the difference between data that can be counted and measured (quantitative) and that which can't, such as the results of interviews (qualitative), before students categorize the research methods. Note that many of the methods could be placed in the overlap between the two, depending on context.

> **Answers**
>
> Largely quantitative: census, lab experiment
>
> Either / both: field work (could be collecting quantitative data or observing behaviour), questionnaire
>
> Largely qualitative: interviews, case study, focus group

3 This activity encourages students to put the largely abstract concepts into a practical context. As an extension, you could elicit typical research methods in students' own discipline areas.

> **Sample answers**
>
> Engineering example – largely quantitative
>
> Economics example – a mixture of both; data about price trends + social, demographic, political, etc. factors
>
> Medicine – largely qualitative
>
> History – a mixture of both; quantitative data such as from carbon dating + observation, expert opinion, etc.

7A **Reading** Expository texts

TASK 1 Critical thinking – evaluating data sources

1 and 2 It is easy to think of data as objective and therefore representing straightforward facts. This task encourages students to think critically about some of the factors that determine how representative data might be and how the way that data is collected (and interpreted) can affect the picture it paints of a situation. Points to consider here include how easy the data in each case would be to collect and analyse, against what the data actually represents. Ask how students assumed that data about crime (which is commonly seen in the media) was collected and why collecting data about crimes committed may not be as straightforward as it first seems.

TASK 2 Identifying purpose and main points

1 and 2 Set students a short time limit, 1–2 minutes, to quickly read Text 1 and establish the basic facts about the text, topic, and purpose. They should be able to use the source data and the first paragraph only to complete the notes in 1 and answer the questions in 2. If students complain that they haven't had enough time to read the whole text, ask whether they need to go beyond the first paragraph. Emphasize that selective reading like this is an important skill. It might also be useful to point out in the source information how a chapter of a book is referenced, where the book is made up of chapters written by different people. You might also note how the British Crime Survey is referred to by its full title at the start of the extract (sentence 2), but thereafter is abbreviated to the BCS, a technique common in academic writing.

> **Sample answers**
>
> 1 **Genre**: academic textbook
> **Date of publication**: 2012
> **Audience**: university criminology students
> **Topic of this section**: the British Crime Survey
> **Main purpose of this section**: to describe the British Crime survey
>
> 2 crime recorded by the police and the BCS (British Crime Survey); to give a fuller picture of crime

3 and 4 This activity revisits the technique of making notes on the main points of a text to use in a summary (see 6B, page 094). By noting down only a few key words and phrases from the text, students are encouraged to synthesize the language of the text, especially those words which cannot easily be paraphrased, with their own voice. Rereading and processing the text for the summary also establishes the main points so that students can move on to the next, more discursive section, Text 2, in the next task. Remind students to include references to the source text as appropriate; it is important for students to get into the habit of acknowledging sources in all their writing.

> **Sample summary** possible words / phrases picked out from the original text shown in bold (88 words).
>
> Maguire (2012) explains that since **2002**, official crime figures for England and Wales have included information from the **British Crime Survey** (BCS) as well as police figures. The BCS started in **1982** to find out about **unreported and unrecorded offences**, sometimes known as the **'dark figure' of crime**. Maguire describes how every year a large sample of people are asked about their experiences of crime during the previous 12 months. This survey includes a **Core Victimization Module** which covers **vehicle and property-related crimes** and **personal crime, mainly assault**.

TASK 3 Quickly identifying writer's stance

1–3 The aim of these activities is to build on techniques for quickly identifying key ideas in a text already practised in previous units (see 2A) and to work further on improving students' reading speed. If students have a stopwatch, for example on a watch or a mobile phone, they could time themselves. Alternatively, you could use a watch or stopwatch and announce when one minute, two minutes, etc. have elapsed. Encourage students to note down how long it took them to read through the text, following the guidelines to read as quickly as possible whilst still picking up the main points. Allow time for students to go at their own speed and stop for feedback when you see that everyone has finished. 3–5 minutes should be a reasonable timeframe for a first reading. As students finish, direct them to complete the table in 3. Encourage them to complete as much as possible from memory and only check back where they are uncertain.

Answers

1 1 heading
   2 a / b details, such as figures / tables; in-text references
   3 d topic sentences, e italics

3

	Police-recorded crime statistics	British Crime Survey
1	no	yes
2	no	no
3	yes	yes
4	no	yes
5	yes	no
6	no	no
7	no	no

4 Ask students how this section of the text differs from the previous extract (Text 1), i.e. Text 1 is more descriptive (expository), simply describing the BCS, whereas Text 2 is more discursive, making comparisons and pointing out strengths and weaknesses. Focus attention back on the title of Text 2 and ask what answer the writer finally comes to: *Which of the statements in 4 best express his stance?*

Answer

Statement 2; the writer seems largely positive about the usefulness of the BCS, but expresses some limitations and reservations.

5 Students could do a written summary here, to follow on from the one they completed in Task 2, or they could compile oral summaries working in pairs or groups.

Points to include

Weaknesses:

1 The BCS does not include all categories of crime.

2 Some of the crimes recorded in the BCS don't map directly onto categories of crime recorded by police (because they are too minor).

Strength: For the comparable subset of crimes, the BCS does provide a fuller picture of crime than police statistics alone.

ACADEMIC LANGUAGE

Evaluation (1) Adverbials

Students have already looked at examples of evaluative language in previous units (see especially 4B page 063). This box focuses on how adverbials (either single adverbs or adverbial phrases) are used to add subtle evaluation. Students read the pairs of sentences and explain how they differ in emphasis. In each case, the second in the pair is the original from the text and shows the writer's emphasis. Ask how emphasis relates to stance. Explain that stance does not always have to be black-and-white, for or against, but can be more subtle in terms of what the writer picks out as more or less significant, especially to support a particular argument. For example, in the first example here, the writer emphasizes the main objective of the BCS, as if to deflect possible criticisms. His point could be paraphrased as: *OK, it doesn't include all these other categories, but it never set out to, that wasn't its main aim.* The use of adverbials in this text could generally be described as slightly defensive, pointing out, but playing down, the weaknesses of the BCS.

TASK 4 Recognizing subtle evaluation

1 Students work together in pairs or threes to explain and discuss how these sentences differ in emphasis depending on the choice of adverbial.

Sample answers

1 *simply* - there's nothing more to read into these findings
   apparently - this looks like the case, but it hasn't been conclusively proven
   to some extent - this is only part of the answer

2 *clearly* - the evidence is clear
   consistently - the same results have been repeated over a number of studies
   convincingly - the evidence is persuasive and difficult to doubt

3 *not necessarily related* - may not be related (but could be, it hasn't been conclusively proven)
   completely unrelated - definitely not related in any way
   apparently unrelated - do not seem to be related (but it hasn't been conclusively proven)

4 *overwhelmingly* - the majority of studies found no evidence
   largely - most (but not all) studies found no evidence
   obviously - they didn't find evidence because the claim is clearly not true

5 *adequately* - the legislation should be better
   fully - some areas are not addressed
   systematically - the legislation is patchy or not consistently applied

TASK 5 Asking critical questions about data

1 This task asks students to respond critically to what they have read, returning to some of the issues raised in Task 1.

2 Encourage students to formulate different questions, if necessary, changing or adding to the prompts suggested.

Sample answers

TASK 6 Comparing perspective and stance across texts

1–2 Again, students start by quickly reading the text to establish what type of text it is and the stance of the writer. Point out that this is not a complete text, but just a few points and that the ellipses (...) represent sections missed out here. The original text, in fact, included six points critiquing the methodology of victim surveys, but this short extract has been chosen to provide a simple point of comparison without adding another long reading text.

Sample answers

1 **Genre**: academic textbook
   Audience: students interested in statistics in criminology – fairly advanced / postgraduate
   Purpose: to highlight problems with victim surveys
   Main perspectives: methodological / research methods
2 The writer focuses on critiquing the methodology of crime victim surveys.

3–5 Give students time to reread the text and note down the three key points, as expressed in the three paragraphs, before they get into groups to discuss the questions in 4 and 5. The main point to highlight in feedback here is that the two writers are tackling the same topic from different perspectives, which affect their emphasis and stance. The writer of Texts 1 and 2 is interested in Criminology more generally and how crime statistics are used, whereas the writer of Text 3 is more specifically interested in research methods and so is bound to examine this angle more rigorously.

Sample answers

3 Three key points as shown in the three paragraphs:
   - The omission of crimes against children, commercial crime, victimless crimes, homicide, and fraud.
   - The sample is not necessarily representative of all households.
   - Questions about how reliable people's memories are.

   Only the first point is explicitly mentioned in Texts 1 / 2, and then not all of these categories are mentioned.

7B Writing Data commentary

TASK 1 Understanding data in visual form

1 This module focuses on how data is presented in academic texts, both visually in the form of graphs, charts, and tables, but also in the surrounding text, sometimes referred to as data commentary. This first task starts with understanding visual data and its accompanying description. Check that students understand the key words here, *ivory* and *poaching*, and elicit a few suggestions about the likely effects of a ban on ivory sales and the type of data that might be associated with the topic. Encourage students to bring in any general knowledge or examples on the topic.

2 and 3 These questions encourage students to look at all the details surrounding the graph and to consider their significance. Point out that they don't need to look up what a 'sigmoidal curve' is as it's already paraphrased in the text as 'S-shaped'. In addition you might ask, if the points don't come up:
- What do the numbers on the vertical (or *y*) axis represent? (Students should notice that they range from positive to negative figures.)
- How are the countries arranged along the horizontal (or *x*) axis? (*arranged from greatest losses to greatest gains*)
- What is the function of the footnote – what does it relate to in the text and on the graph?

Sample answers

2 1 figures for the pre-ban period
   2 1989 to 2007 – from the time of the ban to the time of the study
   3 the key showing which countries the numbers refer to
   4 36 countries
   5 not available – the footnote shows that data was not available for Eritrea, the 37th country
   6 students' own answers
3 b a general summary of what the graph shows

TASK 2 Understanding interpretation of data

1 In this task, students move on to read the interpretation of the data that follows the graph. Firstly they should read the text quickly to identify the three main conclusions. These should be easily spotted by the three discourse markers: *First, Second,* and *Third*. Encourage students to put up their hands as soon as they've picked them out and ask those who raise their hands first how they found the three points. Ask how this section of the text differs from the text that appeared before the graph, i.e. it goes into more detail, analyses and interprets the figures, and relates the data to the real-world context.

Answers

First, it appears the ban helped to increase the overall number of elephants in Africa by about 140,000 between 1989 and 2007.

Second, the ban has been effective at slowing the off-take of elephants from some countries that have continued to lose them.

Third, the international ban has not yet benefited every African country.

2 Note that many of the sentences here fulfil more than one of the functions, 1–6. Encourage students just to pick out one clear example of each.

Sample answers

1 Eighteen countries had increases [...] more than 10,000 animals each.
   Two of the countries, Kenya and Tanzania, are particularly important …
   … slowing the off-take of elephants from some countries …
   a few countries are accounting for much of the total loss …
   elephant loss was concentrated in Central Africa …
   Only two of the seven countries saw population increases …

2 it appears the ban helped to increase …
   the ban has been effective at slowing the off-take …
   Much like the unregulated ivory markets, elephant loss was …
   this is the result of the continued presence of unregulated ivory markets …

3 it appears the ban helped to increase the overall number of elephants in Africa …
   the ban has been effective at slowing the off-take of elephants from …
   the international ban has not yet benefited every African country

4 … important, as they suffered greatly from poaching in pre-ban years
   … was one-fifth of the number of elephants lost in the DRC during the pre-ban period
   As in the pre-ban years, a few countries …

5 … by about 140,000 between 1989 and 2007.
   Eighteen countries had increases [...] more than 10,000 animals each.
   the loss of 60,000 elephants in the DRC (1) between 1989 and 2007 was one-fifth of …
   In fact, since 1989, nearly 180,000 elephants were lost …
   This region lost more than 130,000 elephants in the post-ban years.
   Only two of the seven countries [...] a total of about 4,000 elephants.

6 The following sections will argue this is the result of …

Noun phrases (3) Multiple postmodifiers

This box builds on previous work on noun phrases (see 1B and 2A), looking at complex noun phrases consisting of a head noun followed by several postmodifiers. It is easy to get caught up in terminology here, but what students really need to recognize are the 'chunks' of language that are put together into a noun phrase to describe a single idea. Each 'chunk' modifies or adds extra information about the head noun. Work through the first example on the board to show how each phrase adds information about the head noun, *changes*, to demonstrate how such a long phrase can be broken down into manageable parts.

the **changes** (in what?) *in Africa's populations* (when?) *for the post-ban period* (where?) *for 36 of the 37 elephant range states*

Work through the other examples in a similar way.

TASK 3 Decoding and constructing long noun phrases

1 This activity gives students further practice in breaking nouns phrases down into chunks to decode meaning. Emphasize students' own understanding and explanations of each 'chunk' here rather than identifying grammatical categories.

Sample answers head noun shown in bold

1 a **case study** [of abalone poaching] [in South Africa] and its **impact** [on fisheries management]
   abalone = a species of tuna fish

2 [*ex situ* conservation] **status** [of an endangered Yangtze finless porpoise population] [as measured from microsatellites]
   ex situ refers to conservation where animals are removed from their natural habitat, for example to a zoo - compare with *in situ* (= in place)

3 [the conservation management] **implications** [of potential augmentation] [of the wild population] [with immigrants] [from the captive population]

4 a **criterion** [to evaluate [the effectiveness of] [several conservation measures]] [that have been undertaken or proposed [for the American lobster fishery] [in Newfoundland]]

2 This activity aims to provide free practice and to encourage students to experiment in constructing their own long noun phrases.

TASK 4 Writing a data commentary – the data

1 This is the main productive task of the module. It is broken down into two stages: first students get to grips with the data, then they look at the wider context in which it can be interpreted and evaluated. Give students time to study the pie charts and surrounding information individually and make notes on the main points.

2 Students start by writing sentences to describe features and trends in the data. These will be edited and adapted to use in their final text.

Sample answers
- There has been a significant decrease in the proportion of forested land, including both closed forest and woodland, which has shrunk from just over 30 per cent to less than 20 per cent.
- The amount of open woodland has increased slightly over the period by 4.5 per cent.
- The proportion of grassland has more than doubled from 7 per cent around the time of European colonization to 16 per cent of total land cover in the figures for 1995.
- The percentage of land with no vegetation, whilst small, has also doubled.

3 As students work in pairs to compare and discuss what they have written, encourage them to think about whether they could express any ideas more concisely by combining ideas into noun phrases. Monitor and check understanding of the key ideas and language. Check:
- the meaning of terms such as *circa* and the ~ symbol
- the source of the data (this figure = Bradshaw, 2012, data for 1995 = Barston *et al.*, 2000) – you could at this stage get students to add in-text references to their initial sentences
- the significance of European colonisation of Australia for its landscape and ecology in general terms.

TASK 5 Writing a data commentary – the context

1 and 2 Having started to think about possible reasons for the trends shown in the data, students now read three very short extracts which give a bit more background context to the topic. Texts 3 and 4 relate directly to the issue of deforestation in Australia (note that Text 4 is from the same text as the figure), while Text 5 takes a more global view of issues of changing land use.

3 This task could be set up in class and completed as homework. Make sure that what students need to include is clear before they start. Emphasize that they do not have to include citations from all the sources given here, but should use the material that best supports their points. The aim of the task is to produce a good data commentary; it is not an exercise in combining all the information on the page. However, stress that any citations they do use (both from the figure and the texts) must be correctly attributed and referenced, to provide support for their points and, of course, to avoid plagiarism. If students are able to bring their draft text to the next class in electronic form, on a memory stick or laptop, and use computer facilities in class, this will make the process of proofreading and editing their text in the following task easier.

Sample answer (235 words)
[1]Since European colonization some 200 years ago, Australia has undergone major changes in land usage. [2]Figure 1 (Bradshaw, 2012, p.110) illustrates changes in the overall proportion of vegetation type in Australia between the late eighteenth century and more recent data from 1995. [3]The most striking change has been the decrease in the proportion of forested land, including both closed forest and woodland, which has shrunk from just over 30 per cent to less than 20 per cent. [4]This deforestation has clearly been the result of extensive land clearance to make way for a growing population and demand for agricultural land (Braithwaite, 1996). [5]The figures seem to bear this trend out, showing that grassland, as used for farming cattle, has more than doubled over the period. [6]Whilst these figures may seem to be relatively small, as Bradshaw (2012, p. 114) points out, Australia had little forest cover in the first place. Thus even such apparently small changes can have a marked impact on wildlife, leaving remaining forest habitats 'highly fragmented' and 'ecologically compromised' (Gill & Williams, 1996, cited in Bradshaw, 2012), and so threatening many plant and animal species with extinction. [7]Australia is not alone, however, in terms of such dramatic land-cover changes. Man's activities continue to result in land degradation and deforestation across the globe, with many of the most-populated and rapidly changing areas now in Asia and the tropics (Lepers *et al.*, 2005, p.122).

1 Introduces the background
2 Briefly describes the chart, including in-text ref
3 Highlights a trend
4 Suggests a reason + citation & ref as support
5 Highlights a second trend
6 Evaluates the effects of the trends + citation & refs as support
7 Links to the wider context + citation & ref as support

TASK 6 Proofreading and editing your writing

1 The aim of this task is to encourage students to systematically proofread their text. Stress that they should read the whole text focusing on a single point, rather than trying to look out for everything in one read-through. Allow time for students to work through these stages individually and make any changes.

2 and 3 Encourage students to look at global features of each other's texts, such as the overall organization, points which have been included / left out, as well as the details. It is always tempting when redrafting a text to just deal with small details, when sometimes more major rewriting is needed (reordering, adding new points, deleting something, etc.). If students are able to make changes to electronic documents in class, they could edit and redraft at this point. If they are working on paper, you might want to give them time to take their work away to redraft and submit in the next class.

TASK 7 Independent research – visual data across disciplines

1 and 2 This is another opportunity for students to explore how the ideas in the module apply to their own discipline. If students carry out this task for homework, encourage them to bring hard copies of the page containing the visual to class. This gives them something more concrete to focus on during feedback and also allows them to recheck details that they might miss if just taking notes.

3 Use the visuals that students have brought in and the illustrations on the page to quickly check students' understanding of these terms. Elicit what factors might affect which type of visual is used to represent different types of data.

Note: a *histogram* is a type of bar chart in which the height and width of the bars are used to represent and compare different amounts. Histograms are used in statistics to represent the distribution of data in visual form.

4 After students have compared and discussed their findings in groups, collate the information as a class, for example the number of graphs, charts, and tables found, or the reporting verbs used (*show*, *present*, *illustrate*, etc.). If possible, pick out any differences or trends in different disciplines.

7C Listening
Presentations (3)

TASK 1 Understanding visual data in a presentation

1 In this module, students watch extracts from a presentation. Whilst the delivery of the presentation is fluent and convincing, it is not intended as a model presentation and contains a number of flaws for students to critique. It is divided into two sections, the first part focused around data about working hours and the second looking at more general issues of work–life balance. The aim of this brief discussion task is to establish the topic.

2 ▶7.1 The first short extract provides a brief introduction to the topic and an outline of the presentation.

> **Sample answers**
> Part 1: average *working hours* & general trends in *the labour market*
> Part 2: 'extensification' = pressure to *work outside office hours*

3 and 4 ▶7.2 Explain that this extract contains a lot of detail and that students should focus on noting down key overall points rather than specific details or figures for each slide. Feed back as a class and summarize just the main points.

> **Sample answers**
> 3 Slide 1: There has been a fall in average working hours in the UK in the past two decades.
>   Slide 2: This decrease is partly due to a shift in the economy towards sectors which traditionally work shorter hours, especially from manufacturing to services.
>   Slide 3: There has been an increase in the number of people working part-time, including those who would like to work full-time.
> 4 1 b
>   2 the changing UK economy; part-time working

5 and 6 Give students some time to note down any information they can remember on these topics before watching the extract again. The aim of these activities is for students to consider how the details of the presentation relate to the main points. Check that students can explain the implications of each point in their own words. For example, about the link between part-time working and economic recession, ask why more people might take on part-time jobs during a recession (i.e. because not enough full-time jobs are available). Note that the key phrases in 5 are bolded in the transcript.

> **Sample answers**
> the construction sector: traditionally work long hours – now makes up smaller proportion of workforce
>
> the manufacturing sector: also work long hours – also falling proportion of workforce
>
> the service sector: tend to work shorter hours – now making up a much larger proportion of workforce
>
> agriculture: very small proportion of UK workforce
>
> part-time working: increasing share of employment is part-time – effect is to bring down average working hours
>
> the 1990s recession: increase in number of people working part-time who want to work full-time, this fell as economy recovered and started to rise again with 2008 recession

7 The aim of this activity is to highlight how description and interpretation are often combined. Interpretation can differ greatly depending on the nature of the data and the aims of the presentation. This extract is largely describing and explaining the data (it contains no evaluation), but some examples of interpretation illustrated here include:
- Showing how different sets of data link together: *What's important to understand when considering the fall in average hours is the influence of a changing economy in the UK. To illustrate this, let's look at …*
- Explaining the implications of trends and features: *So if we have more people employed in services and fewer in manufacturing, this will act to reduce the average hours worked overall in the UK workforce.*

  The effect of this, of course, is to bring down the overall average for all those in work.

TASK 2 Critical thinking – looking beyond the data

1 The aim of this task is to encourage students to look beyond the fairly slick presentation of this data and to ask critical questions about the presenter's interpretation of the data, which has so far been very minimal and rather superficial, and about what has not been included. Although the speaker highlights the link between economic recession and a rise in part-time working, he doesn't elaborate on the point. Encourage students to add the interpretation that the speaker misses out on this point.

2 Students again generate critical questions that could be asked about the data (as in 7A page 108), using Checklist K at the back of the book.

Sample answers

Has the presenter offered sufficient evidence to support his arguments?

Is the evidence the most up-to-date available?

Does the evidence logically support the presenter's arguments?

Has the presenter accurately interpreted the data?

TASK 3 Distinguishing between evidence and evaluation

1 and 2 ▶7.3 In this extract from the presentation, the speaker moves on to talk about the main topic, work–life balance, and the concept of extensification. The focus shifts from quantitative data to more qualitative research and discussion. Students watch first to identify and make notes on the key points. By reviewing the context through the examples used by the speaker, they relate the key points to real-world context, rather than focusing on the terminology. Allow students to watch either all or part of the extract again if necessary.

Sample answers

- a flexible & mobile workforce – see example
- 'overflow' & new technologies – workers who bring their laptops / smartphones home from work to do extra work in the evenings
- 'intensification' → 'extensification' – instead of making workers more productive at work, employers try to get more from employees by giving them smartphones so that they are always 'on call'
- 'balance model' → 'depletion model' – instead of balancing their work and home lives, employees now find work takes away from their time with family, etc.

3 and 4 The aim of these tasks is for students to identify how the speaker uses evidence to support his points in this extract, using the transcript.

Answers

3 1 Pratt & Jarvis (2006)
  2 flexible & mobile workforce; overflow
4 1 speaker's own comment – yellow text
  2 supporting evidence from stated source – green text
  3 supporting evidence, no source given – blue text

TASK 4 Critically evaluating the content of a presentation

1 and 2 Students may have already raised concerns about the data and sources used in the presentation. These discussion questions allow them to share and formulate their ideas and criticisms. Stress that when making critical comments, it is important to make your case clearly and strongly, justifying any criticisms with clear reasons. During feedback you could first elicit positive points in the presentation (clear delivery, attractive visuals, good explanation of the data, authoritative sources for some points), before students express any criticisms. Ask students to suggest how the presentation could have been improved (e.g. less focus on the working hours data and more variety of evidence for the main points in the second part).

Suggested points of criticism
- The data commentary section is too long and detailed – many of the points made aren't directly relevant to the topic.
- The working hours figures are specifically for the UK, but the Pratt & Jarvis evidence in the second section is from the US – may not be comparable?
- The references in the second section are not clear enough; the full Pratt & Jarvis reference is not shown on the slide (although may be given at the end) and the study cited about BlackBerry smartphones has no source mentioned.

7D Speaking
Presentations (4)

TASK 1 Critical thinking – evaluating the role of visual data

1 If students have little experience of presenting data, encourage them to think of examples where they have watched data presented, including in the Listening module (7C). Key points to raise during the discussion or feedback:
- The audience will determine the level of assumed knowledge.
- The level of detail will depend on the audience, the topic, and the aim of the presentation; a very detailed graph would not be appropriate to illustrate a general point, but may be right for a specialist technical presentation.

- It's always important to show sources of any data – could be just author's name and date on the slide and full reference details at the end of the presentation.
- Presentation of any data should always be explicitly linked to the main point it's supposed to be supporting.

TASK 2 Planning and researching a short presentation

1–3 In this task, students research and plan a short presentation focused around a single graph, chart, or table. According to the order of steps given in the book, students first select a specific topic of interest and then search for a relevant visual. Alternatively, they might select a very broad subject area within which to search for an interesting visual and then narrow and develop their topic around what they find. In either case, the research and development phase will probably be best set as homework. Alternatively, you could select several visuals yourself for students to choose from and develop a topic around in class. The key aim of this part of the task is for students to think about how a specific visual relates to and illustrates a wider point.

4 This activity encourages students to develop their material in way that will include not just simple description of the data, but elements of interpretation, evaluation, and stance. Stress that in a short presentation like this, the elements of evaluation and stance do not have to be very detailed or sophisticated. They could be quite brief and simple, but should show some evidence of thinking critically about the data and developing a position. Some questions that might be useful in prompting students to evaluate the data they find include:
- To what extent does the set of data presented prove / illustrate a particular point?
- Does it provide strong evidence, some evidence, or point to a more general trend?
- Are there limitations to the data and if so, what other research, data, or evidence might be needed to give a fuller picture?

TASK 3 Rehearsing your presentation

1 and 2 This task gives students time to try out their ideas and to find and address potential problems or weak points in what they have already planned. Ideally if students have prepared slides, such as in PowerPoint, they should look at these in their pairs. This stage could be done in class time, or alternatively, pairs could be allocated and rehearsal time could form part of students' preparation outside of class.

ACADEMIC LANGUAGE

Signposting (3) Referring to visual data

Students have already seen how lecturers use signposting language to help guide their audience (see 1C and 2C). This box highlights some of the types of expressions used to refer to visual data. Ask students which of the expressions are most relevant to their own visual / data or how they could be adapted, e.g. by substituting *graph* for *chart*, etc.

TASK 4 Presenting visual data

1 Students look for some more examples of signposting language to prompt ideas for wording before they do their final preparation.

Sample answers

… **we can see that** there's been a fall in …

If we look at some major sectors in the British economy, **we see some differences** in …

To illustrate this, let's look at the …

What we see is that around 68% was …

Now looking at 2011, what we see is that overall …

If we return to the first slide, we see that …

Looking at this next graph, we can see that …

Another interesting thing to look at is …

2 and 3 Give students some time to finalize their presentations. Stress that students should not prepare a 'script', but instead rehearse expressing specific points and linking them together. This is also an opportunity for students to experiment with different ways of using notes to present, for example notes on a printout of slides or on separate cards. This should then form part of feedback and evaluation; which style of notes worked best, what issues came up, etc.

TASK 5 Evaluating performance

1 and 2 Rather than evaluation and feedback on individual presentations, this task focuses on identifying points of best practice across the class. This is a positive and motivating activity which encourages students to learn from each other. It also means that a student who may feel weak in one area, may get praised for, say, having well designed slides or keeping to time.

3 Students finally reflect on their own performance. This might form part of one-to-one feedback with the teacher if there are opportunities for this.

7E **Vocabulary** Being specific

1 This activity aims to highlight some of the language which is typically used to specify exact details, especially when referring to research and data. The highlighted words and phrases are likely to be a mix of known and unknown vocabulary. By categorizing according to function, students focus on how they are used in this context.

> **Sample answers**
> 1 a 2 b 3 b 4 c 5 c 6 a
> 7 c (could also be b) 8 c

2 The aim of this activity is to focus on using the words and phrases accurately. There is no point in specifying exact details at this level if errors lead to further ambiguity, so identify any specific errors that crop up during feedback and work as a class to correct them. If students opt for the more familiar words and expressions, you might want to work on examples for the less familiar items (*adjust for, discrete*, etc.) as a class.

Research Project (1)
Choosing a topic

This box introduces the task which students will complete over the course of the following units. Make sure that students are clear what is expected of them in general terms, stressing that they will not be carrying out primary research, but using sources, such as academic books and journal articles to research a topic of their choice. The exact nature of the project will depend very much on your own class context; the level of the students (pre-university, undergraduate, or postgraduate), the resources available to them, and the length and requirements of your course. The details of the task have been left intentionally general so that you can specify requirements such as exact length, choice of topic, conventions, and any assessment criteria to fit in with your course. Encourage students to be independent in terms of checking specifications and criteria for themselves rather than expecting to be told everything. This could take the form of a Q&A session in class or where relevant, you could direct them to any information published for your course, for example, in a student handbook or on a website.

If you have time in class, students could note down and discuss their initial broad topic ideas. If you have project titles or topics completed by previous students, these can provide a useful starting point for discussion and help prompt ideas. If you have any time allocated for one-to-one tutorials, you might ask students to bring their initial topic ideas and the first two or three sources they find to your next meeting. At this stage, you may have to steer students away from any topics that are unsuitable because they are too difficult to research (in terms of time or available resources), too vague, or too specialized. Remember that you will have to read and assess their project, probably as a non-expert in their subject area, so the topics should be accessible to an educated, academic, but non-expert reader.

By the end of the following unit, students will need to have a clear topic area decided and some initial research completed, ready to work on narrowing their exact topic down and choosing a working title.

UNIT 8 Influence

ACADEMIC FOCUS: CAUSE, EFFECT, AND ASSOCIATION

INTRODUCTION

Unit 8 examines the frequently complex connections of cause, effect, and association in a wide range of academic texts, within the unit theme of Influence. In many contexts, such as health, clear cause and effect connections are hard to establish, which in turn leads to more complex language choices including tentative language. Students need to learn to recognize complex connections in written and spoken texts, and use appropriate language to express these connections in their writing and speaking. The approach to the unit as a whole reflects widespread academic practice in which skills are integrated. For example, students have to prepare for a lecture by reading a pre-lecture handout.

8A Reading explores complex connections – cause, effect, and association – in a selection of texts on a similar topic. In the process of working out such connections, students analyse and practise using a wide range of relevant language which expresses the degree of certainty intended by the text authors. There is a focus on accuracy throughout the module: students learn to identify the precise connection, and they can subsequently use similar language in their own writing and speaking. The module concludes with a task which reflects the process of academic reading: where the student has a topic and needs to find information on it in multiple texts, which they can then select and use in their own output.

8B Writing focuses on the writing process for a complete essay. The module aims to equip students with analytical skills based on sample plans and texts which they can then apply to their own writing. Students learn to formulate their essay title and plan and present clearly connected connections in their written text, using appropriate and accurate connection language. Such language includes the essential language of cause and effect as well as tentative language to express the strength of the connection. The module works through the essay planning and writing process using a full-length sample student essay as a sample for analysis.

8C Listening builds students' competence in extracting key information from authentic lectures. The module follows an authentic academic sequence starting with a pre-lecture handout. This enables students to effectively access the technical content of the lecture. The material develops the unit academic focus with a particular emphasis on associations, which are widespread in the discipline of the lecture, Medicine.

8D Speaking continues to reflect the academic principle of preparing to listen or speak. Students read a given text to inform their content in a subsequent seminar discussion. The module encourages students to negotiate their content with one or two other students before the actual seminar. This leads to the focus of the module: reaching a consensus through persuasion.

8E Vocabulary is the first of two modules focused around word formation (see also 11E). By understanding how some words are formed using prefixes or compounds, students are better equipped to break down and decode new vocabulary or novel coinages they encounter in their reading.

Research Project (2) guides students through the process of establishing a working title. Guidelines help students to narrow down their initial topic to a more specific working title of appropriate scope for this length of project that they will realistically be able to research and write. It then sets them off on the main research phase of their project.

DISCUSSION

1 and 2 The Discussion aims to activate students' interest in the unit theme of Influence, through a discussion of how different factors can influence a range of given items. This leads naturally to the academic focus of cause, effect, and association. You can add degrees of complexity to the discussion, e.g. by writing up questions such as *How significant is this influence?* and *How far can this influence be avoided?* Remind students to approach the discussion from a range of perspectives, e.g. cultural – *How far do cultural factors influence a person's health?* Ask students to note down the factors as they are raised (one student in each group can be nominated to do this), so that there is a record of the factors to do activity 2. Select one or two as examples, and ask students to say both how (i.e. cause, effect, association) and why it is connected in this way, e.g. certain diets are associated with specific diseases, but not everyone who eats, say, excessive fat develops such diseases; this means it is not strictly a cause and effect connection but a strong association.

8A Reading Complex texts

TASK 1 Identifying connections in a text

1 This task centres on the academic focus of cause, effect, and association, which was raised in the Discussion on page 119. Activity 1 enables students to work out some of the large number of ways in which the given items can be connected. While they do this task, you could note down some of the connection language (cause, effect, association) students use; write it up as a record to show how they can build on this language and use a wider range – which they will use throughout the unit.

2 and 3 The students' exploration of possible connections leads directly into Text 1, which contains the same items. Remind students that their first task on coming across a new text is to contextualize it, i.e. work out the information given in the notes. Students need to learn to do this quite quickly, so set a time limit, e.g. 8 minutes.

Answers

2 Title / date of publication: *The effects on stature of poverty, family size, and birth order: British children in the 1930s / Published 2010*
Genre, Audience, Purpose: *abstract of journal article / students & academics of medicine; and social sciences (sociology, psychology, anthropology, geography, history, economics) / to present a concise summary of the whole journal article, including the aims of the research and its conclusion*
Aim of research: *to determine the effects of socio-economic conditions on the standardized heights and body mass index (BMI) of children in Interwar Britain (i.e. sentence 1)*
Background and context of research: *original data is from Britain in 1937-9; analysis in article is recent (2010)*
Perspectives: *medical, historical, geographical, anthropological, sociological, cultural, psychological, economic*
Main findings: *that household economic factors, e.g. income and number of children, affect children's height (but not their body mass)*

3

Household income
positive effect
↓
Birth order ⌉ *negative* → children's height ← *negative* ⌈ overcrowding
Family size / ⟩ *effect*   *effect* ⟨ disease
No. of children ⌋ ~~no effect~~ → ~~BMI~~   ⌊ hygiene
negative effect
↑
height in adulthood

4 and 5 Stress the need for accuracy in these activities. It may be helpful to explain that cause → effect verbs (e.g. *cause*) are in the active, while effect → cause verbs (e.g. *are caused by*) are mostly in the passive, with the exception of *result from*, which can easily be confused with the cause → effect verb *result in*. Refer students to the Language Reference section on Connection, page 202, which they can study independently. Ask students who finish quickly to write further sentences, and exchange their sentences with other students. Monitor and check for accuracy.

Sample answers

4 1 Birth order & family size *can bring about* shorter children.
Increased household income *influences* height / *can lead to* increased height.
Increased number of children in a family *results in* shorter children.
2 Shorter children *can result from* larger families.
Shorter children *can result from* birth order.
Increased height *can be caused by* a higher household income per capita.
3 Shorter children *are associated with* overcrowding & a lack of cleanliness (hygiene).
Cleanliness *influences* instances of disease.
Instances of disease *are influenced by* the quality of cleanliness.

5 Birth order and family size *do not affect* children's BMI.

TASK 2 Preparing to read a complex text

1 Explain that texts which discuss possible connections can be quite complex, characterized by a wide range of carefully chosen language to express the exact type of connection. However, general tendencies of academic texts still apply, such as the division of ideas and topics into paragraphs. This activity requires students to identify the topic in each paragraph – an activity they will have done before, but this time using a more complex text.

Answers
Paragraph 1: c Paragraph 2: a Paragraph 3: b

2 Ask students what the most obvious differences between the abstract and the conclusion of the text are: the conclusion is longer, and contains some expansion on the main findings. The new information is mainly at the level of greater detail and explanation.

Sample answer
Mostly the information in Text 2 is included in the abstract (Text 1). There is some further explanation, mainly in the long middle paragraph.

3 and 4 Explain that journal articles such as this can be very challenging to read, and it can be advisable to read very carefully certain key parts of the text. Three potentially challenging stretches of text are highlighted, and students should collaboratively work out the meaning. Ask them to write this down in one new sentence – this can be a loose paraphrase or slightly longer explanation. Allow sufficient time for students to compare and discuss the authors' use of such language before checking the answers.

Sample answers
3 (i) The authors find that two factors impact negatively on height, namely birth order and the number of children in a family. These factors do not affect BMI.
(ii) Previous research on child development typically finds that chronic poverty has a long-term negative effect on height, but short-term poverty tends to be associated with reduced BMI.
(iii) The number of children in a family affects child health through two main channels: less food and (less directly) worse household hygiene which can lead to higher levels of disease.

4 The authors use this kind of language in order to:
• express a large amount of information in a limited number of words
• meet expectations of academic style, especially conciseness and nominalization
• make what they are saying sound important and significant.

TASK 3 Identifying connections in a text

1 This task aims to help students extract the key points from the text. Elicit ways of doing this: reprocessing the information in table form (as in this task); using

diagrams and symbols; writing notes; even drawing pictures. Check that students understand the meaning of *connection*: this can refer to a cause → effect, or an association. Students can use dictionaries as necessary while doing the task.

Answers

	Factor 1	Factor 2	Connection
1	birth order & no. of children	height	negative effect
2	birth order & no. of children	BMI	no effect
3	enduring deprivation	height	association
4	short-run privations	BMI	association
5	hygiene	cleanliness	association
6	income per capita	disease	association
7	degree of household crowding	disease	association
8	better quality housing	hygiene	cause → effect
9	hygiene	height	cause → effect
10	reduced food intake	child health status	cause → effect

2 Having focused on paragraphs 1 and 2, students now identify connections in paragraph 3 using their preferred way of recording these, as elicited in 1. When checking, focus particularly on the students' accurate use of connection language.

Sample answers
Poverty, family size, and housing conditions affect adult height & health.

Child height affects future health.

Reduced height is associated with heart disease & stroke.

Heart disease & stroke can result in death.

ACADEMIC LANGUAGE

Connection (1) Confident and tentative interpretations

Explain that Texts 1 and 2 illustrated the complex nature of connections, and that a major academic endeavour is to establish connections between different phenomena, whether in science disciplines such as health, or social sciences. To express such connections, language has to be carefully chosen, particularly to express the strength of the connection. Go through the language in the box, and ask students to refer to the Connection section of the Language Reference section on page 202, which goes into much greater detail.

TASK 4 Recognizing confident and tentative interpretation

1 Allow students plenty of time to work out the connections specified. When checking the answers, draw attention to how the three aspects are closely linked, i.e. the type of connection, how confident it is, and the language used to express it. The authors have carefully worked out these three aspects.

Answers

Type of connection:

1 cause–effect   2 association / influence   3 cause–effect   4 association   5 association

Confidence:

1 confident   2 somewhat tentative   3 tentative
4 tentative   5 confident

Language:

1 Thus ... affect
2 ... support the idea that ... is influenced not only by ... but also by ....
3 ... may have a cumulative effect on ... particularly ....
4 ... are often associated with ... and possibly ... and ...
5 ... there is a strong correlation between ... and ....

2 This activity aims to clarify the issue of whose material is being expressed, which has been covered in earlier units. Ask students how they worked this out in each case: sentences 2 and 5 refer to other research, i.e. cited material which is not that of the authors themselves. The implication is that when citing any of these points, students need to make clear that they are not attributable to the text authors (i.e. Hatton and Martin) but to their original source (e.g. the Boyd Orr research).

Answers

1 own   2 others   3 own   4 own   5 others

3 This activity gives freer practice for students to find their own examples of connection language in Text 2. Students should quickly realize how rich the text is in such language. Encourage them to record it separately to use in their own writing.

Answers

a Paragraph 1: both have strong negative effects; the consequences of; the effects measured here capture the longer-term effects.
   Paragraph 2: does have an independent negative effect; the effect of; affects ... directly through ... via
   Paragraph 3: these effects; affect future health; the major causes of

b Paragraph 1: is typically associated with
   Paragraph 2: be associated with; This in turn is negatively associated with ... and positively with
   Paragraph 3: influenced; is associated with

c Paragraph 1: are consistent with an interpretation that; often interprets ... as reflecting ...
   Paragraph 2: what channels of influence it represents; and one that appears to be associated with ...; is suggestive rather than definitive; a variable that is likely to be associated with ...; seems to reduce the effect of ..., presumably ...; more indirectly though
   Paragraph 3: Although ... is less precise, it appears that ...; that can affect ...

4 In this activity students need to build up the single connections they have so far explored into a coherent text. Explain that students should select their items carefully so that the text does not become a disjointed series of statements but a logically constructed text.

Sample answer

Several factors have a potential impact on the height of children. Hatton and Martin (2010) state that enduring deprivation, or long-term poverty, is associated with reduced height in children. They go on to add that birth order and the number of children in a family are further factors negatively affecting height, although these factors do not appear to impact on BMI. Finally, height is also negatively affected by the level of hygiene in a household.

TASK 5 Understanding complex connection language in a text

1 This task further explores connection language and meaning in a new text on a similar topic. Set a time limit for students to complete their reading and notes, perhaps 12–15 minutes depending on level. As with previous similar tasks, make sure that all students write notes rather than holding the information in their head or highlighting the text.

Sample answer

Title / date of publication: *Child Public Health (2nd Ed.) / Published 2010*

Genre, Audience, Purpose: *university textbook or professional (i.e. medical) text / students & academics of medicine & medical practitioners / to present information on, and a case for, family size and how this relates to child health issues in the UK and globally*

Aim of research: *to synthesize multiple sources into a clear description and argument*

Background and context of research: *long-term changes in the UK and globally*

Perspectives: *medical, geographical, historical, social, cultural, economic*

Main findings: *that family size is decreasing dramatically in industrialized countries such as the UK; developed countries use most of the world's resources* (this could be a 'minor' finding); *women are achieving more independence; divorce levels are rising*

2 and 3 These activities aim to bring out the meaning in the text, first with the four given extracts, and in activity 2 using the students' selected points. Suggest that students focus their discussion by analysing the points from the same perspectives, e.g. economic, political, cultural, geographical, historical. Remind students that in academic contexts personal responses are ideally supported by evidence, examples, and explanation.

Sample answers

2 Families, family size, birth interval, single-parent families / lone-parent families

4 and 5 These activities bring together the aspects of connection, degree of confidence, and specific language. Through this process of analysis, students should learn to recognize the precise meaning of a wide range of language. Ask them to record the language carefully and actively use it in their subsequent writing and speaking.

Sample answers

neutral, <u>tentative (hedged)</u>, or **strong**.

<u>Connecting a cause to an effect / introducing an effect</u>

Families are **a potential influence both on** *a child's genetic constitution* **and**, as we have seen in the last section, **on** their health and related behaviour.

The family **also** constitutes a child's immediate social network **and** has **a vital influence on** the development of socio-emotional health **and** wellbeing.

In industrialized countries, **both of these factors** have changed dramatically over the last century, and these changes have had **a major influence** on the way children are looked after.

Partly as a result of changing gender attitudes and expectations (Table 3.4), **which have given** women greater financial independence, marital breakdown is now very common.

While these changes create problems for many children, (see below) for some they **may be a source of** resilience.

The family **also** constitutes a child's immediate social network and has **a vital influence on** the development of socio-emotional health **and** wellbeing.

<u>Connecting an effect to a cause / introducing a cause</u>

The key factors in *reducing family size in developing countries are increasing income*

Until fairly recently, epidemiological studies of **the influence of** families **on** children's growth and development have concentrated on easily measurable **determinants** such as family size and structure.

Countries such as Kerala (a state of Southern India) and Sri Lanka, which have focused on **these factors**, have had remarkable success in reducing fertility. Family size and short birth interval are **important predictors of** nutritional status, but far more of the earth's resources are used by the small families of the industrialized countries rather than the large families of the poor world.

Marital breakdown is **therefore an important cause of** childhood poverty.

<u>Expressing an association</u>

The latter **are more prone to** *break down than first time marriages*

Becoming a single parent **is almost inevitably associated with** a drop in family income,

TASK 6 Critical thinking – exploring evaluation across texts

1–3 The final task of the module brings together the three texts and asks students to look for instances of the same topic across the texts. This process reflects the academic reading practice of having a topic in mind and locating instances of it in multiple texts. Explain that students can then use this material in their own writing and speaking. Students can briefly compare their findings on the theme of poverty before selecting their own theme. Ideally, put students in groups of three with each student searching for a different theme across the three module texts. Conduct group feedback

simultaneously, with a limit of about five minutes for the students in each group to report back.

4 Students should by now have sufficient material and knowledge of the three texts to process the authors' evaluative material. Stress that there are no right answers, although students should be able to identify whether the evaluation is based on quality citations in each case. Explain that the issue of generalizability is closely associated with certain types of research, such as medical. With other research, e.g. anthropological, there is no reason why findings in, say, Mongolia, should be applicable to different contexts, say Ireland. This observation illustrates the importance of the topic when discussing knowledge and research.

8B **Writing** Cause and effect essays

TASK 1 Speculating on cause and effect relationships

1–3 This task builds students' awareness of how different items can be related through different types of connection, with a particular focus on causes and effects. To illustrate the wide possibilities of possible causes, expand on the example as a whole-class discussion, encouraging students to explore the scenario from different perspectives, e.g. emotional problems, health concerns, family pressures. Check that students have recorded their ideas before moving on to speculating on effects, which students should also record. These activities lead to the evaluative phase, 3, where students can discuss and speculate on their ideas using the questions as prompts.

4 These diagrams should stimulate students to look at types of cause and effect connection, for example a chain – in which a situation (A) becomes a cause of a new situation (B), which is therefore its effect, leading to a further situation (C), meaning that B is both the effect of A and the cause of C. Encourage students to relate these possibilities to their discussions in the previous three activities. At the end of Task 1, point out that students have simply been speculating, and the next step would be to search for evidence and further ideas in published sources.

TASK 2 Writing a cause-effect and evaluation paragraph

1–5 Activity 1 gives students a reason for reading, a straightforward question with a simple answer. Point out the ideas in this paragraph might be similar to the ideas students have just discussed in Task 1, thereby showing the usefulness of discussing a topic in preparation for writing. The first five activities in the task can be done in one stretch before checking answers. By analysing the paragraph, students should see how the paragraph develops the topic stated in sentence 1 by first speculating on possible causes, leading logically to a possible effect and then an evaluative sentence to conclude the paragraph. As is typical in such texts, it is hard to draw very certain conclusions, so there is a significant amount of tentative language. At the end of these activities, ask students to look once again at the sample paragraph in preparation for writing their own.

Answers

1 Scenario 4

2 Three causes relate to her own behaviour (demotivated, insufficient work, emotional problems); one external reason (bullied); plus one medical reason (ADHD)

3 Sentence 2: an example / effect
Sentences 3, 4, 5, 6: speculation on possible causes
Sentence 7: speculation on a possible effect
Sentence 8: evaluation

4 Confident: the writer uses the expression it's never too late to ...

5 **Cause and effect language**
There are a number of possible **causes** of educational underachievement. A **symptom** of such underachievement might be a promising student doing badly in her exams. To explain this failure, the student's poor marks **may result from** her own behaviour. She might have become demotivated and not worked hard enough, or she might have developed emotional problems **as a result of** her relationships with her friends and family. Alternatively there may be another **reason for** her underachievement which is essentially beyond her control, **because** she has been bullied for example. A different category of **explanation for** her academic failure could be medical: in cases of Attention Deficit / Hyperactivity Disorder (ADHD), young people "who show symptoms of inattention, hyperactivity, and impulsivity with or without formal diagnoses of ADHD also show poor academic and educational **outcomes**" (Loe and Feldman, 2007, p.643). While any of these **causes may have led to** the student's underachievement, the **effects** are likely to be similar, whether loss of confidence or a negative cycle of failure and lowered expectations. However, one poor set of exam results **does not necessarily mean** permanent failure; **therefore** it is never too late to change a pattern of behaviour.
Examples of tentative language: *may result from; there may be another reason for; a different category of explanation for x ... could be; any of these causes may have led to*
Examples of neutral language: *a number of possible causes; a symptom; as a result of; because; outcomes*
Examples of confident language: *does not necessarily mean; therefore (it is never too late)*
Note that students may legitimately argue that some of these language items could be in a different category, e.g. 'as a result of' is quite a confident statement.

6 Refer students back to the notes they took in Task 1 as the basis for their paragraph. Explain that they can selectively summarize these points in order to achieve a coherent paragraph like the one in Task 2. The purpose of this is mainly to allow controlled practice of writing a paragraph prior to writing their essay later in the module. Encourage students to include appropriate and accurate connection language. If necessary, look again

at the first Academic Language box in the unit (in the Reading module), and forward to the second one below.

TASK 3 Exploring cause and effect essay structures

1 and 2 The main aim of this task is to enable students to work out which organizational structure is best suited to the purpose of the text. Start off the task with a discussion of the issues. With cause and effect essays (and other texts, such as reports), an essential question to ask is *What is the main focus of the essay?* Answers include, with the essay plans a–d in brackets: the possible causes of something (b); the possible effects of something (d); an examination of how causes and effects / effects and causes are linked (c); a chain of events, where the first situation becomes the cause of the second, which itself becomes the cause of the third, and so on (a). The chain structure has limited application, as only certain situations have such cause–effect chains. The answers to the essay focus question should lead students to the correct essay structure 1–4. Other factors include: the number of causes and effects, e.g. Block 1 has to separate causes each with their own effect, while the Variation identifies multiple causes relating to a single effect. Stress that the Variation given in 4.1 is just one example of a variation – there are of course many other possible variations. A further point is that causes are closely related to problems – a cause is often evaluated as a problem and vice versa.

Emphasize that essay questions often do not explicitly ask for all the elements which are required in the answer. Most importantly, students need to include evaluation: a text does not present causes and effects alone – the purpose of the essay is typically to speculate on how serious the effects are, or how they might in turn affect other things, and other evaluative points like these. Evaluation may be best integrated, or presented as a separate block, especially where causes and effects are very closely linked.

Answers

1 b Block 1 - cause 1, cause 2, effect 1, effect 2, evaluation
c Variation - cause 1, cause 2, effect, evaluation
d Block 2 - effect 1, effect 2, evaluation, causes

2 Structure 1 (Block 1) is a traditional structure and provides a balance between causes and effects, with evaluation 'saved' for the end of the essay. It reflects chronology - causes come first, then effects.
Structure 2 (Block 2) emphasizes the effects, putting these first. Less attention is therefore given to causes, though these are discussed later in the essay.
Structure 3 (Chain) emphasizes how causes lead to effects, which then lead to further effects (and so become causes themselves). This is suited to chronology and process, and chains of events, where one thing leads to another, and so on.
Structure 4 (Variation) allows the writer to vary their structure to suit their content and focus.

Connection (2) Expressing cause and effect coherently

This box builds on the connection language introduced in the Academic Language box in 8A Reading. Remind students that connections always involve at least two items (often more), and working out exactly how such items may be connected is a major concern in academic contexts. Explain the importance of coherence - students need to select appropriate language to correctly express (a) how the two items are connected, and (b) how strong this connection is. Go through the box, focusing on the essential cause and effect language (i.e. point (a) above) in bold black, and the language used to express the strength of the connection (i.e. point (b) above) in bold blue. The Academic Language box focuses mainly on nouns and verbs; point out that these and other structures are covered in much greater detail in the Language Reference section on page 202.

TASK 4 Using cause and effect structures

1-3 This task puts into practice some of the connection language which students will need to use in their cause and effect essay later in the module. Point out that students need to focus on accuracy of use. Activity 1 deals with how two items need to be connected logically (i.e. the causal relationship between the two items needs to make sense), using appropriate and accurate language. Activity 2 enables students to select a word with right meaning for the context. Point out that although one word has a different meaning in each case, the remaining four do not necessarily have exactly the same meaning. Activity 3 focuses on using the items. Give some examples of incorrect use to elicit what is wrong and ask students to correct it, e.g. *The doors will not open due to the train has overrun the station platform*: in this example the speaker is using a preposition (*due to*) instead of a subordinator (e.g. *because / as*). To add further examples, simply pick out some sentences from the texts in this unit and substitute a different cause and effect language item with a different word class. Base students' sentences on those in 1, and as an extension ask them to write their own sentences using the items in 2.

Answers

1 1 typically leads to (c)   2 because (e)   3 is one possible effect of (a)   4 are sometimes associated with (f)   5 owing to (b)   6 can be caused by (d)

2 1 impact   2 association   3 may account for   4 moreover   5 so that   6 in relation to

TASK 5 Analysing a cause and effect essay

1 This task requires students to analyse a sample cause and effect essay so that they can apply the same analytical principles to their own essays in Tasks 6-8. The essay title relates to some of the scenarios which students discussed in Task 1, so students should be familiar with some of the issues raised in the essay notes. Ask students to be selective when using the items in the notes in a suitable essay structure - they can miss out some of the items. Students should focus on coherence and logic, and having one topic per paragraph. Allow time for students to compare their proposed essay structures with other pairs / groups.

2-4 This series of activities analyses the student sample essay. Students compare the essay notes with the finished essay, which illustrates part of the writing process: emphasize that the ideas in the planning stage need further refinement (including cutting) during the writing stage. Finally, say that the student essay is a sample and not a model - it is one way of answering the question and not the only way or the best way. Many of the sections in 4 (particularly d, e, f) are specific to this sample essay.

Answers

2 Structure 4: variation

3 Several points are not included in the sample essay: in the opening statement - the case of an underachieving student / film; in the background and context - money, funding, poor teaching, poor facilities, other disruptive students, ?poor parenting, school curriculum; in key factors - migration, dedication / ability to study independently, distractions e.g. relationships; in the effects - poor facilities.

These may have been excluded in the final essay because: there was insufficient space to develop all these ideas; they are not all as relevant as the ideas actually included; there are too many ideas to write a coherent essay - each paragraph needs to develop one main topic, and the essay becomes less coherent if each paragraph has several ideas which are not very closely related.

4 1 (h) opening statement to gain the reader's interest
2 (c) definition of key term in title
3 (i) reference to the wider context
4 (j) thesis statement
5 (e) discussion of possible socio-economic causes
6 (d) discussion of possible clinical psychological causes
7 (f) discussion of possible personal psychological causes
8 (g) effects
9 (b) conclusion
10 (a) acknowledgement of limitations

5 Explain that evaluation is integrated throughout the sample essay, from the introduction onwards. This approach suits the purpose of the essay, which follows a fairly complex chain structure. Examples of evaluative language from different parts of the essay are given in bold below.

Sample answers

1 This narrative illustrates **the importance of** expectations in achievement.

2 a number of **serious problems** including **poor** employment prospects.

3 Low expectations are **certainly** a contributing factor.

4 This essay investigates two **major** causes

5 Research [...] **does indeed affect** a student's performance. [...] students were '**strongly associated with**' greater success [...] Triventi's **important** research underlines the **important** role

6 Also **of crucial importance** [...] **In some respects it can be problematic** to [...] were '**far less likely**' to graduate

7 **critical** for all students [...] This is **arguably** connected to [...] because of the **likely** correlation between [...] unskilled worker **is unlikely to** aim for [...] Such a goal **would seem unattainable**. [...] are **likely to be important contributors** to [...] child **are likely to be** aligned with ...

8 These are both **likely to lead to** underachievement [...] **This unfortunate cycle of negative effects** is [...] and **may not be directly connected to** the [...] are **negative**.

9 this essay has presented **the importance** of interconnected [...] These factors **appear to play a major role** in

10 **Of course**, other factors [...] **may also come into play to a greater or lesser extent. Most crucially though**, a child's [...] low expectations **typically bringing about disappointing results**. Trying to change this situation is **extremely challenging**, but **a good starting point** would be to

TASK 6 Refining and focusing the title of an essay

1 and 2 This essay gives students their first opportunity in the course to formulate their own title. In other assignments, in particular the research essay (Units 7–12) students will also practise this. Give students time to work with the theme of *influence*; you could set this task for homework and ask students to report back next lesson. Remind students of the use of perspectives in approaching and analysing a written task. Make sure that students focus closely on causes and effects, and demonstrate the connection between items.

TASK 7 Researching and planning a cause and effect essay

1 and 2 Manage this task so that students have sufficient time to search for suitable sources. Some sources can be found online, e.g. using Google Scholar, while others are only available in book-based or paper-based form. Guide students through any local library search facilities, as appropriate. Remind students of the referencing conventions done in earlier units; refer them also to the sections on *Citation, referencing, reporting,*

referring to sources and *Connection: cause, effect, and association* in the Language Reference section on pages 200 and 202. Go through Checklist G on page 210 and encourage students to focus on planning a coherent essay with clearly connected material.

TASK 8 Writing and evaluating a cause and effect essay

1–3 As with the planning stages, part or all of the writing stages can be done independently / collaboratively outside the classroom. Explain that the writing process represents an important opportunity to refine and learn from the process. Optionally, ask students to keep a brief writing diary to record the key stages in their writing process, and most importantly how they can improve. Remind students to pay particular attention to their essay structure and the accurate and appropriate use of cause and effect language. Decide on the degree of collaboration: it may be advisable for students to work individually throughout the writing process, or you could encourage students to give each other critical feedback as they write.

8C Listening Lectures (6)

TASK 1 Preparing – reading a pre-lecture handout

1–3 Explain that the first task replicates the academic practice of preparing for a lecture by reading a prescribed text. Given the technical content of the lecture (strokes), this preparation is particularly important. Reading the pre-lecture handout, then, helps students to access the content of the lecture more effectively than approaching the lecture 'cold' and unprepared. This pre-listening task can be done for homework before the lesson – if so, check students' comprehension before listening. Pay particular attention to the vocabulary in 3 which is used in the lecture: this is a closely related set of words but with different and possibly confusable meanings. Say that these words can also be used more figuratively in non-medical contexts, e.g. *the prognosis for the economy is ...*

Answers

1 Genre: textbook
   Audience: medical students
   Purpose: to present essential information on strokes – what they are, the main types, historical background

2 a Background information
   b Definition
   c People affected
   d Symptoms, process, and diagnosis
   e Causes
   f Specialist information

3 1 impact 2 diagnosis 3 symptom 4 prevention
   5 risk 6 prognosis

TASK 2 Listening for essential factual information

1 and 2 ▶8.1 Point out that the slides offer a useful lead-in to the lecture, and relate to the handout. Extract 1 uses the two slides given in the Student's Book, while in subsequent extracts the lecturer uses a series of quite complex slides in his lecture which represent and clarify aspects of the content in visual form. As a guideline in this task, show the extract once and carry out a visual check of students' notes to make sure they have written down sufficient information relating to the lecture content. You can then show the extracts again, while students read the lecture transcript either on-screen (selecting the 'show transcript' facility) or in the Student's Book.

Answers

1 Aims and content of lecture:
- introduction to stroke – its importance, what it is, what it means to have a stroke, diagnosis, prognosis, impact on people
- treatment of stroke
  - primary prevention
  - secondary prevention
  - acute treatment

2 Definition of stroke; what it means to have a stroke; diagnosis

3–5 ▶8.2, 8.3 Explain that the focus of Extract 2 is on statistical information, and that of Extract 3 on the essential concepts which were introduced in the pre-lecture handout. Activity 4 gives students an opportunity to reprocess this factual information orally, based on their notes. Before starting, check their notes to ensure they are complete, showing Extract 2 again if necessary.

Sample answers

3 **/ 2 seconds** - worldwide sb has stroke
/ 6 secs - sb dies
5.8m - stroke deaths / year; 2007 - WHO report, Geneva
3rd most common cause of death
1 in 3 strokes fatal
1 in 6 people have stroke in lifetime
1 in 6 will have recurrence
2005 - Lancet: vascular disease increases with age
over 65 group - in EU: will increase by 2050 to 29% of population (Social Trends Office for National Statistics)

4 Every two seconds somebody has a stroke worldwide.
Every six seconds somebody dies of a stroke.
There are 5.8m stroke deaths per year, according to the 2007 WHO report published in Geneva.
Stroke is the third most common cause of death.
One in three strokes are fatal.
One in six people will have a stroke in their lifetime.
One in six people will have a second or further stroke.
In 2005 in *The Lancet* it was reported that vascular disease increases with age.
The number of people aged over 65 in EU will increase to 29% of the population by 2050, according to the Social Trends Office for National Statistics.

5 Stroke: *disturbance of cerebral function with symptoms lasting 24+ hours → death, of vascular (blood vessels) origin (WHO); NOT a CVA (cerebral vascular accident)*
Ischemic stroke: a *clot forms along a blood vessel → blood supply is blocked → damage to brain tissue* (most common cause, 80%)
Hemorraghic stroke: *a bleed from a blood vessel (20% of strokes)*

ACADEMIC LANGUAGE

Connection (3) Association, speculation, and degree of certainty

Point out that this is the third Academic Language box showing language expressing connections. Students should by now be familiar with hedging and speculative language: explain that such language is frequently used when expressing cause and effect as these connections are typically not certain. Further information on Hedging and Speculating is on page 205. Explain that this whole area of language is also related to stance - different speakers / writers can assess the likelihood or strength of particular connection in different ways, resulting in different language, e.g. *potentially cause / frequently cause / possibly cause.* Adverbs relating to stance and possibility tend to be placed in the middle of a sentence, before the main verb.

TASK 3 Listening for association and evaluation

1 Set up the activity and monitor to note down any particularly interesting connections. Ask students to use real (or made-up) examples to illustrate the connections. Focus on accurate use of connection language, and encourage other students to correct any language mistakes, e.g. 'high blood pressure can ~~result from~~ *result in* a risk of subsequent strokes'.

2–4 ▶8.4 Say that students' predictions are still valid regardless of whether the lecturer mentioned them or not. Extract 4 illustrates the importance of evaluation: a discussion of possible connections typically leads to evaluation. Ask students to keep a record of the lecturer's evaluative language so that they can use it in their own speaking and writing. Show the extract a second or third time to draw attention to the connection and evaluation language.

Sample answers

2 **Associations**, using the symbols ← → reducing smoking, treating blood pressure, improving diet, promoting exercise ← → stroke prevention
diabetes, high blood pressure ← → at risk of subsequent strokes
aspirin, rehabilitation ← → stroke prevention
Evaluation
Extracts from the lecture (taken from Extract 4):
So, primary prevention in the population group, reducing smoking, treating blood pressure, improving

diet, promoting exercise **is obviously the principle strategy to prevent strokes. In those who have risk factors** and they are diabetes, high to- high blood pressure, previous warnings or TIAs as we've discussed earlier, **these groups of patients benefit from** treatment strategies that are rather more accelerated than the normal population, for example, starting aspirin for treating blood pressure very well, **and these have all been shown to reduce the, the risk of subsequent strokes**. [...] **What's very exciting now** is the acute treatment of stroke with interventions and with rehabilitation, and one mightn't think that rehabilitation is **that exciting but in fact it is, and it is probably the best proven treatment for any stroke patient.**

3 **reducing smoking, treating blood pressure, improving diet, and promoting exercise** are the principle strategies for stroke prevention
aspirin is an older treatment for those at risk of subsequent strokes
rehabilitation is the best proven treatment for any stroke patient

TASK 4 Reprocessing information from a lecture

1 The final task in the module focuses on the content of the lecture. Monitor the pairs in order to assess students' effectiveness in accurately reprocessing the information in the lecture and the pre-lecture text. If students are having difficulties with locating the target information and/or presenting it, suggest that they should practise independently using this and previous lectures in the book.

A useful further resource for authentic lectures is the *Oxford University Open Spires* resource, at:

http://openspires.oucs.ox.ac.uk/index.html

8D **Speaking** Seminars (4)

TASK 1 Reading to gather evidence for a seminar discussion

1 and 2 Like the Listening module (8C), this task reflects the academic speaking process through the study of a preparatory reading text. In earlier units (e.g. Unit 6) students have practised reading abstracts to gain an overview of a research topic; Text 1 is a 300-word abstract which includes headings to help navigation. As with the Listening module, the reading task can be given for homework. One advantage of doing it in class, however, is that you can monitor, focusing on students' effective note-taking. If students start coming up with ideas on solving the problem mentioned in the text, i.e. ideas on promoting physical activity, ask them to note these down to use later in the discussion.

Sample answers

1 Aims: to *quantify the effect of physical inactivity on major non-communicable diseases (e.g. coronary heart disease (CHD), type 2 diabetes, breast & colon cancers); to estimate how much disease could be averted and life expectancy extended*

Main results: *physical inactivity causes 6% of CHD, 7% of type 2 diabetes, 10% of breast and colon cancers, 9% of premature death (i.e. 5.3m of 57m deaths worldwide in 2008)*

Recommendations: *reduce or remove inactivity (an implicit recommendation)*

2 Explicitly mentioned in Text 1: Becoming active, i.e. inactive people becoming active.

General statements in Text 1 to motivate people to become more active: Inactivity increases the risk of coronary heart disease, type 2 diabetes, breast and colon cancers.

Inactivity shortens life expectancy.

Selected more detailed information: Physical inactivity causes 6% of coronary heart disease, 7% of type 2 diabetes, and so on.

ACADEMIC LANGUAGE

Evaluation (2) Defending your argument

Explain that when presenting an argument in a seminar discussion, the speaker needs to defend their argument as it is likely to be critiqued by other participants. The key to this is justifying and evaluative language. In general, the argument is presented in a detached way, e.g. *This argument is [effective] because [...]*, rather than simply using a subjective frame, e.g. *I think / In my opinion* - this last expression is best avoided. Encourage students to provide reasons and support for their argument.

TASK 2 Preparing a case for a seminar discussion

1 Allow plenty of time for this preparation task, so that students are well-prepared for the seminar discussion. Emphasize that in academic seminars, it is advisable to prepare (through reading and thought) rather than simply relying on spontaneous ideas. Focus the discussion on the local situation, or if students are from a number of different countries, these can be used as points of comparison in the discussion. Make sure students think of benefits for each strategy. Students should also think of drawbacks, so that they can be prepared to defend these, e.g. local volunteers reaching target groups through clubs and organizations: this could be very effective as it is at 'grass roots' level. However, there are issues of trust and control – the local volunteers are not employees, and so they could be hard to manage and ensure quality.

2–4 In these activities, students select one strategy from each geographical category (local, national, global) and negotiate a coherent argument involving their chosen strategies. Encourage a critical approach. You could write up critical questions for the specific context, e.g. *How would that lead to increased activity? / How would that strategy work? / Why would inactive people be persuaded by that strategy?* Students should aim for what they consider to be the most effective strategies.

5 In the final activity, students have the opportunity to present their case in a supportive environment, i.e. in pairs, before they do so again in a larger group in Task 3. Check that students fully understand the three stages in the activity; you could write a summary of these on the board: *1 present and justify; 2 evaluate; 3 reach a consensus.* Monitor the pairwork to check that each pair is following this structure. Conduct a brief whole-class feedback stage to check that all pairs reached a consensus (but they do not need to say what this consensus is at this stage).

TASK 3 Presenting a case and reaching consensus

1–3 In the final task students put their preparation into practice by conducting the seminar discussion. As with their pairs / smaller groups, students should aim to use argument and persuasion to reach a consensus. Remind students to offer evidence and examples that apply to the local / selected contexts. Set up the seminar with a time limit, and organize groups as necessary for variety and a mixture of levels in each group. Suggest that each group nominate a student to act as chair in order to monitor the use of time and ensure that all students have the opportunity to present their strategies.

The final stage in the process shifts to writing, so that the whole process gives students the opportunity to be persuasive in both speaking and writing. Refer students back to the Academic Language box for examples of justifying language.

8E Vocabulary Word formation (1)

1 and 2 These are words that students have already encountered in the reading texts in this unit, so they should be familiar with the general meanings. Look at the example as a class to give students an idea how they might categorize the words. As students compare and add to their classifications in groups, check the meaning of suffixes, such as *inter* = between.

Sample answers

Classification	Words from box	Possible additions
Noun from a phrasal verb: verb + particle	*breakdown, follow-up, trade-off*	*takeover, turnover, setup*
Noun from a phrasal verb: particle + verb	*intake, outcome*	*input, output, uptake*
Discipline / perspective prefix + discipline/ perspective adjective	*biophysiological, socio- economic*	See ex. 3
Simple compound noun of two words put together	*dataset, layman, well-being*	*textbook, wrong-doing*
Adjective with negative prefix	*inadequate, unhealthy, non-communicable*	*inconsistent, indirect, unethical*
Addition of a prefix with a general meaning	*interwar, postwar, overcrowding*	*prewar, overestimate, underestimate*

3 This activity focuses on a common set of academic prefixes to describe a field of research, especially a cross-disciplinary field (e.g. *biochemistry*), or a perspective where two factors overlap (e.g. *socio-economic*). Encourage students to think of relevant prefixes or combinations that relate to their own disciplines. Note that these are shown as adjectives, but many can be formed into nouns as well (*neurolinguistics, biomechanics*, etc.). Many prefixes are listed as their own dictionary entries, so encourage students to look any up they are not sure about.

Answers

a **neurolinguistic** - *neuro-* = to do with the brain; *linguistic* = to do with language → to do with the study of how language is processed in the brain

b **biomechanical** - *bio-* = to do with living things and the body; *mechanical* = to do with machines and movement → to do with the study of how the body moves

c **microelectronic** - *micro-* = very small in size/scale → to do with the study of very small scale electronic devices

d **socio-political** - *socio-* = to do with society → to do with the connections between society and politics or involving both social and political factors

e **geophysical** - *geo-* = to do with the land/Earth (*geography*) → to do with the study of physical features of the Earth

Research Project (2)
Establishing a working title

Having chosen a general topic and conducted some initial research, students now need to narrow down their topic and choose a working title in order to focus the main phase of their research. Look at the first example title, which is too narrow, and ask students what problems they might encounter researching the topic. Although micro-credit schemes might be an interesting topic, by focusing so narrowly – on women, in rural areas, in Southern India – it might become difficult to find enough relevant academic resources in English. By dropping one or more of these restrictions, for example, by looking at micro-credit schemes in rural India or micro-credit schemes aimed at women in India, more resources will become relevant. Students should primarily use sources in English for two reasons: firstly as the aim of an EAP course is to practise reading in English, and also so that sources can be more easily verified by the assessor (most likely yourself). You may decide to allow an occasional foreign-language source, for example, official data from the student's home country, but students should clear any non-English sources with you.

Most project topics start off quite broad and need to be narrowed down. Students read through the guidelines for narrowing down a topic, then suggest possible changes to the two example titles. Working in groups they can then look at each other's initial topic ideas, categorize them from most general to most specific, and discuss which need to be narrowed down (or broadened out). Encourage students to try out different possible working titles for their projects, consisting of either a noun phrase or a question, or a combination of the two.

Once students have established their specific focus and working title, they should conduct the main part of their research, and be ready to bring together their ideas to create an outline plan by the end of the next unit. At this stage their working title is not 'set in stone', it may be adjusted depending on research findings, but encourage students not to change their topic completely as they will get behind.

UNIT 9 **Variation**

INTRODUCTION

Unit 9 This unit looks at some of the less obvious forms of academic writing, such as narratives and critical response, which are nonetheless still common across disciplines and which many students are likely to encounter at some point. Under the unit theme, students consider variation in both the real world, and in terms of style and language.

9A Reading has two aims: for students to explore narrative accounts, a common feature across disciplines, and also to understand the different types of academic and non-academic genres they might encounter through their studies and research. With a wide variety of genres available to students online, it is vital that they can recognize and evaluate different genres and understand how they can use them as sources. The module takes an anthropological theme, exploring the idea of variation across peoples and cultures.

9B Writing examines the genre of critical response, also known as critique or review. Students are encouraged to think critically, to recognize different types of evaluation and to practise the language needed to evaluate ideas confidently and tentatively. The module ends with students writing their own critical response to a text.

9C Listening looks at some of the potential differences in lecturing styles that students might encounter during their studies and some practical techniques for dealing effectively with lectures. Inevitably, students will encounter lecturers with different accents and approaches to presenting ideas, and they have to be prepared to deal with these variations. In this module, students watch three short extracts from lectures which employ quite different styles and discuss the factors that affect how easy to follow and memorable a lecture is.

9D Speaking provides an opportunity for students to discuss differences in academic culture, to explore their own expectations about what they might encounter studying abroad, and to highlight any potential differences they might face. In previous modules, students have read texts in preparation for a seminar discussion (see 3D, 6D, and 8D), but in this module, they divide into two groups to read different texts, meaning they have to focus on clearly explaining ideas from sources that others have not seen.

9E Vocabulary highlights some idioms that are common in academic writing. Although the more colourful idioms we think of in conversation and journalism are not typical of academic writing, there are a number of multi-word expressions that are very commonly used and which students need to be able to recognize and decode when reading.

Research Project (3) Having researched their chosen topic area, this section helps students to organize their ideas into an outline plan. Students identify the main themes and ideas which they will focus on and determine a logical structure for their overall project.

DISCUSSION

1 These first Discussion activities introduce the theme of Variation, taking the English language itself as an example. Students don't need to come up with definitive answers, but suggestions from their existing knowledge. Check that students understand the meaning of the term *lingua franca* here (= a shared language of communication used between people whose main languages are different).

2 The aim of this activity is to get students thinking beyond the most obvious varieties of English, not to focus on the meaning of these specific words. Students may spot *color* and *sidewalk* here as being American English. As they check the others in a dictionary, focus attention on the regional labels. These words all appear in the *Oxford Advanced Learner's Dictionary*, but some (such as *sook*) may not appear in other learner's dictionaries.

Definitions from OALD

bairn - *Scottish English, North England English*: a child

biltong - *South African English*: raw dry meat that is eaten in small pieces. Biltong is preserved by being treated with salt

color - *US spelling* of colour

lakh - *Indian English*: a hundred thousand

sidewalk - *North American English*: a flat part at the side of a road for people to walk on (BrE pavement)

sook - *informal, Australian English, New Zealand English, Canadian English*: a person who is not brave

3 The final discussion task moves from looking at regional variations, to variation across genres, the main focus in the following Reading module. You could put up prompts on the board to generate discussion here: *vocabulary, grammar, organization / format*. Rather than going through each genre in feedback, you could take these categories and ask for examples of differences in each one.

Sample answers

The examples below are the extremes, other genres can be placed somewhere in the middle or could arguably vary depending on context; so an undergraduate essay / textbook could be at the simpler end of the scale, whereas an advanced postgraduate essay / textbook could be more complex, technical, and specialist.

Vocabulary: formal (academic journal, PhD thesis) vs informal (an email between students)

Vocabulary: technical / specialized (academic journal, lab report) vs general (popular science magazine)

Vocabulary / Grammar: impersonal (lab report, academic journal) vs personal (email, popular science magazine)

Grammar: long, complex constructions (academic journal, PhD thesis) vs short, simple sentences (email)

Organization: fixed format and structure (lab report) vs no fixed structure (email) / lots of variety (student essay, textbook)

9A **Reading** Different genres

The aim of this module is to provoke discussion about the reliability of different types of sources and how they might (or might not) be used in an academic context. Read through the rationale as a class to establish some of the key terms and concepts here, including **peer review** (already mentioned in 3A) and **popular academic texts** (books, magazines, and online content). If possible, bring in some examples of popular academic books or magazines (such as *National Geographic*, *New Scientist*, or *The Economist*) to help prompt discussion.

TASK 1 Critical thinking - evaluating types of source

1 and 2 The aim of this activity is to get students thinking about different genres they might encounter when researching academic topics, especially in a context where the internet is as likely a source of information as a more carefully curated university library. The key point here is not to make judgements about which sources are 'good' or 'bad', but for students to recognize different genres and their characteristics. As an extension, you might want to talk about how students can evaluate online sources. Many university websites include guides for students to evaluating online sources, which involve asking critical questions about the source and content.

Sample answers

Source	1.1	1.2
1	b	academic
2	a	academic
3	c	popular academic
4	f	popular academic
5	d	non-academic*
6	e	academic (but informal)

* Views about Wikipedia vary widely; some academics would avoid it completely, others treat it with caution. By most it is not considered to be a reliable source and should not be cited in academic writing or discussion. Students may though find it an easy starting point to understand some general concepts, from which they can then go on to read more reliable academic sources.

3 How different genres might be used (or not used) in a particular discipline (or institution or department) will vary greatly. This module takes examples from Anthropology, a discipline which draws from a wide variety of sources. In some disciplines, for example, journalism may be an important source of recent real-world developments (politics, sociology, international development) or examples of how society or the media views an issue. In science and in many professions, such as medicine, it is common for popular magazines to highlight the latest developments and provide a useful source of news, which academics and professionals can then choose to follow up by reading the original research papers. Ask students to research popular sources relevant to their own discipline. The important thing for students to recognize is that while many different genres can be useful in their academic studies, not all are appropriate to cite directly, for example, in an essay. Ask students why non-academic genres may not be appropriate to cite, i.e. they are not written according rigorous academic standards, so they may be simplified and lack important technical details and distinctions, they may not contain references to sources, they may also use a non-academic style of language, and in some cases, they may not be reliable.

> **Sample answers**
> - to cite in an essay: a, b
> - to cite in a seminar discussion: a, b, e, f (maybe c)
> - as background reading: a, c, f, d - but to be treated with caution (see note above)
> - to keep up to date with ideas: e, f

TASK 2 Recognizing narrative in source texts

1 Narratives occur in both published and student academic texts across disciplines. They may be third-person narratives, for example, recounting historical events, as in Texts 1 and 3 here. They may also be first-person narratives recounting an experience, such as the fieldwork in Text 2, or in the case of a student, for example, an account of a work placement. Set students a time limit of 4–5 minutes to read just the boxed sections of the three texts, in order to identify the basic elements of the 'story' in each one.

Text 1 note: the Peace Corps (pronounced /kɔː/) is a US organization that sends young Americans to work in other countries as volunteers with the aim of creating international friendship.

> **Sample answers**
>
> | | Location / host culture | Outsider(s) | Cultural difference |
> | --- | --- | --- | --- |
> | Text 1 | Tswana people in Botswana (southern Africa) | American Peace Corps volunteers | Ideas about spending time alone |
> | Text 2 | Mongolia | The author (Empson) | Beliefs about luck / fortune (keeping hairs from a cow's tail) |
> | Text 3 | Mixtec, Mesoamerican people (from Mexico) | John (a Western visitor / researcher) | Belief in 'coessential' animals |

2 All three texts need to be covered here to allow for comparison later, so check that each of the texts has been chosen by at least one group in the class. As these are quite engaging, vivid accounts, encourage students to express their feelings and reactions to them as part of the discussion.

> **Key concepts described in the three texts**
> Text 1: ethnocentrism
> Text 2: harnessing fortune
> Text 3: coessential animals

3 and 4 These questions aim to draw out the differences between the three texts, especially between those which use a third-person narrative as an example to illustrate a general theory (Texts 1 and 3) and the first-person narrative (Text 2) which is an account of field work carried out by the researcher and which forms the main focus of the text (a monograph). Give students the opportunity to share their personal reactions to the texts as well and any interesting stories or parallels that came out of their discussion.

> **Answers**
> Text 1 & Text 3 - a
> Text 2 - b

5 Examples here might include third-person accounts in case studies (across disciplines including business, law, medicine, engineering, etc.) or accounts of historical events (as background to a current situation). Or first-person accounts in a report on a work placement (common in health sciences and education, but also business or engineering) or reports of field work (as in Text 2).

TASK 3 Identifying different writing styles

1 This task focuses more specifically on different styles of writing, and the language they use, as touched on in the Discussion (page 135). Note that the sources here are the same here as in Task 1 (page 136), but the references have been shortened and the genre stated. As these are very short extracts, students will only be able to identify one or two points per extract.

> **Sample answers**
> A **textbook**: overall fairly formal or neutral
> **vocabulary**: formal & specialized; *ethnocentrism*
> **impersonal language**: *anthropologists* (plural noun for a general group); *one's* (not *your / our*)
> B **monograph**: the most formal academic genre, but also quite personal here as it relates to fieldwork
> **vocabulary**: formal & academic; *actions, practices, attended*
> **grammar**: complex & formal, long sentences, passive structures / impersonal subjects
> **personal language**: *This leads <u>me</u> to consider* ... typical of a researcher's own work as described in a monograph
> C **popular book**: generally simpler and less formal
> **vocabulary**: *a bit far-fetched* - fairly informal / non-expert
> **grammar**: short simple sentences
> **personal language**: *to us* - style tries to relate ideas to the audience (typical of popular books and some textbooks)

D journalism: more colourful and evocative with more marked, non-academic language

vocabulary: colourful / dramatic / emotive & informal – typical of journalism to create interest - _shielded from the outside world, colonial blundering, that shredded other societies_

E academic blog: a new genre with often a mix of very formal academic and informal styles

vocabulary: a mix of specialized academic, _indigenously-produced_, and language more typical of spoken academic discussion than academic writing: _plethora of, heavily weighted towards the informative end of the spectrum_

personal language: very informal, 'spoken aside' in brackets: _at least, the ones I have seen_

ACADEMIC LANGUAGE

Style (3) Marked language

In Linguistics, language is described as **marked** when it is different in style from the language around it, for example, a very informal slang word in the middle of a formal academic essay. There is a danger that students can pick up language from their reading, without realizing it is marked in style, and then use it inappropriately in a more formal or neutral essay. These subtle differences of style, register, and usage can be difficult to learn, and even native speakers will have different feelings about usage. By recognizing different genres though and the ways in which their language might be different (especially popular sources and journalism), students can try to avoid some of these pitfalls.

TASK 4 Recognizing levels of formality and marked language

1 and 2 Working in pairs or small groups, encourage students to match as many of the pairs as possible before they check any words in a dictionary. Draw attention to any register labels shown in dictionaries (_informal, formal,_ etc.).

Sample answers

a bit _informal_	somewhat _quite formal_
blunder _informal_	error _neutral / more formal_
broke _informal_	insolvent _formal / technical_
clear up _informal / neutral_	resolve _formal_
deplete _formal_	use up _informal / neutral_
envelop _literary_	surround _neutral_
far-fetched _neutral_	implausible _formal_
miss out _neutral_	omit _formal_
nimbly _descriptive_	swiftly _also descriptive / literary_

TASK 5 Independent research – recognizing writing styles

1 and 2 Students are most likely to come across textbooks and journal articles, but encourage them

especially to search for popular sources, such as the magazines mentioned in Task 1, or for academic blogs or discussion forums in their own discipline. Professional or academic societies or associations are a good place to look for relevant blogs or discussions (e.g. The Law Society, The Royal Society, etc.). It is worth noting that blog posts and comments, even on the website of a reputable academic organization, may not be as carefully formulated and checked as more formally published sources (academics may try out new ideas or post comments to provoke debate) and so should be treated with caution.

3 Allow some time in the next class for students to report back on their findings, not just about the genres they found, but also the language features they noticed.

9B Writing Critical response

TASK 1 Recognizing types of evaluation

1 Students read the short extracts quickly, making general guesses about any unknown vocabulary.

Sample answers

	Discipline	Topic	Stance
A	Engineering / Computing	A tool / technique (computational simulation models)	neutral but expressing limitations
B	Agriculture / Ecology	A technique (use of non-synthetic pesticides)	critical
C	Law	A section of a law	critical
D	Business	A particular text	supportive
E	Politics* (Sociology / Economics)	A theory (by Esping-Anderson)	critical

*_decommodification_ is a term / theory generally associated with the field of Politics, but students' guesses at Sociology or Economics would be reasonable

2 Having identified each writer's stance, students now consider the language used to make evaluative comments in the extracts. The abstract terms (_precision, extent_, etc.) are less important here than a general understanding of what is being evaluated; encourage students to explain the type of evaluation in their own terms.

Sample answers

A _whilst ... remain a guide_ = extent; _significant uses_ = usefulness; _should not be treated as absolute_ = extent; _have to make assumptions_ = basis; _not entirely consistent with_ = consistency

B _not fully in line with_ = consistency / basis

C _does not account for_ = basis

D _a useful model / easily applied to_ = usefulness

E _can only really / most likely to be_ = extent

3 and 4 These activities encourage students to extend their vocabulary for making evaluative comments, thinking about the basic meaning and connotation of these words, as well as further extension through opposites. Note that the opposites will not always just involve the addition of a negative prefix. These activities can be carried out in pairs or in small groups to pool and share knowledge.

Sample answers

	1.3 Category	1.4 negative / positive	1.4 opposite(s)
assumption	3 basis	largely (but not always) negative	principle / firm basis
compatible	4 consistency	largely positive	incompatible / not compatible
comprehensive	2 extent	largely positive	not comprehensive / limited
conjecture	3 basis	negative	proof / evidence
consistent with	4 consistency	largely positive	inconsistent / not consistent with / contradictory
effective	5 usefulness	positive	ineffective / not effective
error	1 precision	largely negative	correct / accurate
exactly	1 precision	positive	approximately / roughly
limited	2 extent	largely negative (*limited evidence / resources*) sometimes positive depending on context (*limited impact / damage*)	broad / comprehensive / wide-ranging / widespread

TASK 2 Identifying and responding to a writer's evaluation

1 Having looked at isolated examples of evaluation, students now identify evaluative language in the context of a longer text. They start though by identifying the writer's main points. Point out that students only need to read the first paragraph at this stage and that the points are numbered in the text. This activity also provides useful practice in paraphrasing.

Sample answers

1 See example
2 There is often a gap between people's 'intrinsic values' about food; they enjoy eating certain foods, and their 'extrinsic values': the desire to eat healthily.
3 Diet-related health problems often develop gradually so are not immediately apparent.
4 In order to feel the health benefits, people need to change their diet over the long term.
5 Some changes in diet do not appear to have immediate and visible benefits.

2 and 3 Having identified the issues highlighted in paragraph one, students now look at the solutions that

have been tried in paragraph 2 and try to link the ideas to their own experience. You could give feedback on 3 at this stage or allow students to compare and discuss in 5. Students should note down one or two examples of healthy eating campaigns they are familiar with individually; they will discuss these later.

Answers
2 a & b

4 The aim of this question is for students to use the evaluative language to identify the writer's stance.

Answer
b

5 Students work in pairs to summarize the writers' main argument and then discuss their response to the text, using the campaigns they noted in 3 as examples.

ACADEMIC LANGUAGE

Evaluation (3) Confident and tentative language

Ask students where they've come across examples of confident and tentative language before in the book (Hedging – 3B; Maximizing and minimizing language – 5D). Ask what characterizes the two examples of confident language here – do they use maximizing language for emphasis? (No, they are just presented as clear, straightforward statements.) Ask what criticisms could be levelled at the writers if the hedging were removed from the next sets of examples. For example:

Stem cell therapy offers a powerful treatment for inherited disorders. → Criticism: You can't be sure about that, stem cell therapies haven't been fully tested and proven to work yet, there might be problems or side effects we don't know about yet.

Focusing on the vocabulary choices in the final example, note that all these alternatives express criticism, but ask which is the most tentative and which the most confident.

Question is a fairly tentative word choice and is further hedged by the modal, *can.*

Dispute is stronger, but hedged by *sometimes.*

Criticize is also strong and maximized by the strong adjective, *heavily.*

TASK 3 Expressing evaluation confidently and tentatively

1 and 2 Students work individually or in pairs to grade these sets of near synonyms. Allow dictionaries if necessary to check any unknown words. In most cases, it would be difficult to substitute all the words in each set into the same sentence (because the senses diverge too much), but encourage students to use at least two for each one. Collect examples and correct any issues with meaning or usage. In some cases an adjustment, such as an added preposition, may be needed for two words to work in the same sentence.

3 After students have read and identified the writers' stance and use of evaluative language, ask them to evaluate how effective each paragraph is in terms of persuading its readers. Although both put forward a valid perspective, A seems a little too positive and confident, especially as the writer doesn't offer any support (in the form of examples or citations) to back up their assertions. B's claims are not only more tentative (so less open to criticism), they are also supported by an example and citation.

4 and 5 This short writing task gives students practice in expressing their own evaluation on a topic from their own experience. Note how the paragraphs A and B in 3 do not go into detail explaining the healthy eating campaigns but summarize them in very general terms in the first sentence. The paragraph should consist of just three or four sentences (around 80–100 words) and could be written in class to allow for immediate peer feedback. Feedback can be fairly informal and students need not submit their writing as they will complete a more structured writing task at the end of the module.

TASK 4 Responding critically to a text

1 This task introduces the text which students will respond to in their final writing task at the end of the module. This discussion question encourages students to think about the topic of food preferences and which factors might influence an individual's tastes.

2 and 3 First give students a time limit to read through the text quickly and identify the factors mentioned (*taste, exposure to foods,* and *social transmission*). Once these are established, give students more time to make notes on the sources of evidence used to support each point. Note that making notes in a table like this can be a useful way for students to break down the key points in a text.

4 Students work in groups to discuss their initial responses to the ideas in the text. These will help to form the basis of their evaluative comments in the writing task to follow, so encourage students to note down any interesting points that come up.

TASK 5 Writing a critical response to a text

1 and 2 This forms the main writing task of the module, a piece of critical response, which will most likely be completed as homework. Work through the guidelines as a class, emphasizing again that students should not write a full summary of the text, but should only very briefly summarize the main point(s), before adding their evaluative comments. No word limit has been given, but as a guide, the sample response below is 235 words. Explain that academic writing is typically a process of writing, checking, and redrafting, so students should write their initial ideas following the Guidelines, but then use the Checklist to evaluate what they have written and make any changes before they submit their final draft.

This disparate range of subjects, experimental contexts, and food types tested make it difficult to draw direct inferences that can be applied more widely.

Perhaps the most convincing of the three influences put forward by Wardle and Cooke (2010) is the idea that exposure promotes a liking for certain foods. They offer a number of studies, largely in children (Cooke *et al.*, 2004, Sullivan & Birch, 1990, and Wardle *et al.*, 2003) that show repeated exposure to a new food, in both experimental and more natural settings, increases a child's acceptance of it, a finding which intuitively fits with our own experiences of food. Whilst this finding has interesting implications in the area of child health and nutrition, it seems clear, however, that there may be other important influences at work that are not mentioned in this extract, such as genetic, biological, or even cultural factors, that need to be explored to build up a more complete picture.

9C Listening Lectures (7)

TASK 1 Evaluating different lecture styles

1 As students discuss each of the factors, encourage them to give specific examples from their own experience, either from their previous studies (in English or in their first language) or from the lectures they have watched so far during this course. Elicit feedback on which factors make a lecture:

- easy to follow
- memorable
- difficult to follow
- boring / difficult to concentrate on.

2 Quickly run through the lecture titles to establish the probable subject areas. Note that students may recognize the first lecture from Unit 1C.

Answers
1 Education
2 (Political) History
3 Philosophy

3 ▶9.1–9.3 Emphasize that students shouldn't worry about the content of these three extracts, but focus instead on the lecturing style, using the headings in 1 to make brief notes. Give students time after each short extract (3–4 minutes) to compare and discuss their responses to the lecturing styles.

4 and 5 Reformed into their groups, students should not only discuss which styles they preferred but explain why. In feedback, establish which three factors are most useful and which least useful in following a lecture. Ask if there are any points which didn't come up in these extracts which might help or hinder understanding, such as strong regional accents, practical demonstrations, etc.

As an extension, you could identify and watch some short clips of different lectures, perhaps demonstrating different regional accents or that are particularly

appropriate to your own context, via YouTube, TED.com, or iTunesU for students to comment on. Although it is worth noting that some of the lectures available online (such as those on TED.com) are intended for a wider audience and so are likely to be more populist and engaging than the standard course lectures that students might expect to encounter in their own studies.

TASK 2 Techniques for dealing with different lecture styles

1–3 This task is intended to prompt discussion about practical techniques that can help students deal with different lecture styles and generally get the most from lectures. All of the strategies suggested here could be useful, although some have more potential pitfalls than others, in terms of time and practicalities, and all will depend on the individual's context and their preferred learning style. Listening to online lectures, for example, may be more useful for students before they start their university studies, than for those just about to start or already busy with a course. Encourage students to add any other techniques they have found useful.

Sample answers
1 c   2 d   3 d   4 b   5 a   6 e   7 e/a   8 f

TASK 3 Using lecture notes and slides effectively

1 The aim of this task is to explore how students can most effectively combine their own notes with slides or other information made available by the lecturer. Point out that where lecturers make slides available, it is a waste of time for students to carefully copy down all the information on screen during the lecture or to get distracted trying to take photos of the screen. But equally they shouldn't rely on slides as their only record of the lecture. Students start by recalling what they can from the first extract in Task 1. Of course, they were told to focus on style rather than content when they first watched, but it is still interesting to see how much they can remember.

2 and 3 ▶9.1 As students compare notes, try to pick out different styles and approaches to the task, in terms of:

- the amount that students wrote (single words, phrases, or whole sentences)
- what they chose to note down
- whether they used words and phrases from the lecture, their own paraphrases, or translations.

As an extension, you could ask students to find the notes they wrote for a previous lecture, perhaps near the start of the course, to see how useful they are after a period of time has elapsed. Can they read what they wrote? Can they remember the significance of particular notes?

TASK 4 Reflecting on techniques for dealing with lectures

1 The aim of this task is to review the ideas brought up in the module, so that students can decide on particular techniques and strategies they will try to adopt in the future. Emphasize that the lectures in this course give them the opportunity to experiment with different techniques.

2 You could encourage each group to agree on four main pieces of advice (one per student) to present informally to the class. They should explain the technique, why it's effective, any possible disadvantages, contexts where it might be most appropriate, and give examples where possible (e.g. from previous listening activities). As you work round the groups, encourage students whose point has already been made to add to what was said before, perhaps with their own example, rather than just repeating (e.g. *We came up with the same idea as X about Y, I'd just add that you can also …*).

9D Speaking Seminars (5)

TASK 1 Critical thinking - comparing academic cultures

1 ▶9.4 This short extract from the same lecture (seen in 1C and 9C) introduces the idea of differences in academic culture.

> **Answers**
> The key ideas mentioned here are:
> • authority and student-teacher relationships
> • critical thinking and asking critical questions
> • developing your own voice.

2 and 3 The focus of discussion here will depend very much on the backgrounds and mix of nationalities represented in the class, and also their experience so far of 'Western' English-speaking university culture. Some points of difference may already have come up in class and this is an opportunity for students to talk about their experiences and/or expectations.

TASK 2 Reading to prepare for a seminar discussion

1 and 2 Establish the topic for discussion first so that students understand their purpose for reading before dividing the class into A and B groups. Recap previous work on making notes on a text in preparation for discussion. You could provide photocopies of the two extracts if students would like to annotate the texts without writing in their books. Set a time limit for students to read and make notes, 3–4 minutes. Text A is slightly longer, but probably simpler to read, whereas text B is slightly shorter, but denser.

3 Students work together with other students who read the same text to compare their notes and clarify between them any points that were not clear. Depending on the size of the class, this might involve two larger groups or four or more smaller ones (e.g. two A groups, two B groups). Monitor and offer help on any language or ideas in the texts as necessary.

> **ACADEMIC LANGUAGE**
>
> **Discussion** Giving examples
>
> Write the word *example* on the board and ask students to suggest collocations or phrases it can be used in. Encourage them to think beyond the obvious, *for example,* prompting common collocating verbs and prepositions.
> *provide / give / use / consider / take / offer / cite + an example*
> *an example illustrates / shows sth*
> *an example of sth*
> *an example from [a source]*
> *use sth as an example*
> Read through the box and ask what other words and expressions can introduce examples (*Say …, Take …, From my experience …*). You might also add *instance, case,* and *illustration* (*for instance, an interesting case, one illustration of …*).

TASK 3 Giving examples

1 ◀))9.5 These two short audio clips illustrate some different types of example that might be used in a discussion context. Students note down the different types as in the Academic Language box: from a source, general, or personal. Note that each speaker gives several examples.

> **Answers**
> See annotations in transcript page 234.

2 The aim of this activity is for students to practise using the language to introduce examples, but also to think about paraphrasing the ideas from their text. At this point, encourage students to notice the source of their text, so that they can cite examples appropriately: Siemens and Burr for text A or Gallagher for text B. Help with pronunciation of the names if necessary.

3 In this activity students go beyond identifying the main points and examples in the text. They work together to link their text to the overall discussion question and to respond to what they have read critically.

TASK 4 Preparing an oral summary and evaluation of a text

1 Students initially work together still in their same-text groups to prepare an oral summary of their text. This should not be in the form of a written script, but should involve students working together to rehearse the best ways to explain and paraphrase the key ideas.

The guidelines should provide points for discussion: is this based on research? What are the key terms? Which points to include? Which examples are useful?

2 Allow students time to work alone to prepare a more general introduction to their text, including a brief summary plus how it links to the discussion question and their own evaluative comments. Again, students can make notes, but they should not prepare a complete 'script'.

TASK 5 Participating in a seminar discussion

1 and 2 Allocate students to mixed groups, ideally two or three As with two or three Bs. Only two students in each group (one A and one B) will present their text, but other group members who read the same text can answer any questions that come up. So, for example, A1 presents their 1–2-minute introduction, Bs ask questions for clarification, A2 answers them. B1 presents their text, As ask questions, B2 answers. The group then opens up to more general discussion with contributions from all members. Monitor and note particularly how well students introduced what they had read and incorporated ideas from sources with their own ideas and examples in the general discussion, to mention in feedback at the end.

9E **Vocabulary** Idioms in academic writing

1 and 2 Give students a couple of minutes to read and make notes about the idioms highlighted individually. They should not use a dictionary at this stage but make guesses if necessary. In pairs, they then compare their answers and use a dictionary if necessary to check the correct meaning and any other possible variations. Explain that idioms can usually be found under the most salient word, often a noun, verb, or adjective. If an idiom contains a very common word, such as *come*, it will probably be found at the entry for the other key word, i.e. *fore* or *contact*. The entry at which these idioms can be found is shown in bold below.

Answers

1 *come to the **fore*** = to become noticeable
  Also: *bring something to the fore* = to make something noticeable

2 *come into **contact*** (*with*) = to meet or touch somebody / something
  Also: *bring into contact* (*with*) = to cause people or things to meet or touch

3 *at the **expense** of something* = with loss or damage to something
  (no obvious variation)

4 *in the same **vein*** = on the same topic, style or manner
  Also: *in a similar vein*

3 and 4 This activity again illustrates a number of idioms or expressions that are common in academic writing, which students should be able to recognize in reading and might use for themselves.

Answers

1 *to a greater or **lesser** extent* - used to say that something is more or less appropriate or significant in different circumstances
  Also: *to a lesser extent, to a certain extent, to some extent*

2 ***no** matter who* - regardless of who; whoever the person is
  Also: *no matter what / how / whether*

3 ***give** rise to* - cause

4 *paint a disturbing **picture** of* - give a disturbing impression / description of something
  Also: *paint a **picture** of* (= give a clear description of), *paint a grim / vivid / alarming / accurate*, etc. *picture of …*

5 ***came** into force* - (of a rule, law, etc.) to start being used
  Also: *enter into force* and *bring something into force*

6 *followed **suit*** - did the same thing immediately after

Research Project (3)
Making an outline plan

By this stage, students should have completed the bulk of their research and they should be ready to organize their ideas into an outline plan. Stress that it is important that they move forward to this stage now, even if they feel they haven't got very far with their research, otherwise they will fall behind and not have enough time for writing.

Look at the example plan together as a class. Notice that the title is a refinement of one of the suggestions in Unit 8 (page 134). Ask students how the initial idea has developed, i.e. the topic has been narrowed down; from *in language teaching* to *in the English language classroom* and the student has developed an angle from which to view the topic: *aid or distraction?*

As an extension, students write down the key themes to arise from their own research as a mind map. This will allow them to see what they have got, decide what is most useful and relevant to their topic / title, and what points they may have to reject at this stage. You could put the example below on the board and ask which points the student decided to focus on and which to drop:

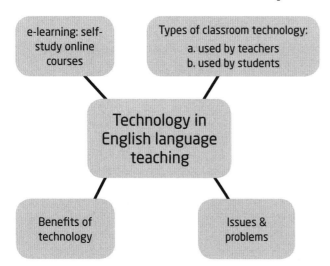

Students can share their ideas and start to discuss possible angles or organization structures that might fit their material / topic. You might ask students to hand in their outline plans, either at this stage, or after they have started adding some detail, so that you can check they are on the right track and offer guidance. They will need to have a firm and detailed plan completed by the end of the following unit so that they can move onto the main writing-up phase.

UNIT 10 Globalization

ACADEMIC FOCUS: PROBLEMS, SOLUTIONS, AND EVALUATION

INTRODUCTION

Unit 10 explores the problem-solution pattern which is very frequent in academic texts. Students learn to extract information relating to these essential elements from a wide range of texts. There is a particular focus on evaluation: students identify the writer's evaluation in texts and relate this to the topic and type of text and to the writer's background. Students also evaluate the presentation of information in both spoken and written texts. They can then apply these analytical principles to their own speaking and writing.

10A Reading aims to familiarize students with problems, solutions, and evaluation in academic texts, so that they can recognize and interpret these in a wide range of texts. The module covers four texts related to the unit theme of Globalization. Through a guided process of text analysis and language analysis, students reach the stage where they are able to select and synthesize material from multiple texts to use as support for their own arguments. There is a focus on personal responses to the issues raised in the texts, and a more analytical and critical approach, for example through identifying assumptions in a text and analysing how the authors' background can influence their content and argument.

10B Writing focuses on planning and writing a problem-solution essay. Students add solutions and evaluation to given ideas presented in an essay plan. The module aims to develop students' voice and flow by working on logic, coherence, and individual evaluative responses to the solutions they propose. As with the reading module, the writing module particularly relates the unit theme of Globalization to the topic of education. In writing their essay, students put into practice many of the academic skills and language they have studied throughout the course.

10C Listening introduces a more public type of presentation: conference presentations. Many students may aspire to presenting at conferences, which means that they can reach a wider, more public audience than at a single educational institution. The module works through the main elements of conference presentations, moving from the presentation abstract through the presentation itself to the post-presentation written summary which is typically written up in the conference proceedings publication. During the presentation itself, students learn to identify the presenter's coverage of the problems and solutions, and their integrated evaluation. In the process, students evaluate the presentation itself, including the written components (abstract and summary), so that they can apply this process to their own presentation work in the future.

10D Speaking brings together the work done on presentations in Units 4, 7, and 10. Students put into practice what they have learnt, focusing on the planning stages and working towards delivering their presentation without relying too closely on a script. The planning stages incorporate developing the topic and title, which reflects academic practice in spoken and written work. There is an emphasis on advice and self-evaluation in order to constantly improve beyond the course.

10E Vocabulary looks at an important area for students across disciplines to consider: using language which reflects an appropriate tone and does not cause offence. Many academic disciplines touch on socially and culturally sensitive topics and this module aims to raise students' awareness about vocabulary connotations, the importance of noticing how language is used in the literature, and also of how appropriate terminology may change over time.

Research Project (4) gives students advice about how to get started on their first draft. It looks at the process of writing drafts, receiving feedback and editing, as well as how to manage your time when conducting an extended project.

DISCUSSION

1–4 The Discussion incorporates strategies done in previous units, such as investigating causes which may be also be characterized as problems (in Unit 8). The discussion develops the unit academic focus by focusing first on problems and their possible causes, followed by solutions and evaluation. The first two activities require students to speculate on causes, and relate these to global issues and trends. In the second two activities, suggest that students use a range of perspectives, e.g. educational, political, economic, to propose solutions based on their chosen issue. Finally, students can use these and other perspectives to evaluate the solutions. During the discussion, suggest that students make notes on their proposed solutions, etc. in order to use later in other work.

10A Reading Textbooks (2)

TASK 1 Identifying problems and solutions in a text

1 and 2 The first module task examines a text which only presents problems and solutions. Ask students what they understand by the two terms, and to give examples of particular countries and sectors which might be involved, e.g. the medical sector: doctors and nurses emigrating from certain countries to others. This brief discussion and prediction leads into Text 1, which looks at the problem and presents example solutions from two South American countries. As with other tasks in this module, monitor to make sure students make effective notes while reading. Stick to time limits for the tasks and texts in this module to encourage more efficient reading.

> **Answers**
> 1 Brain drain: the movement of highly skilled and qualified people to a country where they can work in better conditions and earn more money.
> Brain gain: the opposite, i.e. the same thing from point of view of the receiving country.

2 The context / situation (time, place, people involved)
- International students gaining a higher education qualification and skills from abroad - language skills, technical knowledge, networking.

The problem(s) identified in the text
- Such students often do not return home, due to better employment prospects in the host country - this can be at the expense of economic growth in the home country.
- It is not easy to stop such students going abroad.
- The challenge of how a government in a home country can best make use of its students studying abroad.

The solutions proposed
- The CONACYT programme in Mexico enables PhD students to return home; also to offer higher pay for productive researchers to encourage them to remain in Mexico, and also to increase their productivity.
- The COLFUTURO programme in Colombia pays students to study, but requires them to return home afterwards.
- To build bridges between researchers in Colombia and those in the US.

3 Having looked at the meaning, the task focus now shifts to language. Encourage students to look for words with related meanings, e.g. *problems*, *concerns*, and then add to these, e.g. *issues*, *challenges*. Ask students to identify the other words surrounding such words, and stress the usefulness of looking at language in phrases / chunks, e.g. *a cost-effective way to improve*, rather than single words, e.g. *way*. Draw attention to the tentative language which forms part of some of the phrases, e.g. *may be a cost-effective way*.

> **Answers**
> 3
>
> | Problems | Solutions |
> |---|---|
> | Often, **however**, we observe that those individuals who migrate as students, or as temporary workers, do not return home. | **In fact**, from a policy point of view, and at least in the short run, promoting emigration by workers and students (the latter probably more than the former) in order to acquire higher levels of education and skills **may very well be a cost-efficient way to improve the quality of** domestic human capital, as opposed to establishing, say, universities or research institutes in the source country. |
> | The ever-increasing number of skilled emigrants, as well as the increase in the number of students studying abroad, **is raising concerns of brain drain** for developing nations. | The programme **has a repatriating component for scientists** (i.e. recent PhDs). |
> | **But this may be to the detriment of** growth and development in the source country. | CONACYT also **implements** a separate **initiative**, called the *Sistema Nacional de Investigatores*, in order to provide higher pay for productive researchers, **in order to make it more attractive for them** to remain at home (and, more generally, **in order to encourage their research productivity**). |

It also prevents the **acquisition** by these individuals, and to some extent by the source country **of knowledge** available abroad.

Preventing outflows of workers and students **is not easy**.

The students **receive a stipend** that allows them to pay for part of their studies, but in return they must come back home after the completion of their study.

In this third programme, **the objective is to build bridges between** those undertaking research at home and Colombian nationals residing in the US, for example, in universities.

4 Ask students to base their summary on their notes on Text 1, re-reading the text as necessary. Stress that students should not simply lift parts of the text and put it together into a new text, but use their own language as far as possible. In order to do this, students need to understand and be able to explain the main points in the original text. As their notes should show, these points are centred on problems and solutions. Optionally, show the sample answer and invite students to make comparisons between this and the original text.

Sample answer

International students are increasingly choosing to remain in their host country, rather than returning abroad to their country of origin. This can be for several reasons, including better career opportunities in the host country. Rather than preventing their students from studying abroad, which is difficult, home countries can adopt policies to maximize the potential of foreign-educated students. Typically, such solutions involve encouraging students to return home after their studies through incentives such as increased pay. The CONACYT programme in Mexico, for example, facilitates the return of PhD students, and offers higher pay to encourage productive research. In Colombia, the COLFUTURO programme pays students to study abroad, but requires them to return home afterwards. Colombia also aims to build links between researchers in Colombia and the US.

TASK 2 Identifying evaluation in a problem-solution text

1 Ask students if they have heard of the term *global commons*, and ask if they can suggest what it refers to. Set a time limit of 1–2 minutes for students to read the first paragraph to establish this information.

Answers

a   fragile global resources that are important to large numbers of countries

b   climate change, fisheries, water resources, food security, pandemic threats, biodiversity, human security

2 This reading activity is one of a series in this module to encourage purposeful reading and efficient note-taking. Give a short time limit, e.g. 5 minutes, and monitor for accuracy.

Answers

Problem	Solution
1 environmental issues	multilateral environmental agreements (MEAs)
2 impact of climate change on the developing world	*international cooperation to protect vulnerable people and restructure emerging energy systems in the developing world*
3 food security	*related to climate change; reinvigorating the Consultative Group on International Agricultural Research (CGIAR)*
4 pandemic threats	*the World Health Organization (WHO)*

3 and 4 As with the previous text, the focus shifts from meaning to language. Ask students whether the authors' evaluation is integrated or blocked (it is integrated throughout). Explain that the authors' evaluation is closely linked to their argument, and is essential to the message of the text.

Sample answers

*Confident evaluative language in **bold**:*

Problems

By global commons, we mean **fragile** global resources that are **important** to large numbers of countries; global management of economic systems is **vital** and how the existing institutional framework is **unfit for this purpose**; **Important** emerging global commons; Each poses **a difficult public policy problem** in its own right; With regard to pandemic threats, the **oft-forgotten** case of the 'Great Influenza' of 1918 stands as **a cautionary tale**; hundreds of millions, **health deprivation on a vast scale**. The **daunting nature of the task** cannot be **an excuse for inaction, however**. If it is, history **will not look kindly on** the current generation.

Solutions

it will become increasingly clear that a positive relationship between globalization and development depends on **the effective management** of the global commons; A **first best approach** to managing global commons issues is via multilateral agreements. These are **not easy to reach**, but **successes** in the area of multilateral environmental agreements (MEAs) suggest that **difficulties can indeed be overcome**; If we are to overcome parochialism to achieve global cooperation, **it is necessary that** the threats of non-cooperation **be made explicit**, that **any significant** economic losses inherent in cooperation be addressed; emerging food security issues **will be contingent on** international cooperation on climate change; **ignored for too long**; This is **insufficient preparation**.

Other writers' ideas

Schelling (2009) **rightly** pointed out; this is an issue of global cooperation in which '**parochialism interacts with globalization**'.

*Tentative evaluative language in **bold**:*

Problems

The issue of global commons management is **not necessarily or primarily** economic; The global commons agenda is **admittedly huge and perhaps overwhelming**.

5 Ask students to work either individually or collaboratively, and ask them to take notes. They can then briefly present their reasons, using their notes as prompts.

Sample answer

The style of Text 1 is more measured / tentative, while Text 2 is quite confident in style: most of the evaluative language and argument is stated quite strongly in Text 2. This arguably reflects the aim of the writers of Text 2, who seem to want to state their case and argument clearly and robustly as a wake-up call for action.

ACADEMIC LANGUAGE

Sentence patterns (1) Identifying subject + verb to work out meaning

Knowledge of basic sentence patterns is assumed at this level; this Academic Language box examines cases where it can be difficult to work out meaning. Explain that in such cases it is helpful to identify the grammatical subject and verb. If students cannot do so, they may misinterpret the sentence. For example, in the first sentence *With regard to pandemic threats, the oft-forgotten case of the 'Great Influenza' of 1918 stands as a cautionary tale*, the subject is not 'pandemic threats' or 'Great influenza', but the noun phrase built round the head noun 'case': this is the only interpretation of the sentence which makes sense. For further information, refer students to the relevant language reference section on page 206.

TASK 3 Working out meaning in complex sentences

1–3 This task applies the information in the Academic Language box to sample sentences from academic texts. Analyse one or two sentences as a whole-class activity to draw attention to the difficulties: in many examples there are several nouns before the main verb, only one of which controls the verb, e.g. sentence 1 has five – *estimates, panel, data, countries, period*. Also, there are two head nouns in 2 and 3, joined by a coordinator *and*. Explain that some noun phrases can have two (or even more) head nouns joined by a coordinator: *and, but, or*.

The second activity looks at the reason for the separation of head noun and main verb: elicit that the 'extra information' can be the post-modification in the noun phrase (sentences 1, 3, and 4), or adverbial(s) (sentence 2).

Answers

1 The subject of each **bold** verb in sentences 1-4 is highlighted in grey; the head noun is underlined. In sentences 2 and 3 there are two nouns in the head noun, joined by a coordinator (and).
 1 Estimates based on panel data for fifty countries over the period 1990-99 **provide** some limited evidence on brain drain or gain.
 2 In a process more akin to 'brain circulation' than 'brain drain', these US-educated engineers and entrepreneurs, aided by the lowered transaction costs associated with digitization, **are transferring** technical and institutional know-how between distant regional economies faster and more flexibly than most large corporations.
 3 The interdependency of socio-ecological systems and the increased reach of human activity **have led** to major political and scientific challenges in the governance of environmental resources.
 4 The global environmental processes commencing from the Stockholm Summit of 1972, the Rio Summit of 1992, and the Rio and non-Rio conventions of climate change, biodiversity, ozone depletion, the Basel Convention, and the POPS (Persistent Organic Pollutants) Convention **offer** many lessons on how to manage global goods.

2 1 a 2 b 3 a 4 a

3 **Sample answers**
 2 Engineers and entrepreneurs educated in the US are acting more nimbly than large companies in transferring knowledge globally.
 3 Social and economic systems are now interdependent, leading to a number of environmental problems.
 4 There is much that can be learnt from the 1972 Stockholm Summit in terms of environmentally sound ways of managing global goods.

TASK 4 Recognizing the influence of perspective in texts

1 Students should be familiar with *perspective*. Explain that writers draw on perspectives to fulfil their purpose: in Text 3 the authors are analysing an educational problem from a western perspective, informed by global, historical, economic, political, linguistic, and business perspectives. Point out that book covers, including many academic books, can send a strong message about the content. This example contains negative language, e.g. *broken promises*, which presumably reflects the authors' stance.

Sample answers

The most likely intended audience for the book: policy makers; researchers in education; students; lecturers.

The stance of the writers in relation to globalization: possibly negative ('broken promises').

How the background of writers and audience might influence the ideas in the book: through their western background, the authors may feel negatively towards threats from other regions, e.g. Asia.

2 As with the other texts, set a time limit, e.g. 3–4 minutes depending on the level of the class. During these timed reading activities, ask students not to look up vocabulary; rather, they should focus on what they know.

Answer

b: The striking example of China represents the main point of paragraph 1, while the text extract goes on to offer more globalized background information and evaluation. The example, then, is a detail of the text rather than the main point.

3 and 4 These activities focus on the problems, solutions, and evaluation in Text 3, and require students to explain how the authors' background informed this content. Encourage students to ask critical questions to help them explain this relationship. Examples of such questions, with suggested answers in brackets, include: *Why is a whole paragraph given to describing one example?* (the example of the new education city in China is seen as very large-scale, and therefore threatening to western countries); *Why do the authors talk about 'China's ambition,' 'ambitious plans,' and 'major challenge'?* (this language expresses the authors' likely fear of China – together with other countries that are not traditionally seen as being culturally close to America, i.e. India, Russia, Brazil, Hungary, Lithuania, Ukraine, the UAE, and Saudi Arabia); *What is the function of the metaphorical language, i.e. trickle down, tsunami, flood?* (it illustrates the content of the text more vividly – a trickle is gentle, while a tsunami and a flood are frightening, threatening, and beyond our control). In response to this last question, draw students' attention to the metaphorical language, which is typical of such texts.

Sample answers

3 Problems: the growth and investment in education in emerging economies poses a threat to the knowledge supremacy of developed nations (the US, Western Europe, Japan).

Solutions & evaluation: the huge flood of knowledge to emerging economies has led to a global abundance of skilled and educated workers. This is leading to increased competitiveness in emerging economies. Western universities and companies have greatly assisted in the process of global education and competition.

4 The writers' western perspective informs the negative tone of the argument in the text, i.e. fearful of emerging economy expansion in education and competitiveness, and the crucial role of western countries in this process.

TASK 5 Linking evaluative language and stance in texts

1 For the fourth text in the module, set up the reading activity with a time limit, e.g. 8–10 minutes including note-taking time. Students should now be quite practised in identifying the essential elements of problems, solutions, and evaluation in academic texts.

Sample answers

Problems
- Students are abandoning STEM subjects in favour of non-science subjects potentially leading to knowledge-based economy jobs in financial services and the creative industries.
- People working in the City (i.e. the financial district of London / New York) contribute to the huge wage gap in jobs.
- More students are doing business studies / media studies / journalism, etc., rather than engineering - as in the past.

Solutions
- Put STEM subjects at the core of education, as happens in some Asian countries, e.g. Singapore.
- Provide government support for such a focus, especially mathematics.

Evaluation
- The global distribution of key (STEM) expertise is obvious when taking account of the number of students studying such subjects in different countries: 37% in China down to 5% in the US.

2 The focus of this activity is a detailed analysis of the authors' stance in Text 4, with students working in groups to achieve this. The identification of assumptions is a particularly useful activity for students (Unit 6A Reading Task 5 practised identifying assumptions in texts). For example, there is an assumption in the text that students studying STEM subjects leads to innovation and economic growth. However, no evidence is offered to support this, and it is open to question. Invite students to think of arguments against this assumption, e.g. arguably, allowing students to study what they want (including journalism, media studies, art, or whatever) is an effective way of fostering innovation and economic growth. Explain that approaching a text with critical responses like these can enable students to understand academic texts – and the motivations of the writers behind them – more deeply.

Sample answers

a essentially negative - critical of the decline in the number of US / UK students studying STEM subjects, and opting for subjects such as journalism instead

b Statistical evidence (not referenced) provides support for numbers of students studying particular subjects; the then governor of the Bank of England, Mervyn King, adds weight to the writers' argument, while the policy of the Singapore government (unreferenced) provides further support.

c assumptions include:
- students studying STEM subjects leads to innovation and economic growth
- talented students avoid studying STEM subjects due to the influence of celebrity culture and the desire for financial reward
- banking jobs are better paid than engineering jobs
- STEM subjects are less highly regarded in western countries than they used to be, and than they are in Asian countries
- a diversified economy requires not only STEM subjects but other subjects as well

- studying engineering is important for the knowledge economy.

d Explicit evaluation: (as in 5.1 above): The global distribution of key (STEM) expertise is obvious when taking account of the number of students studying such subjects in different countries: 37% in China down to 5% in the US.

Implicit evaluation: (closely related to the assumptions in (c) above): the US / UK are making a mistake in having so few students study STEM subjects, especially engineering. The US / UK should increase its number of students studying such subjects in order to maintain competitiveness.

TASK 6 Critical thinking – responding to texts

1 and 2 The focus of this task is on students' personal responses and reflections on the texts, particularly Texts 3 and 4. Encourage students to put forward their own motivations in studying, based on the points given, e.g. future career prospects. They should relate these points to the material in the texts, e.g. *Studying STEM subjects should (or may not) enhance my future career prospects, as Text 4 argues.* These responses lead to activity 2, where students need to provide their own examples and experience to respond to the authors' arguments. Students' critical work in Task 5 should support them in this task.

3 and 4 Explain that, to some extent, a reader takes what they want from a text, and this is not necessarily the same message as the writer of the text originally intended. For example, an American reader of Text 4 with similar views to the authors may accept their stance as it reinforces their own. In contrast, a reader coming from a different culture, e.g. Asia, may interpret the text differently – seeing instead confirmation that Asian investment in STEM subjects is vindicated by arguments in the text. Monitor to check that students are able to organize their material in response to the question in 3. Give prompts where appropriate, as in the American / Asian example above. A key question to raise is to what extent reading a text can lead you to modify your stance on an issue.

TASK 7 Synthesizing material from texts to use in a discussion

1–4 This task brings together the four texts in the module. The issues are closely related to the unit theme of Globalization, and require students to take a stance. As with written texts, ensure that students support their argument using evidence from the texts. Through collaborating in groups, students can further develop their arguments in preparation for the discussion in 3. Emphasize that students can apply the evaluative questions in 4 to their subsequent discussions and contributions in seminars.

10B Writing Problem-solution essays

TASK 1 Defining problems

1–4 This task explores the unit theme of Globalization through a given situation, and requires students to propose and evaluate further problems arising from this situation. Elicit perspectives through which the situation can be further analysed, e.g. global, economic, financial, cultural, linguistic, ethnic, anthropological, business, intellectual, logistical, moral, psychological, technical, commercial. Write these up for students to refer to through the task and unit, so that students can become more familiar with using perspectives to approach and analyse a situation. As a challenge, ask students (in groups or individually) to come up with at least one problem for each perspective. Also, encourage students to approach the problem from the point of view of different agents, e.g. students, academic staff, management and support staff, national governments, publishers, employers / business. Emphasize the importance of the evaluation stage in 3, which reflects the academic practice of evaluating problems; later in the module students will evaluate solutions. In the summary stage, either ask students to write one bullet point for each point they have made, or a more formalized summary in the form of a paragraph.

TASK 2 Proposing and evaluating solutions

1 and 2 This task leads on logically from Task 1. Keep students in the same groups, or for variety and new ideas re-form the groups. Further evaluative questions can be found in many of the Checklists, pages 209–213. Use some of the perspectives from Task 1, especially financial, logistical, cultural, linguistic, and others. Ask students to note down their solutions. Time permitting, ask students to briefly present their solutions to other groups.

ACADEMIC LANGUAGE

Evaluation (4) Collocation and connotation

Evaluative language has been covered quite extensively, and this Academic Language box examines it from the aspects of collocation and connotation. These concepts are central to a language, and students can only achieve proficiency in them through extensive reading and listening (there are too many collocations and connotations to study in isolation, for example using a collocation dictionary). Explain that the given meaning (technically known as the denotative meaning) of many evaluative words is already either positive (e.g. *success, impressive*) or negative (e.g. *failure, problematic*). Other words are more neutral, e.g. *issue*, and these words can take on a more positive or negative meaning through the addition of further words, e.g. adjectives such as *important / crucial / major*. Also, the connotation of many words depends on how they are used in the text.

TASK 3 Refining your evaluations

1–3 These activities put into practice the principles of collocation and connotation using sets of related words in different combinations. Check students' understanding of countable / uncountable nouns, using examples from the words given. Many words can be both, e.g. *impact* can be countable, as in *have a significant impact on*, or uncountable, as in *have little impact on*. Encourage students to 'play' with the words in different combinations, and apply these to their proposed solutions from Task 2, e.g. the cost of international study *primarily affects* students, their future, and their families.

Sample answers

1 a significant / serious / minor **problem**; a serious **crisis**; a significant / serious / considerable **challenge**
2 a quick / simple / practical / possible / definitive **solution**; a quick / simple **fix**; a quick / simple / practical / possible / definitive **answer**
3 a(n) adverse / positive / potential **outcome**; a(n) adverse / positive / serious / potential **impact**; a(n) adverse / positive / serious / potential **repercussion**
4 directly / successfully / effectively / explicitly **address**; successfully / effectively / explicitly **tackle**; directly / successfully / effectively **confront**
5 easily / largely / completely **solve**; easily / largely / completely **overcome**; easily / largely / completely **alleviate**
6 potentially / seriously / adversely / primarily **affect**; seriously **threaten**; potentially / seriously / primarily **attack**

TASK 4 Incorporating voice in an essay

1 Explain that in this task students need to come up with appropriate evaluation based on the material in the essay plan. 'Voice' is related to a writer's stance and evaluation, and also to how they express these. As the texts in the 10A Reading module show, different writers can present their arguments more forcefully, or more tentatively. Also related to voice is the writer's choice of supporting material – is it based around 'hard' facts, or 'softer' arguments and exemplification based around people's experiences? In the initial activity, ask students to evaluate the plan itself using questions such as *Is there sufficient material? Is it relevant to the essay title? How logical and coherent is the plan?* These questions lead to the possible evaluation that can be included. Stress that this evaluation needs to arise from specific points, and can be positioned following each paragraph.

Sample answers

Essay plan: 1 material is relevant to title; 2 there is sufficient material; 3 generally it is logical and coherent.

Paragraph 1 Evaluation: work towards recalibrating university rankings metrics to include *all* languages, in order to end possible bias towards English (the language of many of the most prestigious journals).

Paragraph 2 Evaluation: only national political intervention can protect minority languages, as market forces favour a monoculture (cf. Latin in middle ages).

Paragraph 3 Evaluation: potential barriers to international agreement, e.g. by English-speaking countries with vested interest (UK, USA, etc.); only international intervention can be effective in limiting the monoculture of English.

2 This activity requires students to express their argument very concisely, in one sentence. Use familiar, conversational language to elicit this, e.g. *How would you solve the problems that face minority languages in our globalized higher education sector?* The single-sentence summary needs to accommodate the various issues in the essay plan, so it should not be too specific.

3–4 For the rest of the task, ask students to organize their material from the tasks leading up to this. The key point about a conclusion is that it should be clear – it should clearly express the writer's main argument and stance, and the resolution to the argument, e.g. to what extent it is true.

TASK 5 Planning a problem-solution essay

1–4 Allow students a few minutes to analyse the new essay title. If necessary, remind them about the parts of an essay question given in Unit 4B Writing, Task 1: main topic, instruction, limitation. Students should have a number of relevant ideas based on their work in this module and the information in the texts in 10A Reading. As with earlier tasks, students should start with the given situation and then follow the sequence problems – solutions – evaluation. Students can do part of their planning independently, although doing this in class allows you to monitor: look for an appropriate number of points and amount of material (as a guide, one new topic per paragraph). If students try to include too many points they will not have sufficient space to develop these points. Encourage students to engage with their material so that their stance and voice can come through. They can do this by: giving reasons and examples to support their arguments; selecting examples from familiar cultures which can illustrate the main points; integrating evaluation throughout the essay using personally constructed language (such as that in the Academic Language box in this module); finding their own way of presenting and ordering the material. Depending on time available and local conditions, allow students an agreed amount of time to further research their essay by looking for relevant sources.

TASK 6 Drafting to refine voice and flow

1–3 The final task enables students to work on their material with a particular focus on logical organization, development, and flow. Some or all of this task can be done independently; however, it can be useful to devote some class time to writing. As a variation, set up a timed writing activity in class, where students have to write a paragraph of their essay based on their plan. State that they have to write this in the given time (e.g. 10–15 minutes). In this way, students' writing fluency should improve and they can learn not to spend an excessive amount of time on, say, one sentence. It can also help their examination technique. Following their writing, encourage students to reflect and note down specific areas to work on for their next written piece of work.

10C Listening
Presentations (5)

TASK 1 Reading a presentation abstract to predict content

1–2 Explain that this module replicates a conference presentation from the point of view of the participant. The first stage for the participant in a conference is to read through the abstracts, normally published in the conference programme. The presenter can use these to decide which presentations to attend, and to learn more about the presenter's expected coverage of the topic. In this task students work through the essential elements in the text (problems and solutions), plus the evaluative language and presenter's stance.

> **Answers**
> 1 Main problems: The current pharmaceutical market has widespread monopolies, poorly-informed consumers, limited competition, and highly variable demand.
>
> Solutions: Address the financing of medicines and increase the use of policies such as using generic drugs, involving both governments and private providers.
>
> Evaluation: A greater balance is achievable.
>
> 2 1 Confident evaluative language in **bold**:
> *Characterized by **widespread** monopolies, **poorly-informed** consumers, **limited** competition, and **highly variable** demand, the global pharmaceutical market is **currently imperfect and imbalanced**. Given **extreme variations** in pharmaceutical expenditure across different income countries and **rising per capita expenditure**, solutions need to involve both governments and private providers.*
> Tentative evaluative language in **bold**:
> *This presentation [...] offers **possible solutions**. [...] Through strategic planning in public financing, health insurance, and user fees, the pharmaceutical market **can achieve a better balance**.*
>
> 2 Presenter's stance: critical of the current state of the global pharmaceutical market; supportive of active government intervention.

3 Explain that many conferences are characterized by accommodating both highly experienced and less experienced participants (sometimes known as delegates). From the abstract and other information in the conference programme, it should be possible to work out whether a particular presentation is appropriate for an experienced or inexperienced delegate. This abstract appears to be accessible for a less experienced audience,

with further possible audience profile information, depending on the type and level of the conference, given below.

> **Sample answers**
> • students, researchers, and academics within the discipline of pharmacology and related disciplines such as medicine
> • professionals in pharmaceutical corporations
> • government ministers involved in health policymaking
> • NGOs and charities involved in global healthcare provision
> • other stakeholders, e.g. pressure groups, legal teams involved in healthcare provision

TASK 2 Listening to and evaluating a presentation

1–4 ▶10.1 This task covers the presentation itself by focusing on note-taking and evaluation. Remind students that it is essential to take notes during a presentation – if not, they will not be able to recall the content later; also, taking notes can help process and understand the content while it is being delivered. Monitor while students are listening, and encourage them to make full notes, particularly relating to specific points such as statistical support or proposed solutions. During the subsequent listening, ask students to switch their focus to evaluation using the given criteria. The final activity again reflects a real conference presentation by inviting students to think of relevant questions to ask; they should aim to do this with any presentation.

> **Sample answers** (these notes are presented in full detail; students may write less)
> The presentation topic and main aim is to present the challenges facing the global pharmaceutical market today, and how these can be addressed.
> **Situation (background and wider context)**
> The pharmaceutical market is not a perfect market where supply perfectly balances demand. And this leads us to the situation we have today.
> 1990 and 2000 expenditure figures WHO (published in 2011):
> • private expenditure on pharmaceuticals outweighs government expenditure in all income categories – high, middle, and low
> • total expenditure increased very substantially between 1990 & 2000: 50% overall, with higher increases in middle-income countries
> • extremely wide variation between countries with different incomes, e.g. in 2000 governments of low-income countries spent just over $1 on pharmaceuticals, vs high-income countries at $167
> • per capita pharmaceutical expenditure has been increasing steadily for many years: 2005 to 2006 $7.61 US dollars in low-income countries & $431.6 dollars in high-income countries
> • highest rate of increase is in low- and middle-income countries

- 16% of the world population currently live in high-income countries, which account for over 78 per cent of global medicine expenditure
- the *proportion* of total health expenditure which is spent on medicines in low-income countries is higher
- total pharmaceutical expenditure referred to as TPE
- since 1995 the *private* share of TPE has been increasing in low- and middle-income countries, but not high-income countries

Problems

The pharmaceutical market is not a perfect market where supply perfectly balances demand (source: Walley and Wright)

- Consumers are not well-informed about the medical products they are using, e.g. their quality, safety, efficacy, & appropriateness
- Not much competition: vast number of consumers, but rather few providers: health care providers, purchasers, and manufacturers
- The issue of monopoly: manufacturers create a monopoly through their use of patents; also brand loyalty, achieved through intensive marketing; market segmentation by introducing therapeutic subclasses; many cases of price-fixing by producer cartels in order to keep market prices high
- Externalities exist: treatment for some conditions, e.g. communicable diseases like tuberculosis and sexually transmitted diseases, benefits not only the patient but also the wider public – who will as a result have a reduced chance of themselves contracting the disease

Evaluation of problems

- The pharmaceutical market is far from perfect.
- It's quite unlike many other markets.
- It's a failed market.
- A key point is that the financing of medicines plays a critical role in the market.
- Governments are key players.

Solutions

- Medicine costs need to be kept down, and national governments have a key role to play in drawing up principled lists of medicines which people can be reimbursed for, including mainly cost-effective medicines
- Market competition can be increased, through generic medicines – the generic market can be promoted, and pharmacists can substitute more expensive branded drugs with the equivalent generic ones
- Therapeutic substitution is also possible, i.e. adapting a patient's therapy with a lower-cost programme
- Governments can promote medicine pricing policies using their buying power to negotiate with the manufacturer on prices, and comparing medicines on the market
- Parallel imports – where patented medicines are bought from countries in which they cost less
- Compulsory licencing – where a local manufacturer is licenced to produce a patented drug under licence & usually at a lower price, allowed by WTO under certain conditions

Evaluation of solutions

- These measures illustrate the choices available to stimulate local & global pharmaceutical markets.
- Any health financing system must be sustainable
- Health financing systems need to promote equity, efficiency and rational use of medicines.

Overall evaluation

Public financing
- raised through taxation
- advantages are:
  - medicine supplies can be better selected and targeted to those who need it most
  - the government can control the quality of the medicine
  - achieve economies of scale by buying in large quantities
  - cost of payment is effectively shifted to a wide base of the population, i.e. taxpayers, & those earning higher salaries pay more

Health insurance (a mechanism for sharing risk among a section of a population)

- has an important role to play in many countries
- health insurance schemes may be public / private; compulsory / voluntary
- common in developed countries (not USA); rare in developing countries
- an attractive option for developing countries as medicines account for a large share of total household expenses
- risks include over-prescription, abuse, and fraud
- to be effective, such schemes need cost control measures

User fees – in developing countries, = 2/3 of expenditure on medicine, mainly private
- Cost recovery schemes – where people have to pay back the cost of their medicines
- These fees are then ploughed back into general medical expenditure
- User fees can improve medicine availability and efficiency & reduce over-consumption, & allow public funds to be targeted
- The needs of the poorest are often not met
- Checks and balances needed, e.g. exemptions for those least able to pay

Final evaluation

- In short, the pharmaceutical market is an imperfect and imbalanced market, but there are a range of more or less successful options to improve it.

ACADEMIC LANGUAGE

Sentence patterns (2) Known and new information

Go through the box and clarify the main patterns in English sentences: known information typically comes first in order to contextualize, refer back to previously mentioned information, and/or frame the new information, which comes last. Give an example which has different versions – one or two following this pattern and one opposing it, e.g. *Today I'd like to focus on finding workable solutions to the problems facing the pharmaceutical industry / What I'd like to focus on today are solutions to the problems facing the pharmaceutical industry / Finding workable solutions to the problems facing the pharmaceutical industry is the focus of my presentation today.* Students should be able to work out that the first two are more effective; the third is more difficult to process and leaves nothing new to say at the end of the sentence (we can see that the speaker is giving a presentation today, so there is no point putting that information at the end of the sentence). You can mention also the tendency in English to put longer structures at the end; refer students to the Language Reference section on Sentence structure on page 206.

TASK 3 Recognizing known and new information

1–3 This task puts into practice the information in the box above, enabling students to understand what makes information 'known', and how known and new information can be presented in sentences.

Answers

1 Sentence (a) is 3 (it has been mentioned before in the presentation)
  Sentence (c) is 1 (it can be seen in the visuals)
  Sentence (e) is 2 (it is assumed / general knowledge or common sense)

2 **Known information**; background / new information:
  a **The WHO** is the world's most visible global health organization, with a 193-country membership which means it operates at both a global and local level.
  b **This global reach** means that they are able to collect data from more countries than any other organization.
  c As we can see, this table shows the private and government per capita expenditure on pharmaceuticals in 1990 and 2000.
  d First, private expenditure on pharmaceuticals outweighs government expenditure in all income categories …
  e **Most parties agree that medicine costs need to be kept down**, so national governments have a key role to play in drawing up principled lists of cost-effective medicines.
  f **Governments can use their buying power** to negotiate with the manufacturer on prices.
  g **They can do this** effectively by comparing the medicines with other similar medicines on the market.

TASK 4 Evaluating the summary of a presentation

1 The final stage in this sequence of tasks offers students the opportunity to critically evaluate the sample summary. Explain that presentation summaries are typically 'blind' reviewed to determine whether they are acceptable for publication, i.e. the details of the presenter are deleted so that the reviewer is not influenced by these. By evaluating a summary, students can adopt this critical approach for their own summary writing. In activity 2, ask students to refer to their notes on the presentation to work out how coherent, relevant, and complete the presenter's material is.

Sample answer

The summary meets these six criteria satisfactorily.

10D Speaking
Presentations (6)

TASK 1 Advice on giving a presentation

1–3 Explain that this module puts into practice what students have learnt in previous units (in particular 4, 7, and 10). Ask students to review the material in those units before the lesson. Stress the importance to students of developing their own material based on their own topic and title. This process of development is similar to that of the research essay strand which runs alongside the final units of the book. Monitor the stages in this task to encourage students' responses to the given material and to extend it with their own advice.

Answers

1 1 topic 2 research 3 content and structure
  4 visuals 5 practice 6 abstract 7 delivery
  8 post-presentation

TASK 2 Pre- to post-presentation planning

1 Decide on the most appropriate way of managing this task; students can do a lot of the work independently, but it is advisable to give regular deadlines to check up on their progress so that they do not leave everything to the end. If necessary, provide further examples of narrowing down the topic into a statement or question: you can base these on presentations from previous classes, or even your own presentations. You and/or the students may wish to adapt the stages; note down any changes and make all students aware of them as necessary. Students may value your own experience, so talk through any presentations you have done, giving your own advice. This may be particularly welcome on how to practise effectively, and move away from dependence on your prepared script.

TASK 3 Working towards script independence

1 Explain that script independence means being able to deliver the presentation without reading from a script, but that prompts and notes are perfectly acceptable. You and/or the students can add further suggestions to those given for achieving script independence. Ask students where they want to be on the scale of prepared using prompts to spontaneous delivery. Remind students that, as with the conference presentation in 10C Listening, it is important to stick to the agreed topic and title, and not to deliver unrelated content as this will not meet audience expectations. As with all skills, practice generally improves performance, so encourage students to try their presentations out in small settings with friends; in this way they can get useful developmental feedback.

TASK 4 Giving and evaluating a presentation

1–3 The module concludes with the presentations themselves. Negotiate a timetable in advance, and ensure that students stick closely to their time. Stress the importance of peer-evaluation while watching, as students can learn from each other. Also, ask students to think of questions to ask the presenter. If possible, allow a set time (e.g. 5 minutes) for questions following each presentation. An important final stage is to collate feedback on the presentations generally, and write this up for students to refer to in their future presentations. It can be put up on the institutional learner management system and adapted in the light of new advice.

10E Vocabulary Sensitive language

1 and 2 Having already looked at the concept of connotation in the unit (see 10B, page 159), these short extracts introduce students to the issue of language choices to describe sensitive topics. The key point to highlight here is that these extracts are taken from very different times (1970, 1985, and 2009 respectively) and show how terminology often changes over time as social attitudes to different groups or topics change. Explain that inappropriate or old-fashioned vocabulary choices may be seen as offensive. Ask students how they can decide which is the most appropriate term to use in a particular context; i.e. which term is most currently used, in recent literature, by lecturers, etc. Remind students to always check dates of sources for currency and especially before noting down or citing terminology.

Note: Students might also notice in these extracts the shift from *adjective + person* (*mentally retarded patient, mentally handicapped child*) which some see as defining these people by their condition / disability, towards *person + with condition* (*people with learning difficulties*), which puts the person first and the condition second – a trend reflected in lots of areas of health; *people with disabilities, patients with mental health problems*, etc.

3 and 4 These examples provide an opportunity to explore and discuss other potentially sensitive topics. Explain that in some cases, choice of vocabulary may also depend on context, see notes below. This is also an opportunity to broaden out the discussion, bearing in mind the cultural context of your own class and students, to ask about how sensitivities differ in different cultures or what sort of topics students might encounter in their own disciplines.

Sample answers

3

a **crippled** - now very offensive about people, but used more widely metaphorically to describe, for example, an economy that is badly damaged; **handicapped** - now dated and considered offensive by some; **disabled** - the more acceptable term, although see note above about *people with disabilities*

b **an old lady** - slightly old-fashioned, might be considered polite in conversation (*the old lady who lives next door*), but not appropriate in an academic context (note: '*lady*' is now considered slightly offensive or patronizing by many women); **an elderly woman** - appropriate to describe an individual; **older women** - appropriate to describe a general group

c **a lady doctor** - this would now be considered dated and offensive / patronizing in most contexts (see note above about 'lady'): **a woman doctor** - appropriate in conversation and some academic contexts (especially referring to people's attitudes); **a female doctor** - a more neutral term would be likely in an academic context

d **a poor country** - 'poor' is an emotive word and has negative connotations, so this would be used to make a point persuasively (for example, describing the exploitation of *poor countries by rich nations*), but would be less likely to refer to a specific country; **a Third World country** - 'Third World' increasingly has similar negative connotations to 'poor' and so, would only be used in a similar context as above; **a developing country** - this has more neutral or positive connotations and would be the appropriate term to use when referring to specific countries (*in developing countries like Uganda*)

e **a child from a poor family** - again 'poor' has emotive, negative connotations, especially to refer to an individual child or family; **children from deprived areas** - 'deprived' still has negative connotations, but suggests a wider, external problem rather than a fault of the family; **children from disadvantaged backgrounds** - 'disadvantaged' also has negative connotations, but doesn't attach blame to the family, it covers a wider range of situations than 'deprived' (deprived = lack of money, resources; disadvantaged = lack of money, education, stable family life, etc.)

4

- generally more emotive, dated, or even offensive language might be found in the context of fictional or historical characters or contexts, for example, in the study of literature, film and media studies, history, classics, etc.
- writers are generally more careful to use sensitive language which avoids offence, stigma, or stereotyping when referring to real individuals
- less carefully hedged language may sometimes be used when referring to a general group rather than specific individuals - compare *poor countries* vs *X is a developing country*

Research Project (4)
Writing a first draft

Students are often daunted at the prospect of such a long piece of writing. It is important to emphasize the process of writing and explain that the first draft is not the final piece of work. A first draft is more than just notes, it should involve getting all the ideas from their reading and planning 'down on paper' following their plan, in a form that resembles a final project, but which students will work on, using feedback and editing to produce the final draft. A first draft will not normally include a title page, abstract, and contents page, but you should encourage students to build up their bibliography as they go along, even if it isn't perfectly formatted at this stage.

It can be helpful to discuss strategies for tackling a first draft, such as whether to start with the introduction and write through to the conclusion or to write up different sections, not necessarily in order, and piece them together later. Discuss whether students work just from their notes or work with copies of their sources open as they write. Each approach has both advantages and disadvantages, but by discussing them in groups or as a class, students can share ideas and best practice.

This is also a good point at which to establish any practicalities, for example, if students are to submit their drafts electronically, do they need to save it in a particular format (e.g. a particular version of Word)? It is better for students to use the correct format from the start rather than having the stress of problems and changes later. Make deadlines clear, such as when they should submit their first draft for feedback, what you will check and what you won't, whether they can leave comments or questions in their manuscript for specific feedback, etc.

By the end of the next unit, students should have a more-or-less complete first draft which they will develop and refine before they submit it for feedback. Alternatively, depending on the time available, you may want students to submit first drafts for feedback before the end of the next unit to allow more time for marking and revisions.

UNIT 11 Observation

INTRODUCTION

Unit 11 examines the unit theme and central concept of Observation across a range of texts. By the end of the unit students should be familiar with case study and process, which occupy an important place in academic contexts. Students learn to access information relating to these in complex texts, and practise reprocessing and explaining this information. The language work in the unit covers sophisticated ways of presenting information in texts, and there is a focus throughout the unit on building knowledge from the content in texts.

11A Reading emphasizes the importance of knowledge and content in texts. The module positions students at the centre of the reading process by starting with what they know, developing what they want to know, and reflecting on what they have learnt. Students practise purposeful note-taking while reading, and develop their awareness of generic language which frames and introduces the content of a text. The first textbook extract deals with the topic of case study, which builds students' knowledge of the topic, while the second text presents an example of a case study, to which students can apply what they have learnt.

11B Writing examines complex descriptions of processes. These are characterized by partial but not strict chronological order, as the writer of a text needs to organize the information to suit their purpose. Students learn to work out the actual chronological order in such texts, and build on the rhetorical structure of a given text to construct their own text. There is a focus on chronology language to aid the reader in navigating the text, and students further develop sophistication in language by using a variety of verb-based, noun-based (nominalized), and adverbial structures in their writing.

11C Listening brings in a large number of slides to illustrate the content of a lecture. Students work with the slides to predict and clarify content. Through the module students select appropriate note-taking techniques, and apply these to different extracts of the lecture. Students have the opportunity to review their progress and ability in using different techniques. They have to rely on the effectiveness of their listening and note-taking techniques in order to present and explain the content of the lecture after listening.

11D Speaking aims to increase students' confidence and specific skills in seminar discussions. The module puts into practice the work done on seminars and discussions through the course. Students select and discuss a process which is familiar to them, which enables them to focus on key seminar skills including fluency and interaction. A reading text provides inspiration rather than specific content, as students develop their own content.

11E Vocabulary revisits the topic of word formation, this time looking at suffixes, or word endings. Recognizing how different parts of speech are typically formed can help students to decode unknown words or novel coinages, such as *Manhattanization*, in their reading and improve their writing style by using vocabulary more flexibly.

Research Project (5) looks at ways that students can achieve coherence and cohesion in their research project. It guides students thorough the process of refining a rough first draft by looking critically at what they have written so far and evaluating how it contributes to the overall presentation of their argument.

DISCUSSION

1–4 The Discussion centres on the unit theme of Observation, and asks students to consider how observation can relate to different disciplines and contexts. Encourage students to offer plenty of detail in their responses, including relevant examples and explanations. Check the meaning of key technical terms, e.g. quantitative and qualitative, which were first introduced in Unit 1C. Refer students to the appropriate Glossary entry as appropriate, on page 199. By the end of the discussion students should be familiar with how observation is central to any discipline, and can take many forms for different purposes.

11A Reading Case studies

TASK 1 Understanding the case study genre

1 Start by asking students what they know about case studies. The lesson can then develop along the 'KWL' pattern: *What do I know?* → *What do I want to know?* → *What have I learnt?* The definition is taken from the same source as Texts 1 and 2 (page 712). This activity requires students to consider the characteristics of specific research questions, and assess their suitability to a case study approach.

> **Sample answer**
> 4   To formulate a new beauty product to reduce the visual effects of facial wrinkles.
> *Because this research aim is broad in scope and application and requires an objective (e.g. laboratory-based) research programme to meet the needs of a wide range of people with different skin types. So it's not suited to a case study.*

2 Students should be familiar with extracting the main contextual information from a text using the prompts in the table to guide them. Remind students of the importance of establishing this information: in this text the authors can assume that their audience have an interest in case studies in a business context.

> **Answers**
> GAP: *university textbook extract, aimed at students of business, to present an initial overview of case study design and research*
> Definition of case study: *the detailed and intensive analysis of a single case (essential point) – concerned with the complexity of the particular case (further detail)*
> Types of case: *single organization; single location; person; single event*
> Selected examples: *corporation (e.g. ICI, BBC); event (NASA space shuttle disaster)*

3 and 4 Ask students to explain how the examples in 3 match the types of case in 1, e.g. research aim 1 in 1.1 clearly refers to a single organization, i.e. a bank. Activity

4 checks students' progress in the KWL lesson structure: keep the three questions (*What do I know?*, etc.) written up throughout the class.

> **Answers**
> 1 single organization   2 a person   3 a single event
> 4 *N/A*   5 a single location

TASK 2 Using a glossary to understand detail in a text

1 Explain that this task aims to reflect the academic reading process of consulting a glossary to clarify meanings of technical terms. Textbooks typically present a glossary of technical terms in a dedicated section at the back; remind students that the Student's Book contains a glossary of technical terms. Set up the activity so that students read in a focused way, i.e. reading to find out the answers to their 'want to know' items from Task 1. Give a time limit for this first reading, e.g. 8 minutes. Conduct feedback to establish the remaining unanswered questions, and invite suggestions on how students could answer them, e.g. locate the textbook in the library; search for further introductions to research in this area; carry out online searches for reliable sources to explain the information. Invite students who are studying business to find these out and report back to the whole class.

2–3 Allow plenty of time for the second reading, as students need to read the text intensively while assimilating the meaning of complex technical terms. Stress that it can take quite a long time to learn these meanings, and that students need not expect to fully understand them by the end of the reading. The terms are strongly associated with research, and are of more relevance to students planning to do research and/or postgraduate degrees.

4–5 These activities encourage students to reflect on the reading process so far. Emphasize that students should not expect to fully understand every word in every text they read – to do this would take too long and therefore limit the amount of text they have time to read. Remind students that they have been reading for a purpose, as is typical in academic contexts, and it is acceptable to ignore a certain amount of vocabulary. The guidelines spell out this message.

> **ACADEMIC LANGUAGE**
>
> **Cohesion (2)** Expressing relationships using generic language
> Explain that cohesion in a text amounts to much more than a sprinkling of linking words like *however* and *furthermore*. In fact, it is advisable to limit the use of such words and focus instead on generic language. This refers to the language that supports technical content across academic disciplines: the technical content varies according to the discipline, but the generic language remains similar. This generic language accounts for about 40% of the words

in the sample text (taken from the opening paragraph of Text 2), so it is extremely useful for students to learn to use effectively. It includes verbs, especially prepositional verbs such as *focuses on, is associated with,* nouns such as *emphasis,* and adjectives, e.g. *typical.* Point out that the topic itself, which in this text is *case study,* tends to be repeated as often as necessary, while the generic language introduces and frames the new information which is also highlighted in the sample text.

TASK 3 Using generic language to express relationships

1 Start by eliciting the information students need to complete the text using the given generic language items: grammatical knowledge; understanding of the meaning of the language items; understanding of the surrounding text. In the second activity, ask students to analyse the text in the same way as that in the Academic Language box. Check carefully that they have identified not only the words *longitudinal design* but also the words which refer to it, i.e. the pronoun *it.*

Answers

1 1 represents 2 that is typically used to
   3 has emphasized the importance of
   4 through which 5 Such a 6 involves
   7 is relatively little used in 8 based on
   9 can allow 10 therefore

2 **Key: topic: <u>underlined</u>; generic language: bolded; characteristics / related features: highlighted.**
   What is <u>longitudinal design</u>?
   The <u>longitudinal design</u> **represents** a distinct form of research design **that is typically used to** map change in business and management research. Pettigrew (1990) **has emphasized the importance of** <u>longitudinal study</u> in understanding organizations as a way of providing data on the mechanisms and processes **through which** changes are created. **Such a** 'contextualist' <u>research design</u> **involves** drawing on 'phenomena at vertical and horizontal levels of analysis and the interconnections between those levels through time' (1990: 269). However, partly because of the time and cost involved, <u>longitudinal design</u> **is relatively little used in** business and management research. In the form in which it is typically found, it is usually an extension of social survey research **based on** self-completion questionnaire or structured interview research within a cross-sectional design. Consequently, in terms of reliability, replication, and validity, <u>the longitudinal design</u> is little different from cross-sectional research. However, <u>a longitudinal design</u> can allow some insight into the time order of variables and **therefore** may be more able to allow causal inferences to be made.

As an extension, ask students to make notes from the text using the topic *Longitudinal design* as the main heading. Elicit or explain that the generic language typically introduces new information relating to the topic.

Sample answers to extension task, with generic language in **bold**

Longitudinal design
- **a distinct form** of research design
- **typically used to** map change in business and management research
- **used in** understanding organizations as a way of providing data on the mechanisms and processes through which changes are created
- 'contextualist'
- **draws on** 'phenomena at vertical and horizontal levels of analysis and the interconnections between those levels through time'
- **relatively little used in** business and management research
- **usually an extension of** social survey research
- **based on** self-completion questionnaire or structured interview research within a cross-sectional design
- **little different from** cross-sectional research
- **can allow** some insight into the time order of variables
- **may allow** causal inferences to be made

As a further extension or independent study task, ask students to select one paragraph from Text 2 and highlight the generic language in that paragraph. Students can then present their findings and compare with other students.

TASK 4 Making detailed notes to use for writing

1 and 2 Remind students of the importance of making notes while reading. They can use their knowledge of generic language to help them identify the new information in the text. Ask students to write their own notes rather than going through the text with a pen or highlighter: they may read library books (where this practice is obviously inappropriate), and it is more efficient to keep notes, carefully filed (in paper-based or electronic form) rather than stacks of photocopied highlighted texts. Explain that the purpose of making notes is to identify and record information to use in students' new texts, both written and spoken (e.g. presentations). Activity 2 serves as a useful comprehension check: you can read students' one-sentence summaries to determine how effectively they have understood the text.

TASK 5 Taking notes on a summary of a case study

1 and 2 The first activity activates students' knowledge of the topic of Text 3: data capture. Ask students to use what they know to provide examples of data capture, e.g. by asking employees at a local company about their employer. Collate and write up all the different ways of data capture before extending this list when students have read the text.

Answers

2 Data capture methods in Text 3:
- (qualitative phase):
  - group discussions with public (esp. motorists)
  - in-depth interviews (e.g. vehicle dealerships, journalists [press])
- pilot surveys
  - quantitative questionnaires
- quantitative surveys
  - samples of key groups (e.g. motorists, employees), asking questions such as reliability, individuality
  - second survey undertaken 3 years later to monitor changes in perception

3 and 4 These activities encourage students to experiment in their note-taking styles. Before starting, elicit different styles, e.g. spider diagrams, mind maps, annotated text, bullet points, flow charts, multiple headings (i.e. *main heading → sub heading A → sub heading B*, etc.), images. The suggested headings in 3 should remind students of the conventional structure of a report, and lead directly to the summary stage, 4, in which students need to ensure that they have included the main points relevant to each heading.

Sample answers

3
- the context of the research
  - UK & Ireland
  - motor industry - General Motors subsidiary Vauxhall
  - employees, general public, journalists, unionists
  - from 1983 onwards (follow-up research took place three years later)
- the aim of the research
  - to investigate the benefits of making GM companies such as AC Spark Plug more visibly part of the GM group
  - to provide information on awareness of GM
- the implications of the research
  - to inform future company strategy
- the main findings, conclusion, and evaluation
  - a successful research project
  - much new information found, e.g. that people who knew more about Vauxhall (i.e. that it was part of the American GM group) viewed it more favourably
  - Vauxhall was repositioned as a result

4

The Vauxhall research project (1983) aimed to determine whether it would be more beneficial to more visibly position its various UK-based motor companies as part of its US parent company, General Motors. Using a mix of data capture methods including qualitative and quantitative research, the project identified considerable new information, notably that people who were aware of Vauxhall's American heritage viewed the company more favourably. As a result of this successful research project, the Vauxhall brand was repositioned. (*78 words*)

TASK 6 Evaluating and applying information on case studies

1–3 Remind students that the final task represents the final stage in the KWL cycle: *What have I learnt?* In activity 1, elicit criteria for evaluating note-taking styles, e.g. their completeness, ease of carrying out while-reading, time-efficiency, space-efficiency, and ease of use post-reading. Activity 2 centres on knowledge gained, while activity 3 looks ahead to what students can do to extend their knowledge. Ask students to apply this cycle of learning to their own discipline and context; use questions such as *What can I do to extend my knowledge of [...]? How can I find reliable sources to use? What specific goal-oriented plan can I come up with to achieve my aims?* Conduct whole-class feedback and collate the most effective responses.

11B **Writing** Complex descriptions

TASK 1 Analysing and describing types of process

1–3 The aim of the first task is to extend students' understanding of how different processes work, in particular by considering the role of humans in bringing about these processes. Ask students to give reasons for their answers, plus examples. In activity 2, elicit reasons for representing a process in visual form: it makes the information clearer to access for the reader; it uses fewer words and less space; it clarifies how the process works. You could allow students to represent other processes not mentioned if this is helpful for students. Optionally, ask students to volunteer to present their process to the whole class, using their visuals.

Sample answers

Process	One-off	Recurrent	Natural	Human-driven	Local	Global
1 photosynthesis		✓	✓			✓
2 desertification		✓	✓	✓	✓	✓
3 the global financial crisis of 2007/8	✓			✓		✓
4 passing a new law in a specific country		✓		✓	✓	
5 building employee trust in a company		✓		✓	✓	
6 industrialization in post-war Japan	✓			✓	✓	
7 designing a new public space	✓			✓	✓	
8 research and development of a new drug		✓	✓	✓		✓

TASK 2 Analysing a process and identifying evaluation

1 and 2 Introduce the process described in Text 1, the global financial crisis, and either elicit what students know as a whole class, or ask them to pool information in groups. Some students may not know much, but others should be able to add to their knowledge, particularly students of business and finance. Explain any difficult concepts, or ask students to do so. Alternatively, avoid explaining them, saying that they might be explained in the text. Again students should use an appropriate visual to represent their information.

3 and 4 Give a time limit for the first reading, e.g. 8–10 minutes, and check that students read for the two purposes stated in 3. Check the answers to these points, then elicit answers to 4; students do not need to read the text again to answer this.

Sample answer

4 c Political systems - because the text extract (Text 1) does not coherently explain or exemplify an aspect of a political system. It is clearly closely related to (a) and (b), while (d) is also related, offering an environmental perspective.

5–6 Allow plenty of time for these activities. Students now need to read the text more intensively in order to work out the actual chronological order of the process. Students should realize that Text 1 is more complex than it may at first appear, as the order of events as presented in the text is somewhat different to the actual chronological order. This difference has implications for students when they write their own chronology texts: they should aim for a more sophisticated text structure than process texts at lower levels (e.g. *First x, then y, after that z, finally …*).

As a variation, the text analysis task (activity 6) can be done collaboratively – students could divide up the task into working out the order of the stages, and identifying the evaluation. Another variation, which would help students with certain learning styles (e.g. visual, kinaesthetic), would be to copy and cut up all the stages for students to re-order. This would make the task easier, but doing it as instructed in the Student's Book requires students to summarize each stage as a noun phrase (as in the Sample answers below), which is a useful skill.

Sample answers

6: order given numerically by each stage

Stage in the process	Evaluation
=14 The 2007-8 global financial crisis began	→ the biggest economic shock since the 1929 Great Depression
=14 Asset values crashed	→ sent shock waves through global economy
=14 Sub-prime crisis emerged in US in 2007	→ warning signs of the coming crash
2 Financial institutions made home loans to low-income people	→ an egregious business practice
5 US house prices fell	→ borrowers and lenders later became losers
3 Home loan debts were repackaged as securities called 'collateralized debt obligations'	→ these were more risky than people believed
7 The mortgage default problem spread	→ a devastating process
4 Companies, banks, governments bought CDOs	→ these groups had false confidence / became widely recognized as a hazardous process
6 Big credit ratings agencies gave reassurances on these debts	→ these assurances were inappropriate
8 The extent of the actual risks was revealed	
9 Financial institutions wanted to sell their CDOs	
10 Prices fell	→ this was inevitable
11 The institutions' holdings were near-worthless	
12 Stock market values of the institutions also fell	
13 These institutions began to collapse	
=14 A financial crisis emerged	→ the US sub-prime crisis became a generalized global financial crash
15 Global growth stopped	→ this was inevitable
1 There was strong economic growth in the 1990s & 2000s	→ This was debt-fuelled rather than based on sound sustainable finance
16 Governments used bailouts to restore confidence	→ this did not work
17 The downturn spread from financial markets to the real economy	
18 A global recession followed as a result	→ this was severe and prolonged
19 Economists do not agree on what caused the global financial crisis (GFC)	→ this is not surprising
	Political economic analysis identify neoliberal economic ideas as part of the cause of the GFC
	The GFC was major blow to the claims of free market economists
	Economic instability is rife / endemic in capitalism
	Role of the state in crisis management & stability is contentious

Chronology language Expressing events in time using verbs, nouns, and adverbials

Students should be familiar with narrative verb tenses to express chronological relations, e.g. the past tense, the past perfect, and so on. This Academic Language box aims to extend students' range of chronology language, which can make their writing more sophisticated through more varied style and structure. Point out that the writers of Text 1 use a range of language structures. Elicit or explain that: verb-based forms can constitute a whole sentence (in a SVO pattern) or part of a sentence; nominalized forms typically function as subject or object in a sentence; and adverbials are likely to be positioned at the start or end of a sentence depending on their meaning.

TASK 3 Using chronology language

1–3 This task may be challenging for some students as a number of grammatical changes need to be made in some cases – the changes are not mechanical. Point out that the original extracts from Text 1 are in normal type, and the alternatives are in italics. Ask students to find the original extracts in the text in order to see them in context, which will help them write their equivalent forms. Stress the importance of activity 2: students need to (a) produce the form correctly (i.e. verb-based, nominalized, or adverbial), and (b) use this form correctly in a sentence. In activity 3, ask students to read the three alternatives aloud in order to determine which version sounds best.

Sample answers

1

	Verb-based form	Nominalized form	Adverbial
1	Asset values crashed	The crash in asset values	with crashing asset values
2	sent shock waves through the global economy	global economic shock waves	sending shock waves through the global economy
3	An economic recession developed	The development of an economic recession	developing into an economic recession
4	Incomes fell and unemployment rose	The fall in incomes and rise in unemployment	with falling incomes and rising unemployment
5	People sent warning signals about the coming crash	The warning signs of the coming crash	with warning signs of the coming crash (becoming evident)
6	The 'sub-prime crisis' emerged	the emergence of the 'sub-prime crisis'	with the emerging 'sub-prime crisis'
7	the US housing price bubble burst and prices started to fall	the burst of the US housing price bubble and falling prices	with the burst of the US housing price bubble and falling prices

2

(three alternatives are given for each sentence, but further answers may be possible)

Original sentence with events underlined:

1 **The warning signs of the coming crash** <u>became evident</u> during **the emergence of the 'sub-prime crisis' in the United States in 2007.**
    1 **The 'sub-prime crisis'** emerged in the United States in 2007, <u>leading to warning signs of the coming crash</u>.
    1 The 'sub-prime crisis' emerged in the United States in 2007, warning signs followed, and the global crash came.
    1 <u>With the 'sub-prime crisis' emerging in the United States in 2007</u>, the global crash came <u>amid</u> warning signs.

Original sentence with events underlined:

2 <u>The financial institutions had been making loans</u> to **low-income people wishing to buy houses**.
    2 Low-income people had wished to buy houses, so the financial institutions had been making loans to them.
    2 <u>Wishing to buy houses</u>, low-income people had been given loans by the financial institutions.
    2 **Low-income people wishing to buy houses** had been given loans by the financial institutions.

Original sentence with events underlined:

3 <u>Both borrowers and lenders would become losers</u> when <u>the US housing price bubble burst</u> and <u>prices started to fall</u>.
    3 <u>With the burst of the US housing price bubble and falling prices</u>, both borrowers and lenders became losers.
    3 <u>The US housing price bubble burst and prices started to fall</u>, with both borrowers and lenders becoming losers.
    3 **The burst of the US housing price bubble** led to falling prices and **both borrowers and lenders as losers**.

3 **Evaluation**

In isolation, any of the above alternatives are valid. In a text, *variety* is important, partly to avoid monotonous structures, and partly to organize and present the information.

TASK 4 Describing a process based on notes from reading

1–3 The aim of this task is for students to be able to write a description of a complex process based on their notes from reading a text. Stress the importance of not referring to the original text, so that they avoid copying parts of the text. Students' notes in table form from Task 3 should be sufficient. Encourage students to use the language structures from Task 3 where appropriate. Ask students to evaluate their own and other students' texts using criteria such as: *Is the text within the suggested word count (100–150 words)? Does it include all the main stages in the process? Is there a variety of language structures? Is the chronological sequencing of the events clear to the reader?*

TASK 5 Researching and writing a description of a process

1–4 This task offers a freer practice opportunity which students can personalize according to their discipline. Decide how much of the work is to be done outside the classroom. Researching the material can take a long time, depending on locally available text resources. You can offer some suitable texts to help students as appropriate; textbook extracts are likely to work well. Remind students of the importance of taking notes while reading, in order to use these notes as a basis for their written text, as in Task 4.

TASK 6 Evaluating a written text

1 The final task encourages students to practise peer-evaluation, which can greatly enhance their writing in the future. As with Task 5, they can use Checklist H. Students are also likely to appreciate your own evaluation, so use similar criteria to give individual and/or collective feedback on their writing.

11C **Listening** Lectures (8)

TASK 1 Using visuals to understand and explain key concepts

1 This module focuses on natural processes within the disciplines of ecology and biology. Remind students that predicting content should help them access and understand the content more effectively when they subsequently listen to the lecture. Point out that the purpose is not to learn the subject-specific vocabulary (e.g. *ecological community / abiotic factors*), but to enable comprehension of a technical subject. In reality the subject matter should be reasonably familiar to most students.

2–3 🖵**11.1** Encourage students to use the Lecture Overview form whenever they listen to lectures. This can help to focus their notes. Monitor while students explain the key terms to assess how effectively they have taken notes and can use these to give effective explanations. As a variation, do the explanation stage on a later day – this will underline the need to take effective notes, as students' memories of the lecture content will have faded after a day or two.

Sample answers

Lecture Overview form

PART A General information on the lecture

Lecture title *An introduction to community ecology*

Lecturer *Dr Kerry Lock*

Comments *(student-specific responses)*

Discipline *Biology / ecology / continuing education*

Topic / main focus *Ecology, life forms, environments – in a global context (no locality is mentioned, and as it's ecology, a global context is logical)*

Rationale & aims *To describe community ecology – the study of interactions between organisms and their environments*

Limitations *No stated limitations – small to large (molecular to landscape)*

Key terms & definitions
- *organism (not defined)*
- *abiotic – non-living (e.g. water)*
- *population – individuals of a single species living together in one geographical location at the same time*
- *habitat – the physical area in which species live, e.g. a pond*
- *community – two or more populations*
- *resource partitioning – different areas or 'ecological niches', which are different in physical or temperature terms*
- *niche separation – a situation where different species coexist in the same place, separated by differences in the physical environment*

Supporting information
- ☐ pre-reading *unknown*
- ☐ handouts *unknown*
- ☐ slides *yes*
- ☐ other *no*

3 This information is based on the notes under the *Key terms and definitions* section above.

TASK 2 Taking notes on multiple related processes

1 This activity adds an informative visual dimension to enable students to work out the stages in the process. Ask students to try this first without using a dictionary, relying instead on the information in the slides plus their own existing knowledge.

2 This activity reviews a number of important listening and note-taking techniques and aims to raise students' awareness of which techniques to use for their own purposes. Elicit examples of symbols and abbreviations, which can save valuable time while-listening. Point out that summarizing the content of a lecture or reprocessing it, e.g. by explaining it to someone, can greatly aid students' comprehension.

3 and 4 ▶11.2, 11.3 After showing the two extracts, do a visual check of students' notes, if possible asking them about their effectiveness. The listening itself is not particularly demanding, and is well-supported by visuals, so students should be able to write a reasonable amount of detail.

Sample answers

3

(given as bullet points – other note-taking systems welcome)
- Community structure
  - species richness – different types and amounts of various species
  - physical characteristics of organisms – e.g. plants with thick leaves in arid (dry) areas to reduce evaporation
- Energy transfer
  - trophic (food) relationships – green plants captures solar energy through chlorophyll; & using CO_2 & H_2O through photosynthesis → generate carbohydrate, an energy source
  - food chains – fighter plankton at base of 'food web' (they contain chlorophyll) → fed on by krill
- Herbivory
  - krill are herbivores & primary consumers; also epilobian species → eaten by hawk moth caterpillar (primary consumer); also water vole (herbivore) → eaten by American mink (secondary consumer)
- Predation
  - krill are fed on by leopard seal (a predator & carnivore); the third title is a secondary consumer
  - only 10% of the energy is passed on at each stage → limitation on number of steps in a food chain (usually up to 3 or 4)
- Parasitism
  - a symbiotic interaction in which the parasite derives all / part of its nourishment from its host (harmed / killed in the process)
  - hemiparasitic plants, e.g. yellow rattle, latches onto competitive grasses & impedes their growth – which is 'fantastic' as this technique can enable less competitive species to break through
  - parasitic hymenoptera: this wasp can paralyse a tarantula, lay eggs on it, which will kill it
- Mutualism
  - interaction between two different species → mutual benefit for both, e.g. large blue butterfly & red ant: the ants feed on the caterpillar's honeydew & the caterpillar feeds on the ants' eggs; the butterfly hibernates with the ants, & survives partly through mimicking the ants' noises and smells. The ants take it up to the surface ready for its first flight
- Competition
  - e.g. the Natterjack toad & the common frog – the latter's faecal matter contains a unicellular organism which inhibits the growth of Natterjack tadpoles – which are then more vulnerable to predators for longer → fewer Natterjacks (a protected species)

4
- Eco-systems are vital to our survival.
- The global millennium eco-system assessment of 2001 & 2005 assessed the consequences of eco-system change across 95 countries – the largest assessment of the health of eco-systems in the UK.
- Eco-system services are the benefits that human beings gain from eco-system processes (i.e. nutrient cycling, primary production, solar energy, provisioning (i.e. gaining food and fuel), regulating (i.e. food & flood regulation), water purification, cultural aspects / aesthetics.
- These systems are very vulnerable – because of the level humans rely upon them, it is our responsibility to maintain them and to ensure their continuity.
- The future focus is reconnecting our fragmented landscape – vital in terms of continuing & maintaining these vital ecological processes and eco-system services.

5–6 This mini-presentation activity demonstrates the benefit of having to explain a concept / process using students' own notes. If these notes are insufficient (not enough detail / unclear), students should see that they need to take more effective notes in subsequent listening.

TASK 3 Assessing personal progress in listening

1 and 2 The final task invites students to look back at their progress through the course by relating the listening techniques in 2.2 to their progress. Ask students to formulate a plan to improve any areas of weakness. Elicit ways of doing this for students to select from, e.g. listen *regularly*, ideally daily, to good quality texts in English. Some open resources for lectures include:

University of Oxford: http://openspires.oucs.ox.ac.uk/

University of Yale: http://oyc.yale.edu/

University of Reading: http://www.reading.ac.uk/SACLL/UniversityofReadingLectures/SACLL-UniofReadingLectures.aspx

Technology Entertainment Design: http://www.ted.com/

11D Speaking Seminars (6)

TASK 1 Analysing a process text to prepare for a discussion

1 This task is based around an academic text describing a process; the text is in a slightly different style to other texts in this unit – more informal, with more literary and vivid language. The first activity draws out what students already know, and gives them the opportunity to display this knowledge. You could extend the activity by asking students to give a mini-presentation (e.g. 2 minutes each) on a process of change in their chosen city. Emphasize the importance of approaching the description from several perspectives. Ask students to note these down in order to use in activity 2.

2 Ask students to tick off the perspectives on their list which are mentioned (explicitly or implicitly) in the text, while adding new ones. As with any academic text, the range and choice of perspectives is determined by the writer's purpose. The perspectives reflect their analytical approach to their material.

Answers

Perspectives covered in Text 1: geographical (global / local), historical, cultural, anthropological, economic, financial, commercial, architectural, social, environmental, aesthetic, technological

3–5 These activities require students to analyse the essential content of the text, i.e. the processes being described. The author's language is often quite informal / literary / dramatic, but students should be able to identify her evaluative language using contextual clues. Activity 5 should be an attractive task for more visual students – encourage pictures, diagrams, flow charts, and any other appropriate visual representations.

Sample answers (author's evaluation in **bold**)

Renewal of city centres:

*Erasing bricks-and-mortar **history** to build a **shiny** vision of the future.*

*Clearing out the rundown alleys; **removing** longtime residents; **replacing** small, old houses with expensive apartments and new skyscrapers.*

Perspectives: historical, architectural, cultural.

Changing use of buildings:

*Liverpool and Bilbao have **torn down** their **abandoned** waterfronts and turned **aging** docks and warehouses into **modern** art museums.*

*In London, Paris, and New York, **artists** and **gentrifiers** move into old immigrant areas, praising the working class bars and take-out joints but **overwhelming** them with new cafés and boutiques, which are soon followed by brand-name chain stores.*

Growth of city centres:

*A universal rhetoric of upscale growth, based on both the economic power of capital and the state and the cultural power of the media and consumer tastes, is driving these changes and exposing a **conflict** between city dwellers' desire for authentic origins – **a traditional, mythical desire for roots** – and their new beginnings: the **continuous reinvention** of communities.*

'Manhattanization':

*... signifies everything in a city that is **not thought to be authentic**: **high-rise** buildings that grow taller every year, **dense** crowds where **no one knows your name**, **high prices** for inferior living conditions, and **intense competition** to be in style.*

Changing nature of authenticity:

*Lately, though, authenticity **has taken on a different meaning** that has **little to do with origins and a lot to do with style**. The concept has migrated from a quality of people to a quality of things, and **most recently to a quality of experiences**.*

*This is done **by preserving** historic buildings and districts, **encouraging the development of small-scale** boutiques and cafés, and branding neighbourhoods in terms of **distinctive cultural identities**.*

TASK 2 Developing material to use in a discussion

1 and 2 The students' analysis of the process in Task 1 should prepare them to select their own material to present. Explain that the focus is not on researching new information, but organizing material that they are already familiar with. If necessary, provide further prompts to develop their material, e.g. *What impact have the changes had on specific social groups living in the city?* Point out that this task provides an opportunity to trial their material, while Task 3 represents the seminar itself.

TASK 3 Participating in a seminar

1 and 2 Set the parameters of the seminar, i.e. the student roles in 1, and the time limits. Decide whether you will participate or observe: on occasion it can be beneficial for students if you participate, so that they can interact on an equal level and gain different insights and input. Explain that a major aim of the seminar is fluency – students are discussing familiar material, so they should be able to focus on using interesting language, offering original content, and speaking with a good degree of familiarity and authority. You yourself, as well as those students with specific roles, can review the seminar. As a follow-up task, invite students to reflect on their progress, as in the listening module (11C, Task 3), and come up with a plan to improve their performance.

11E **Vocabulary** Word formation (2)

1 and 2 Students work individually to categorize words from the unit into three broad groups according to their general reference. Explain that an 'actor' can be a person, a group, or a thing (such as a machine) which performs an action. They then work in pairs, focusing on suffixes, to establish which general concepts the endings refer to and which word forms they can be applied to. In feedback, discuss which endings can vary in spelling but express generally the same concept, e.g. *-tion* and *-sion* both describe a process, whereas *-ation* and especially *-ization* typically describe a more active, ongoing process. Elicit how the verbs and nouns to describe processes follow similar patterns (e.g. *accumulate – accumulation*).

Sample answers

a Process		b Quality / Characteristic	c Person/Actor	
Verbs	Nouns	Adjectives	Nouns	Nouns
accumul**ate**, facilit**ate**	identific**ation**, Manhattan**ization**	distinct**ive**	authentic**ity**, complex**ity**	borrow**er**
general**ize**	promo**tion** transmis**sion**		instab**ility**	motor**ist**, theor**ist**
				particip**ant**, respond**ent**

3 Students complete the table, using the ideas from 1 and 2 about suffixes and their general background knowledge. Don't allow the use of dictionaries at this stage, although students could check forms for themselves during feedback. Discuss particularly any cases which do not follow the expected pattern (*respond / response*) or where more than one form is possible, elicit the differences in meaning and usage.

As an extension, students select one set of words from the table (i.e. one row) and write examples to demonstrate how they might be used in context. Alternatively, they could research the words in use using an academic search engine to find appropriate academic examples.

Sample answers

Process		Quality / Characteristic	Person/Actor
participate	participation	participatory	participant
investigate	**investigation**	**investigative**	**investigator**
compete	competition	**competitive**	**competitor**
respond	**response**	responsive (responsiveness)	**respondent**
extend	extension	**extensive**	–
generate	**generation**	**generative**	**generator**
collaborate	**collaboration**	collaborative	**collaborator**
produce	**production**	**productive / productivity**	producer / **product**
stabilize	**stabilization**	stable/stability	**stabilizer**

Research Project (5)
Making a clear argument

This short extract from a research methodology book aimed at students, provides an alternative (i.e. non-EAP) view of the importance of argument in writing a research project. By this stage, students should have rough first draft of their project, which they need to refine and edit to make a coherent, cohesive complete text. It is easy for students to lose sight of their main argument or to be drawn off at tangents in the process of writing, and this is an opportunity for them to step back and look at their project as a whole. After students have read the extract, elicit what questions they should be asking about their own writing. Suggestions:
- Is it just a series of unconnected points?
- (How) Do all my points contribute to the overall argument?
- What is the key message I want to get across to my reader?
- Is there a clear thread of an argument that runs through my writing?

Look at the suggested ways that students can improve their draft to make both their argument more coherent (in terms of ideas) and cohesive (in terms of how these ideas are expressed through language). Explain that it is easy for students to feel that their argument is clear, because it is clear in their own mind, but that it must also be clear and explicitly expressed for their reader.

Depending on your context and time available, you may want students to submit their first drafts before or after this refining stage. Sometimes it is difficult for inexperienced academic writers to step back from their work and spot problems with coherence and cohesion, so feedback on these points may be helpful to help them with redrafting. Either way they should receive feedback on their draft before the end of the next unit so that they can respond to the feedback and carry out final checks and refinements. Depending on time and the number of students, feedback may vary in the level of detail you provide. One option is to 'close-mark' a short section, say 500 words, of the draft (perhaps selected by the student), including detailed comments and corrections, and to just give general comments on the remainder of the draft.

UNIT 12 **Research**

ACADEMIC FOCUS: RESEARCH AND REPORTING

INTRODUCTION

Unit 12 gives students the opportunity to try out the various techniques and strategies they have learnt throughout the course with minimal support. In the Reading and Listening modules, there is an overall task set out at the start of the module and students are encouraged to think about how to approach each task, choosing the best strategy to achieve their aim effectively and efficiently, preparing them to be independent learners, both in their subject area and also as users of academic English. In the Writing and Speaking modules, students focus on preparing a final piece of work for submission and assessment. The theme of the final unit also reflects the idea of looking ahead to future academic careers by focusing on academic research.

12A Reading follows a typical academic process in which students read different texts, all on the topic of research methodology, which they report on and discuss. Finally, as a team, they prepare a summary (written or oral) of their discussion. At each stage, they need to choose for themselves how to approach the task, bearing the aims and outcomes in mind, and organizing and managing themselves.

12B Writing focuses on the final stage of the writing process: proofreading, checking, and redrafting written work. Students practise revising texts for language errors, checking citations for accuracy, and responding to more general feedback on organization and flow. They work on sample student texts and review examples of their own writing to identify areas still to work on.

12C Listening follows a similar process to the Reading module, in which students listen to an extended lecture extract and make notes to prepare short oral summaries of specific points, they then discuss points raised in groups. Again, students are encouraged to work independently to negotiate each stage of the task. The lecture extract is on the topic of research methods for a general student audience and raises a number of key concepts and issues around academic research for students to react to.

12D Speaking builds on the work on presentation skills in earlier units (see 4D, 7D, and 10D) with a final extended presentation, either based on their Research Project or another research-based piece of work. Students are encouraged to think about the best way to present their research, how to introduce their topic effectively, and how to make their presentation accessible to their audience. At the end of the module, students deliver their final presentation to the class.

12E Vocabulary reviews the aspects of vocabulary explored in previous units through a small-scale piece of language research, in which students research and present information about a set of common academic words from a particular perspective (e.g. collocation, word formation, etc.).

Research Project (6) helps students to compile a checklist to work through in finalizing their project before submission. They check through final details such as format, bibliography, abstract, contents page, etc.

DISCUSSION

1 and 2 The topic of Research has been touched on throughout the book and students have already come across terminology such as *quantitative* and *qualitative* research (see Unit 7), *case studies* and *longitudinal studies* (Unit 11). This Discussion task aims to bring some of these threads together by taking a specific example of research and looking at the different aspects involved. Students decide on an example of research they have looked at during the course and together note down as much information as they can under each of the headings. If there are some gaps, encourage them to speculate, using appropriate hedging language (e.g. *The text didn't include any implications, but it seems likely that …*).

Texts reporting on research include: Texts 1 & 2 – 3A; Text 1 – 6A; Texts 1 & 3 – 6B; Texts 1 & 2 – 7B; Texts 1 & 2 – 8A; Text 1 – 8D; Text 2 – 9A; Text 3 – 11A.

3 and 4 Again working in their groups, students pool knowledge about each of these topics, speculating where they are unsure. These topics will come up in the Listening module (12C), so you can leave some questions open to be answered later. If students are already studying in a particular discipline, they may know something about typical research methods; those preparing to study can speculate about what they might expect within their chosen area.

12A Reading Independent reading

TASK 1 Critical thinking – establishing reading purpose

1 and 2 The aim of this module is to give students practice in choosing appropriate strategies to approach a reading text with minimal support. The first step in deciding how to approach a reading text is to establish the purpose for reading; understanding what they need to achieve as a result of reading. Students read the steps set out to identify their purpose and outcomes; i.e. to report on reading (note that students will be reading different texts), to compare and discuss texts, and to produce a summary of the discussion. You may want to specify whether the final summary task will involve a written summary or a short oral presentation, or you could leave it up to individual groups to choose. Note that students will give oral presentations as part of the Listening and Speaking modules in this unit.

TASK 2 Employing appropriate reading techniques

1 This is an opportunity for students to review the reading techniques they have practised throughout the course, such as identifying the genre, audience,

and purpose of a text (1A), identifying main points and supporting evidence (2A, 5A), establishing the writer's stance (2A, 7A), asking critical questions (6A) and responding to a text critically (9A & B).

2 and 3 Allow students five minutes to read their text and make some initial notes. Signal when the time limit is up and give students another five minutes to organize their notes and prepare to report on their text. As in previous tasks, students should use their notes to report rather than preparing a detailed script. Monitor progress but resist intervening to answer questions or give explanations, leave students to deal with the texts on their own. All of the texts are aimed at an undergraduate student audience, so should be fairly accessible.

TASK 3 Reporting on and discussing reading texts

1 and 2 Students re-form into their groups; ideally one student who has read each text, A, B, and C. Briefly read the instructions for this stage of the task as a class, but leave students to organize and manage their own discussions as much as possible. Allow 10–15 minutes for discussion, again monitoring and making notes for feedback at the end. Signal when time is up and direct students to agree on the main points to emerge from their discussion.

Sample points to mention in discussion of texts

Text A: Populations
- description of a technical aspect of research
- focus on quantitative research
- discipline here is Biosciences, but applicable to other Sciences and to some Social Sciences

Text B: Focus groups
- discussion of a specific research method (focus groups)
- focus on qualitative research
- mentions advantages and disadvantages
- discipline here is Health/Medicine, but could apply to other Social Sciences involving people

Text C: The Hawthorne effect
- practical issue/consideration for researchers; potential bias, reliability
- experimental/observation type of research (could be quantitative or qualitative)
- discipline here is Business, but applicable to any research involving people, so Social Sciences, Medicine, etc.

TASK 4 Summarizing a discussion of reading

1 and 2 The aim of this task is for students to work together as a team to prepare a final summary of their discussion (not of the reading texts). Remind students at this point whether they should prepare a written or oral summary, or whether they can make a choice. This stage of the task could be carried out in class or set as homework for students to present in the next lesson. Again, leave students to read the instructions for themselves, only answering relevant questions for clarification. The aim is to replicate a real-world situation in which a subject tutor may not be available to give a lot of individual support and students may be expected to get on with tasks independently.

3 If you have asked students to write a summary, these can be exchanged between groups for comment, evaluation, and peer feedback. If students have prepared oral summaries, they can be presented to the class, again followed by questions and comments from the rest of the class. If you have given students a choice of format, you could divide the class up for this stage, pairing written groups together and presentation groups together. After all the groups have presented and given feedback on their summaries, ask how successful they felt the whole process of reading, reporting, discussing, and summarizing was. Encourage students to identify stages that were successful and any problems or issues that came up. Give feedback from any notes you have made whilst monitoring, focusing especially on approaches, management, and teamwork rather than on content.

TASK 5 Designing a strategy to improve reading skills

1 and 2 This is an opportunity for students to look back at how their reading skills have improved throughout the course. Give students time to reflect on their own progress before they discuss in groups. Encourage them to add any points that are not mentioned on the list and to share experiences and ideas for further improving.

3 Encourage students to set themselves specific goals here with time limits that they can monitor. Make sure that their goals are realistic and achievable. If possible, encourage students to keep in touch with each other after the end of their course and to support each other in achieving their goals.

12B **Writing** Research writing

TASK 1 Critical thinking – evaluating writing skills

1 This task aims to help students evaluate how their writing skills have progressed and identify which areas they still need to work on. They start by considering a number of 'can do' statements, revisiting ideas discussed at the start of the book (1B Task 1) and reviewing the different aspects of writing they have worked on through the course.

2 and 3 All too often teachers give detailed feedback on students' writing only for it to be skimmed through then put away in a folder. This activity aims to review feedback over a period of time so that students can identify areas that have improved or persistent issues. You may need to ask students in advance to bring past examples of their written work to class for this task. If you use a regular

marking code or system, start by relating this to the areas highlighted (i.e. which of these points might be in the form of correction codes and which might be in comments at the end). If there are any other areas that you have specifically been highlighting with the class, monitor and check that these get picked up.

4 Encourage students to set specific and achievable goals here and to set a realistic time frame.

TASK 2 Using feedback to edit a text for language accuracy

1 and 2 The rest of this module focuses on responding to feedback on a draft text, and editing and checking a text before submission of a final draft. This task starts by looking at dealing with language errors, using a sample student text. First ask students to quickly read the text and elicit the topic of the essay. You might want to focus students' attention on the tutor's comments and ask students how they are similar to or different from your own feedback on their writing; both in terms of format and perhaps also in terms of the type of errors that crop up. Some of the errors here may occur across language backgrounds (missing articles, problems with uncountable nouns), others are more specific to the writer's L1 (in this case, Spanish – especially the use of the inflected *s* on the adjective *actives*). Allow students some time individually to correct the errors before putting them into small groups to compare and discuss their solutions.

Sample answer - corrections in **bold**

According to Abutalebi **et al**. (2009: 9) **'the*** bilingual brain is a special brain' and there **is** some **evidence** that **demonstrates** that. For example, higher activity has been found in memory and other areas of the brain when someone is **performing / completing / undertaking** a multilingual task (ibid). Other studies suggest that **a unique control structure exists in bilinguals that lets** them choose the right language to use, because both languages are always **active** in the brain, and this fact improves **a** bilingual's attention and cognitive control, giving them the ability to solve problems in **non-verbal** tasks as well as verbal ones (Bialystok **et al**., 2004, Costa **et al**., 2007). Further still, this superior stimulation of the brain across **the / a / their** lifetime is thought to be good protection against cognitive decline due to aging (Bialystok, 2009).

*As students are not able to check the original quote (which does in fact include the article), a 'safer' option would be to add the article outside the quotation marks ... the 'bilingual brain ...'

---

3 and 4 The aim of this task is for students to focus on checking text in detail for errors, but also to think about how individuals tend to make repeated language errors. If an individual is aware of which errors they are prone to, they can systematically check for them when proofreading, a point developed in the next task.

Sample answers – corrections in **bold**

1 It is essential to **recognize / understand / distinguish** the difference between early **bilinguals**, who learn two languages at the same time, and late **bilinguals**, who learn a second language once the first is known.

Or ... between **the / an** early bilingual, who **learns** two languages at the same time, and **the / a** late bilingual, who **learns** a second language once the first is known.

2 Considerably more work will need to be done to determine how the human brain works, although '**the** neuroscience of multilingualism' (Abutalebi **et al.**, 2009) is a growing field.

Note: As above, without being able to check the quote, students could add the article outside the quotation marks. ... *although the 'neuroscience of ...'*

Error 1: Errors with articles before nouns
Solution 1: Check all general nouns – do they need an article?

Error 2: Missing punctuation after *et al.*
Solution 2: Use a computer 'find' facility to find and correct all instances of *et al*

Error 3: verb + noun collocations
Solution 3: Check verb + noun collocations in a dictionary – use 'find' as above for recurring uses

TASK 3 Developing a personal proofreading checklist

1 Students often read their own writing, reading over and not spotting errors. By developing a personal checklist, they can make their proofreading more focused and stand more chance of spotting and correcting mistakes. Students could reuse the examples of past work they reviewed in Task 1 to create their own checklists. Emphasize that it is better to choose a handful of specific points to check rather than either very vague categories or a very long list of specifics. You might want to suggest some specific areas for inclusion that you have identified in marking your students' written work.

2 and 3 This activity gives students a chance to discuss the practicalities of proofreading and share suggestions and experiences. Encourage them to add any other tips and techniques.

TASK 4 Checking citations and references

1 and 2 You could do the first example here as a class and then leave students to check b and c individually and make corrections.

3 As students compare answers, explain that they should look beyond the surface conventions to evaluate the use of citation and identify examples of plagiarism. Students work in pairs to make any further necessary changes and arrive at a final acceptable form.

Sample answers (changes shown in **bold**):

a **Masden et al.** (2009) conducted one of the few comparative studies to look at bird movement both before and after the construction of a wind farm.
Flaws: Spelling errors in the authors' names; no need to show more than three authors in an in-text reference (should use *et al.*)
Good practice: Good, clear, concise summary, appropriate for a literature review
Note: Some institutions may even view minor errors in references, such as spelling mistakes, as plagiarism.

b Whilst the economic burden of an ageing population is a cause for concern in many developed countries, research by **Bloom, Canning, and Fink (2010)** suggests that in **non-OECD** countries falling fertility rates will lead to a greater proportion of working-age people within the population, offsetting increases in the older age group and so **not significantly impeding / slowing** economic growth.
Flaws: By putting the reference at the end of a long sentence, it is unclear which ideas are the student's own and which are from the source – not blatant plagiarism, but not clear attribution. Factual / copying error – should be **non**-OECD countries.
Incorrect in-text reference – all three authors' names should be given; it could include a page reference.
Misrepresentation – the text does not say the demographic changes will 'encourage' economic growth, just that they will 'not significantly impede' it.
Good practice: Some of the paraphrasing does show an understanding of the key ideas in the source text. e.g. 'a greater proportion of working age people within the population'.

c Heal (2012: 154) describes how in the modern world, 'we have built up our intellectual and physical capital [...] while at the same time we have run down our natural capital'. He suggests that we have gained many of our material comforts at the expense of unique and irreplaceable wildlife and habitats that have been destroyed in the process of human development.
Flaws: Plagiarism – the whole of this section comes from the source text, so should all be attributed. Much of the language in the first sentence is also copied exactly – it needs to be either paraphrased or quoted. There is no clear input to demonstrate understanding from the student.
Quotation – copying error with 'built/build' – words missed out without ellipsis – needs a page number.
Note: there are several possible ways to approach rewriting this but it should show some element of the student's own understanding / interpretation.

TASK 5 Acting on feedback

1 In this task, students look at more global issues highlighted in feedback. The comments here are intended to represent feedback from a subject tutor rather than a language teacher. Point out the mix of specific comments and general remarks at the end. What students can expect in terms of feedback on writing from subject tutors may vary greatly and this might be an opportunity to discuss any experiences students have already had in this area, either in their home country

or in their host university. Allow students some time to read the text and identify the topic (Business / Tourism) before categorizing the tutor comments as a class.

2 and 3 Point out that the tutor's comments do not necessarily cover all language errors, so in this task students should be acting on the feedback and looking out for any other details that might need changing. Students compare their completed drafts and discuss the task. Encourage them to relate it to their experience of editing their own work. You could compare their versions to the sample draft below, picking out any points they may have missed, but stressing there is not one correct 'answer'.

Sample answer
2.2 A profile of Chinese leisure tourists

Since the start of the Visit Japan Project in 2004, the Japanese Tourist Authority (JTA) has been surveying the consumption trends of foreign tourists. These surveys reveal some interesting figures regarding Chinese leisure tourists and their consumption behaviour. Over the period 2004-2010, 51.4 per cent of Chinese tourists came to Japan for leisure and their average expenditure on shopping during their trip was 95,239 Japanese Yen per person, the highest for any nationality and twice the overall average (JTA, 2010). In seeking explanations for this trend, we can look to Mok and Iverson's study of Taiwanese tourists, in which they describe how shopping abroad fulfilled an important cultural role in 'maintaining social relationships through the giving of gifts' (Mok and Iverson 2000 cited in Lehto et al. 2004, p.321). Although the Taiwanese context is slightly different, the same cultural ideas may be true for the current wave of tourists from the Chinese mainland, so that money spent on souvenirs during their trip has come to have an important social value through the giving of gifts to friends and family on their return home.

The JTA survey (2010) also found that many Chinese tourists (65.2%) were attracted to luxury retail outlets such as prestige department stores, raising questions about why Chinese tourists prefer these more expensive, high-end, stores to other retail shops in Japan. Moeran (1983), in his study into the habits of Japanese tourists, identified that they did not just buy souvenirs as a reminder of their travel, but as a status symbol that came from having been abroad. He pointed out that they placed particular importance on the country of origin of their souvenirs, as an indicator of their ability to purchase the goods in their country of origin (ibid). At that time, Japan could be described as a 'bubble economy', an economic situation similar to that in contemporary China. Thus, it seems that Chinese tourists, living in a rapidly expanding economy where demonstrations of economic status are becoming increasingly important socially, may be drawn to Japanese department stores for their 'Made in Japan' products, gift-wrapped in paper with the store's logo, which verifies their status as authentic Japanese goods.

TASK 6 Redrafting a written text

1 and 2 If students are completing the Research Project, they could work on a section of their project (1-2 pages) for this task. Alternatively, they could rework part of an essay or other recent written task. This could be set as homework, especially if students want to work on their project in electronic form, however, allocate a set time for them to spend on the task, say 20 minutes. Otherwise, some students will read through quickly without systematically going through the text, and others will spend too long agonizing over details that don't need changing. Explain that students should use any feedback on their writing as well as the personal proofreading checklist they developed in Task 3. Suggest they do several sweeps through the text looking at only one aspect at a time, rather than trying to look for everything in one read-through. After pair feedback, encourage students to repeat the same process with the rest of their project before final submission.

TASK 7 Independent research – writing assessment

1 and 2 This task focuses on understanding and using assessment criteria. Many institutions publish criteria for students' written work in some form and it is important that students read these and take them into account when producing work for assessment. Explain that it is useful to read through any criteria both before they start work, so they understand what is expected, and again before submission to check that they have fulfilled all the criteria and address any weak points. The example from the University of Oxford website demonstrates some of the typical categories and language used. You could match some of the criteria to skills and concepts practised throughout the course, such as using evidence from sources, evaluation, developing a coherent argument, etc.

3 This is an opportunity to review any criteria for your own course and also for students to explore any criteria available for their subject courses.

12C Listening Lectures (9)

TASK 1 Preparing to listen – note-taking and purpose

1 This activity revisits the terms from the opening Discussion to the unit (page 183) and links them to the questions to be explored in the lecture extract.

Sample answers

What are we trying to find out? = answering research questions

What's already known? = literature review; selecting search terms

What is the role of theory?

Could the research do any harm? = research ethics

How can data be gathered and analysed? = research processes; gathering data; selecting a sample; randomization

How can research findings be combined? = combining multiple research studies

---

2 As with reading, students need to think about their purpose for listening. Sometimes this will be quite general (e.g. to learn about a new topic), but sometimes it will be more focused (e.g. to find possibly useful information to use in a piece of research writing). Throughout this module, students work towards giving a short presentation on one aspect of a lecture on research methods, which will then lead into a group discussion. Stress that students will not know which aspect they will report on until a later stage, so they should make notes on the whole lecture extract. As students read through the instructions, encourage discussion, in pairs or groups, about techniques that may be relevant. They might consider using the terms in 1 as headings, they could use the questions on the opening slide. They could use mind maps or other visual techniques, tables, or bullet points.

TASK 2 Noting relevant information from a long extract

1 ▶12.1 Explain that this is a relatively long lecture extract, around eleven minutes, which students will watch only once. Note that it comprises two extracts from a longer lecture, and does not begin at the start of the lecture, so it does not cover all of the questions and points on the opening slide. Allow a couple of minutes at the end of the lecture for students to finish making notes while ideas are fresh in their minds, but do not discuss the content of the lecture at this stage.

ACADEMIC LANGUAGE

Style (4) Informal and idiomatic language

Ask students for their reactions to the lecturer's style: *How easy was it to follow? How helpful were the examples? How clear and accessible was the language?* Draw students' attention back to the title of the lecture and ask who the intended audience was (i.e. any students studying Social Sciences). Explain that the lecturer's style was fairly informal and his use of language was intended to make his topic accessible to a fairly wide audience. Look at the examples of informal and idiomatic language picked out in the box. Ask what the effect of this language might be on native-speaker and non-native-speaker students.

TASK 3 Using lecture notes to prepare for a presentation

1 Divide students into groups of four or five. Ideally allow students to select and allocate their own topics to present from the lecture, although if they are clearly struggling, you could offer some guidance. Possible topics to select / group together:
- literature reviews (including systematic reviews)
- combining multiple studies & selecting search terms
- research ethics and research outcomes
- gathering data, selecting a sample, and randomization.

2 Refer students back to the stages in Task 1.3 and allow some time, 5–10 minutes, for individual preparation. Again, students should not prepare a 'script', but prepare to speak from their notes. They should use the own notes only and not refer to the transcript at the back of the book.

TASK 4 Discussing and extending ideas from a lecture

1 Students reform into their groups and take turns to deliver their short, informal presentations, so that each topic from the lecture is reviewed. Point out before they start that they should listen to each other and adapt their own presentations where possible to pick out points where they overlap (e.g. *As Naomi mentioned before …; Maria talked about …, well, that leads nicely into …*). Monitor and note down good examples of listening and referring to others.

2 After all the students in a group have presented, they open up a discussion reacting to the ideas raised in the lecture. The prompt questions here have been left intentionally vague to allow for students' own responses. Allow another 10 minutes for general discussion and not down any interesting questions raised or good points or examples given. After all groups have finished, ask students what the most interesting points were to arise from the lecture and their discussion.

12D Speaking
Presentations (7)

TASK 1 Understanding the presentation task

1 and 2 This module gives students the opportunity to give a longer presentation based on their own work. If students have carried out the research project, they should give an oral presentation of their project. Otherwise, students should select another piece of research-based writing they have carried out to present. Give students time to consider, note down, and discuss with other students in pairs or small groups, how they might approach presenting their project orally. You could pose the following questions:
- What potential problems are there in summarizing your whole project? (A summary could be too general, skimmed over and lack substance or interest.)
- What problems might there be focusing on a specific aspect of your project? (It could be too technical for a general audience and could feel decontextualized.)

Note that these are initial ideas that students will develop through the module.

3 Students prepare specific questions to ask as either part of a Q&A session or, if relevant, during one-to-one tutorials.

TASK 2 Considering your audience

1 ◀)) 12.2 Students often complain that their topic will be 'too boring' to present to other students, especially in mixed discipline groups. These two short listening extracts provide some ideas for relating a topic to your audience and bringing a potentially dry, academic topic to life a little. You could note how the lecturer in 12C used real-world examples (e.g. choosing search terms to research 'happiness') to make theoretical concepts more accessible to his audience. Elicit examples of how other lecturers seen throughout the course have tried to relate their topics to their audience, using examples, case studies, pictures, etc.

Sample answers

Student A: Use of a hypothetical example which the audience can relate to (an *Amazon* parcel) to illustrate the legal process and potential problems. Use of relevant pictures to help illustrate the process and make it more visually appealing.

Student B: Focus on the most interesting, 'new' information, i.e. the case studies. Also mention of own experiences as an intern to make it more personal and screenshots of websites to make it more visually interesting. Audience of students from same / similar discipline so less need to explain the theoretical background.

2 As students place their own project topic and audience on the scales, explain that even a student with quite a specialized topic to present to an audience not familiar with their discipline can make it accessible through careful choice of what and how they present.

3 Ideally pair students with partners from different discipline backgrounds for this task to represent their 'most challenging' audience member. This will help reveal any points that the presenter will need to make more accessible or explain more carefully.

ACADEMIC LANGUAGE

Introducing a topic Giving reasons and examples

This box suggests a few different techniques for introducing a topic at the start of a presentation. Explain that the opening remarks of a presentation are important for the audience to understand the topic of the presentation and to become accustomed to the presenter's voice and style. Some presenters will say a little about their choice of topic before they outline the structure of their presentation, others will give the title and the outline before saying more about the topic. Ask students which style they prefer and why.

TASK 3 Preparing and giving a research presentation

1 ◀)) 12.3 Following on from the Academic Language box, these short extracts illustrate how some of the techniques and expressions for introducing a topic might be used in practice. The extracts are quite short – you could either listen to both students together or stop after each one for feedback. Ask students which introduction they prefer and why.

Sample answers

Student A: Personal reasons - link to own home country; significance of topic - importance of exports to Chinese companies

Student B: Relevance/currency of topic - link to recent figures in the news; significance of topic - important for retailers to be competitive

2 Pairs from the previous task (2.3) reform to discuss how they might introduce their own presentations.

3 and 4 Students will probably want to prepare their presentations for homework, especially if they are to form part of their final assessment. At this stage, make sure they are clear about what they should do in terms of timing, visuals, etc. and in terms of what they should expect when they give their presentation: equipment available, time for rehearsal in the presentation room, audience, questions at the end of their presentation, etc.

As an extension, you could review some of the practicalities of giving a presentation, drawing on students' previous presentations and perhaps demonstrating good and bad practice yourself. Points to mention might include:

- Producing clear visuals – with text in a large, clear font, not too much information on one slide, clear colours and background, no inappropriate backgrounds or graphics, no distracting sounds and animations, etc.
- Checking equipment – students should check and if possible, rehearse using any equipment
- Posture and positioning – where to stand so as not to block any visuals, maintaining eye contact with the audience and not facing the screen or looking down too much at notes
- Notes – how will students use notes, will they hold them or place them on a desk? Cards or a single page?
- Delivery – speed and volume of voice, remember to pause and take breaths, especially between points, check and practise pronunciation of any 'tricky' words
- Timing – students should rehearse their presentation right through to check timing, possibilities for monitoring timing on the day.

5 Students take turns to give their presentation in front of the whole class. Explain whether you will stop students if they go too far over the time limit. Also say whether there will be a question and answer session after each presentation. If so, encourage the rest of the class / audience to contribute with questions.

TASK 4 Critical thinking – learning from experience

1 and 2 If possible after the whole class have given their presentations, allow students time to work in groups to 'debrief' and discuss their experience. To finish on a positive note, encourage students to pick out their favourite points from the presentations they have seen. These could be about content, interesting topics, engaging examples, delivery, visuals, response to questions, etc.

12E Vocabulary Review and research

1 This task reviews some of the aspects of vocabulary covered in the book and encourages students to do some independent language research using the resources they have encountered during the course. This might include dictionaries (paper, electronic, and online), other language references such as a thesaurus or specialist dictionary, and any other online resources they have come across, such as using an academic search engine to research collocates and usage. Make clear that students will choose one of the perspectives (e.g. *collocation*) and research three of the words in the box from this perspective (e.g. *demonstrate, significant, and interaction*). They may decide to research more than three words initially (say four or five) and select the three which produce the most interesting results to present. This could be done as a relatively quick activity in class using just dictionaries or set as homework for students to research more fully.

2 Students work in groups (of 3–5) to present their findings to the group. They could use simple visuals, such as a flip chart to write on, and should be encouraged to give examples wherever possible.

Research Project (6)
Finalizing your work

This final box helps students to think about what they need to do to finalize their research project before submission. In class, students could work in groups to read through and discuss each of the points. Add any extra points relevant to your particular course requirements. Students should reach a consensus on points they are sure about and formulate questions about anything they are not. If appropriate, they could then use a resource such as a student handbook to check any queries. Alternatively, you could conduct a Q&A session to clear up any outstanding points. As a class, create a final checklist for students to work through before submitting their final draft.

AUDIO CD TRACK LISTING 🔊

TRACK NUMBER	UNIT NUMBER	TRANSCRIPT AND EXTRACT NUMBER
1	2D Speaking	2.6
2	5D Speaking	5.5 Extract 1
3	5D Speaking	5.6 Extract 2
4	6D Speaking	6.7 Clips 1–4
5	9D Speaking	9.5
6	12D Speaking	12.2 Extract 1
7	12D Speaking	12.3 Extract 2